NEBRASKA
Admitted
1867

- - - - Pony Express
T T T T Telegraph
x x x x Overland Stage
- · - · - Mormon Trail
- · · - · · Oregon Trail
+--+ Union Pacific

Reedstrom

Missouri River

Elkhorn River

Omaha

Kanesville

Omaha

River

Ft. Kearny

EMPIRE ON THE PLATTE

EMPIRE ON THE PLATTE

BY RICHARD CRABB

ILLUSTRATED BY ERNEST L. REEDSTROM

THE WORLD PUBLISHING COMPANY
CLEVELAND AND NEW YORK

Published by The World Publishing Company
2231 West 110th Street, Cleveland, Ohio 44102

Published simultaneously in Canada by
Nelson, Foster & Scott Ltd.

First Edition

Library of Congress Catalog Card Number: 67–15227

INTRODUCTION

THE LITERATURE on the Platte Valley is considerable. Nonetheless, I hope in *Empire on the Platte* to place the river and its valley in better focus than does any other book that has come to my attention.

Most Nebraskans think of the Platte Valley as that firm, level strip of land along the river, ranging in width from a few hundred yards to several miles. The area is almost devoid of trees, rock formations, and undergrowth. In *Empire on the Platte,* I consider not only the level Platte bottom land but also the river's complete watershed embracing roughly 50 per cent of the State of Nebraska, in addition to important areas of Colorado and Wyoming.

For many years, Nebraskans living along the Platte have referred to their homeland as "The Empire Of The Platte." The reference is rooted in justification as well as in pride. When its historical role and its present-day contribution are added together, the Platte is a stream of national, even international, importance. There never was a satisfactory alternative to this Platte route in crossing the Central Plains. Today, the railroad streamliners and the jetliners follow the Platte just as the wagon trains did a century ago.

Most Americans know much more about what has taken place along the Platte than they realize; yet, few know the name of the stream that made it all possible. The Platte has been a valley of decision; this was so before recorded history. Throughout the centuries, Indian tribes fought to control it, knowing that control determined their safety and security on the Great Plains for hundreds of miles in any direction. The buffalo throughout this vast area was doomed once the big brown shaggy animals were denied the rich Platte feeding grounds.

The Oregon Trail is one of the best-known institutions in all America. Yet it is one of Nebraska's best-kept secrets that the famous trail, as well as the California Trail and the Pony Express, moved up the Platte. In traveling the Oregon Trail, the white man was making his first major use of the Platte.

The mass western migration began when thousands of Mormons migrated from Nauvoo, Illinois, to the Utah wilderness. They, too, traveled the length of the Platte Valley. The camps of the Mormons, as they moved west, were the early roots of many modern cities. Omaha, in the Platte Valley, located near the point at which the Platte River empties into the Missouri, is an example.

Almost every well-known person associated with the "Winning of the West" traveled the Platte Valley: Kit Carson, Jim Bridger, Wild Bill Hickok, Calamity Jane—in addition to the most famous of them all, Colonel William F. Cody, known to the world as Buffalo Bill. He knew the Platte mile by mile.

The east-west lifeline of the United States was, and is, through the Platte Valley. This was as true in the 1960s when the new interstate freeway, U.S. Route 80, was located there as it was when the first pioneers chose to locate the Oregon Trail along the Platte. The importance that historian Francis Parkman assigned to the Platte is still valid today. His book, *The Oregon Trail*, was published nearly 120 years ago.

President Abraham Lincoln confirmed the vital role the Platte Valley has played in the building of America when he decided to send the nation's first transcontinental railroad the full length of the Platte.

The Platte Valley has always been a catalyst to American progress. But the building of the Union Pacific Railroad injected tremendous change all along the Platte. Many of the railroad work camps became towns. One of these settlements, Cheyenne, had a population of 10,000 before the town was even named. The railroad unleashed economic developments that reached across the nation. The railroad made the Platte Valley a center for great change and rapid progress on the Plains.

There is no more dramatic example of the power of the trans-continental railroad to bring about change than the sudden formation of the Great Plains cattle industry. The legendary Chisholm or Texas Trail was actually brought into existence by the Union Pacific's run up the Platte Valley and across northern Kansas. Over this trail millions of longhorn cattle and thousands of Texans traveled north to the Platte railheads, to exchange their cattle for gold coins by the saddlebag full, money that brought the cattle industry to the Great Plains and the Platte country. At the same time, the Union Pacific carried tens of thousands of homesteaders from the Midwest and the East. The Texans coming up the big trail to the Platte were largely out of the old Confederacy. The homesteaders were mostly Union veterans. But the confrontation was not solely rooted in the Confederacy and Union identities. Even if the Civil War had not been fought, the problem would have existed. The stage was set for trouble.

The Texans who populated the plains did not possess a tradition of law and order. Under the conditions of the open frontier, they made their own rules, and enforced them with their own guns. They were determined to keep the Platte watershed a free range. The homesteaders wanted to farm the land. In the clash that followed, shootings, lootings, and killings raged across the valley for more than a decade.

Nebraska became a state in 1867. Twelve years later, when both the number of Texas cattlemen and Union veteran home-steaders had greatly increased, it was clear that a showdown had to come.

At this point, the Texas Olive family moved tens of thousands of cattle and horses onto the range just north of the Platte. They challenged homesteaders to bring their plows into that area. These Texans had trouble with many homesteaders but they ran into their greatest difficulty when they tried to destroy the homesteading operations of Luther Mitchell and Ami Ketchum.

Print Olive was a Confederate war veteran. Luther Mitchell was a Union veteran. Into this impasse moved two Nebraska governors: Silas Garber and Albinus Nance. Governors Garber and Nance were determined to end the lawlessness. These constant skirmishes might easily touch off a continuing violence between cattlemen and homesteaders that could sweep across the plains.

The State of Nebraska put up the money to bring the Olives to justice. Governor Nance called for U.S. Army troops to stabilize the situation. As a result of research done in writing *Empire on the Platte*, we now know that Governor Nance obtained the cooperation of the federal government through the direct intervention of the President of the United States.

The result was a triumph for law and order. Solving the Plate problem set a pattern that became the blueprint for similar problems across the American plains. This has often been the role of the Platte in the plains culture and economy.

Settling of the cattlemen-homesteader difficulties opened the way for agricultural and industrial development. As irrigation and modern farming were introduced, the region became unique for its high food production. The world is a little less hungry because of this. The Oregon Trail, the Pony Express, the first telegraph and railroad to cross the nation, the hammering out of new patterns of cooperation between strong-minded cattlemen and determined homesteaders, all played their part.

RICHARD CRABB

February 1967

CONTENTS

CONTENTS

IN THE BEGINNING

"SHOOT HIM!" someone bellowed from the mob below. The man on the roof of Turner Hall in downtown St. Joseph, Missouri, moved on toward the American flag flying from its staff, heedless of the clicking hammers of six-shooters up and down Charles Street. In the threatening crowd, dozens of revolvers were trained on the figure on the roof, but no shot was fired. Robert Bradshaw, his confidence rising with every step, continued his walk toward the flagpole. Reaching its base, he gave three cheers for the American flag and fired all six shots from his own revolver into the air in a salute to the colors. Then he reverently lowered the last American flag to fly over St. Joseph for some years. The date was May 23, 1861.

Long before that day, St. Joseph had been caught in the cross fire between proslavery and antislavery factions in both the Kansas Territory and the State of Missouri. Feelings ran so high that in early May, in an effort to reduce the danger of riot, the city council of St. Joseph had passed an ordinance forbidding the public display of either the United States flag or the flag of the Confederacy by private organizations. Turner Society members, Union sympathizers, had defied the city council's order, the only case of such defiance in the city.

Shortly after noon on May 23, an unruly group of men led by Jeff Thompson, who later became a Confederate officer, went to the post office, pulled down the American flag, and tore it to pieces. Only a direct order from Postmaster John L. Bittinger, speaking from behind a drawn gun, prevented the shreds from being publicly burned.

Thwarted at the post office, the mob responded when someone yelled, "Now for the dirty rag on the Turner Hall!" By the time the inflamed throng reached the Turner Hall, seven blocks away, its numbers had swelled to approximately five hundred men, most of them armed.

Bradshaw, a member of the Turner Society, happened onto the Thompson mob at the post office and instantly grasped the seriousness of the situation. Taking shortcuts and running as fast as he could, he arrived at the Turner headquarters ahead of the raiders. He found only a clean-up boy in the building and sent him to report to other members that a "secession mob" was bearing down on the hall.

Locking the back and side doors, Bradshaw took up a position in front of the main entrance on Charles Street. He did not have long to wait. The rioters crossed Sixth Street, which intersected with Charles less than half a block away. About forty feet from the building Thompson halted his followers, and after a brief consultation two men, Alonzo W. Slayback and Thomas Thourghman, approached the beleaguered building. These two, both reasonable men, were taking part in Thompson's march in the hope that they could find some way to avert bloodshed. Slayback, in a plea for the peace and welfare of St. Joseph, asked Bradshaw to take down the American flag. Bradshaw refused.

"Jeff Thompson is drunk," Slayback told Bradshaw, "and no one can tell what a mob under a drunken leader will do."

Bradshaw was still protesting when Judge Miller, the justice of the peace, reached the scene and joined the parley. He demanded in the name of "the mayor and city council" that the flag be taken down immediately. He threatened to arrest Bradshaw, as a representative of the Turners, for violation of the new ordinance.

Faced with this threat in an already highly charged atmosphere, Robert Bradshaw agreed to go to the roof and take down the flag if Slayback would take his place at the front door and prevent anyone from entering while he was on his mission. Slayback agreed. Bradshaw's only other request was that he be permitted to salute the flag before lowering it. Though Slayback thought this was toying with the temper of the crowd, he consented to try to keep order at the door.

There was some murmuring and confusion as Bradshaw started across the roof, but for the most part the mob remained calm. Suddenly, when Bradshaw was about halfway between the roof door and the flagstaff, the cry "Shoot him" rang out. Bradshaw, showing little regard for his life, stopped to address the throng below. In keeping with the demand of the mayor and the city council, he told them, he would take down the American flag. But, he added, no mob could compel him to do so, and he would salute the flag before lowering it. He concluded, "I will take down the American flag, knowing full well that ere long it will float in triumph over every seceding state."

This brought renewed cries of "Shoot him" as hammers clicked to the ready. Jeff Thompson and his followers hesitated. They had within the hour desecrated the American flag, but firing on a fellow townsman meant murder. Nor would it cease with the killing of only one man. On the Kansas-Nebraska border only a spark was needed to start a conflagration that could lay waste the region, and every man knew it.

Into this taut situation stepped Alonzo Slayback. He shouted, "I will kill the first man who fires a shot at Bradshaw."

In the hush that followed, Bradshaw completed his mission.

That evening a short account of the day's events in St. Joseph was flashed by telegraph to Washington and relayed to the newspapers in major cities throughout the Union. Later, Postmaster Bittinger made a full report. By twilight on May 23, 1861, the future of St. Joseph as a rail terminus and Midwest capital had dimmed. Its luster would never again approach the first magnitude.

Before this tense day in 1861, St. Joseph, the largest city on the Missouri River west of St. Louis, seemed certain to become the eastern port of entry to the entire Central Plains, perhaps even to replace St. Louis as the "gateway to the West." There was no Kansas City nor Omaha to contest St. Joseph's claim; Kansas City did not yet exist, and Omaha was a small village established less than five years before.

In the 1850s, as in earlier decades, availability of a water-level route had encouraged America's westward thrust. The northernmost route by which passengers and traffic could be moved on schedule and in volume was along the Ohio, Mississippi, and Missouri rivers. St. Joseph was the western junction of this great route, the point where the river boats and wagon trains or stagecoaches exchanged their cargoes and passengers, water moving them east, wheels bearing them westward to California and Oregon. In the river era, circumstances pointed to St. Joseph as a major city in mid-America's future.

Now the United States was well into a fabulous new era, the era of the railroad, whose fast, dependable, relatively inexpensive transportation would provide the major impetus to convert the United States, within a few decades, into an entirely new kind of nation. Before the coming of the railroad, men and ideas could travel overland only as fast as a man could walk or a horse could run. Now the steam engine had begun to harness the almost unlimited energy to be found in wood and coal.

The first steam train to begin regular service in the United States originated, not in New York or Philadelphia, but in Charleston, South Carolina, in November of 1830. In 1832, the Baltimore and Ohio brought in the first steam train to serve Washington, D.C. Within the next ten years numerous short lines linked the cities of the eastern seaboard, and by the 1840s railroad building had begun west of the Allegheny Mountains. From western New York State and Pennsylvania, from Ohio and southern Michigan, the iron rails began spreading into Indiana and Illinois, until by 1860 almost every important town east of the Mississippi River and north of the Ohio was located on a railroad line. California also became dotted with railroad towns.

In between stood the plains, which did not invite settlement because they were too dry for the type of farming carried on back East, they were devoid of forests, and they were populated by hostile Indians. No railroads spanned these barren lands, so pioneers followed the Oregon Trail through the Platte country en route to the more hospitable West.

The mood in which Americans were building railroads is illustrated by the first Chicago-based company, the Union and Galena. With its tracks laid only a short distance out of Chicago to a town less than twenty years old, the railroad's name indicated that its terminus was the small river town of Galena. These fragmentary and tentative beginnings gave little clue to the pivotal role Chicago was to play in linking the western grain fields with the factories of the East.

Another Chicago-based railroad company, the Rock Island, completed its first bridge across the Mississippi in 1856. But the builders had been so confident that they could span the mighty river that they had already laid tracks in Iowa, from Davenport to Iowa City, sledding engines and equipment across the river on the winter's ice. The bridge represented a major engineering triumph, but railroad-building Americans scarcely paused. Men only forty years old could remember when there had not been a single steam-powered train on the entire North American continent; yet they were sure that the biggest railroad of them all, the one to span the continent east to west, could be built— and their generation would build it.

From the moment the trains began rolling across the Mississippi River bridge linking Rock Island, Illinois, and Davenport, Iowa, without even reducing their speed, no serious doubt demained that completion of a transcontinental railroad was only a matter of time. Two factors, both closely linked to the impending war, were to delay the project for nearly ten years, however —the route and the cost. Most men regarded a transcontinental railroad as a project so vast that only one such facility could be undertaken in their lifetime. Hence the choice of route was all important. And the cost would be so great that government support of some kind would be essential.

As political tensions increased between North and South, members of Congress from the two sections stalemated one another. Southerners wanted the route to start from a point on the Mississippi somewhere between New Orleans and Memphis, crossing Texas and terminating in southern California. Stephen A. Douglas of Illinois had long advocated a route through the Platte River Valley, and it was chiefly to this end that as early as 1844 he had introduced a bill in the House of Representatives for the creation of the Nebraska Territory. Although by 1854 passage of the Kansas-Nebraska Act assumed major importance because it removed the limitations on the spread of slavery through repeal of the Missouri Compromise, Douglas had first proposed it to "serve notice to the War Department not to locate any more Indians" on the plains which would further complicate the problem of locating the railroad there. With the outbreak of the Civil War, the long-contested issue of the route was partially resolved. Once the members from the seceding states withdrew from Congress, that body could get on with the matter of deciding particulars of a northern route. It would begin somewhere on the Missouri River and, like the Oregon Trail, cross the Central Plains and follow the Platte to the mountains.

Until May of 1861 many factors had favored St. Joseph as the eastern terminus of the railroad. It was here that Buffalo Bill Cody and others had started westward, riding the Pony Express. This route from St. Joseph to Sacramento, California, had proven to be the soundest route geographically. And along this route, in the 1850s, young Buffalo Bill had fought Indians, outsmarted holdup men, braved tempestuous winter storms, and won for himself the reputation that was to make him, in later years, a spectacular circus attraction. From the spring of 1860 until the coming of the telegraph, St. Joseph and Sacramento were linked solely by a handful of brave young men who made the run on horseback in ten days in good weather and fifteen days in bad.

Engineering studies confirmed that the topography lent itself to the building of a railroad from that point too, since grading was an important consideration when every ton of earth had to be moved by muscle power, whether of men or of draft animals.

6

The fact that St. Joseph was linked by telegraph to all the important Atlantic coast cities had been a prime consideration in selecting St. Joseph for the starting point of the Pony Express, for messages flashed into the city by wire could, within minutes, be on their way to California. Privately financed, work on the telegraph lines westward had come to a halt at St. Joseph. It had been generally recognized that their extension would be too costly to be undertaken privately, and the United States government had shown no inclination to underwrite the cost. Instead, the wagon-train-operating firm of Russell, Majors, and Waddell had been induced to establish the Pony Express. The company, which had distinguished itself for efficient long-distance hauling, could have stretched the wires from St. Joseph to Sacramento for the sums they invested in setting up and operating the Pony Express, as things turned out. Promises were made to the firm that were never kept; and before government subsidies were forthcoming, the company had been allowed to drift into bankruptcy.

The telegraph was completed across the country much more quickly than most people thought possible when the Pony Express began operations on April 3, 1860. Just seventy-four days later, President James Buchanan signed into law an act providing a subsidy of $40,000 to anyone who would build the first transcontinental telegraph from the "border of Missouri to San Francisco" by July 31, 1862. Only two years and six weeks were allowed for its completion. Western Union, the only organization qualified and equipped to do the job, began the line in St. Joseph, as expected; but instead of moving with the trail to California and Oregon across the thinly populated Kansas plains and into the central Platte Valley, the company's chief, Hiram Sibley, took the line up the Missouri River to Omaha. Thus the new line could serve not only Council Bluffs and Omaha, but also bustling Nebraska City, the big staging base for Russell, Majors, and Waddell wagon trains. From Omaha the line then followed the full length of the Platte Valley, the Mormon route, now dotted with additional settlements.

Construction began within thirty days of the signing of the

7

authorization. By September 5, 1860, the telegraph line had reached Omaha, and by the first Tuesday in November, the news that Abraham Lincoln had been elected President of the United States could be flashed all the way to Fort Kearny in the Nebraska Territory.

Hiram Sibley and his men were determined to finish the job in 1861. Less than two weeks after President Lincoln was elected, Edward Creighton of Omaha, Western Union's chief representative in the Platte region, boarded a stagecoach for Utah. There he enlisted the cooperation of Brigham Young, who had begun his own great building project, Salt Lake City, only a dozen years before. Since there was no stagecoach service over the five hundred miles to California during the winter, Creighton, at great personal risk, pushed forward on horseback, organizing in San Francisco a company that would begin at once to build the telegraph line east toward Salt Lake City.

In the spring Creighton was back in the Platte Valley to direct the westward push, and by June 16, 1861, W. H. Stebbins, the foreman, and his men had reached almost to the Jules Reni Ranch on the South Platte River near present-day Julesburg, Colorado. Creighton saw that even under the most favorable circumstances one crew alone could not build the telegraph line into Salt Lake City by the end of 1861, the target set for completion of the eastbound section from San Francisco. He therefore instructed Stebbins to divide his experienced men to form the nucleus of two teams, Stebbins taking one to Salt Lake City and building east toward the Reni Ranch, Creighton and the second crew urging the line westward to meet them.

Although Creighton's crew had to haul some poles nearly 250 miles, and both teams had to improvise frequently—and fend off Indians—Stebbins and Creighton finished their branch of the system on October 17, 1861. A week later, more than nine months ahead of the deadline set by Congress, the California company brought its lines into Salt Lake City, and the transcontinental telegraph had been completed. That day, October 24, Chief Justice Stephen J. Field of California sent the first message across the nation to President Lincoln:

. . . The people of California desire to congratulate you upon the completion of this great work. They believe it will be the means of strengthening the attachment which binds both the West and East to the Union, and they desire in this, the first message across the continent, to express their loyalty to the Union and their determination to stand by its government in this, its day of trial. They regard the government with affection and will adhere to it under all fortunes.

Along with its river traffic, St. Joseph had already been linked to eastern Missouri by the tracks of the Hannibal and St. Joseph Railroad that ran almost directly east and west between the two towns. Neither downstream toward Independence nor upstream toward Omaha and Sioux City was there another railroad within hundreds of miles of the Kansas-Nebraska border. And now St. Joseph had the telegraph. Its future as a junction seemed assured as the matter of the transcontinental railroad continued to be studied in Washington. The lifeline to California was seen as both an economic and a military necessity, and a bill was drafted that set the wheels in motion literally.

As the Pacific Railroad Act of 1862 emerged, its language clearly implied that there would be but one transcontinental railroad. While it did not specifically rule out others in the future, its entire discourse focused upon an agreement to be reached with one or more organizations engaged in building *the* railroad. Congress was prepared to go to generous lengths to encourage such an organization, offering ten sections of public lands for each mile of track laid and establishing a sliding scale of loans based on the terrain: $16,000 per mile completed on the plains, $32,000 per mile in the foothills, and $48,000 per mile of mountain track. The Pacific Railroad Act of 1862 was specific on every vital point save one—the route.

In the early months of 1862 the political and military situation on the Missouri River was too uncertain to permit an easy

9

decision. The St. Joseph rebel mob had raised substantial suspicion in Congress and at the White House that that city had become too great a security risk to be the principal hinge of the transcontinental railroad. The Act of 1862 stated that it would be the responsibility of the President of the United States, at such time as he deemed necessary, to determine the exact route to be followed. During 1861 and early 1862 the President had been careful not to express any personal preference as to the Missouri River terminus. Some important persons along the river further east were going to be disappointed regardless of the route chosen, and their contributions to the war effort could be adversely affected. The President knew the terrain as he knew the military implications. He was also aware of the considerations weighed by Hiram Sibley and Western Union when they decided to run the "talking wires" the full length of the Platte Valley. But by autumn the President still had said nothing.

On September 2, two months after the Act of 1862 had been passed, the Union Pacific Railroad Company was formed in Chicago for the purpose of building the road from the Missouri River toward California, although later the plan was altered somewhat when the Central Pacific Railroad Company, headed by California's Governor Leland Stanford, was organized to start laying track east from California. Tracks of the two companies would meet "somewhere in the Utah mountains." But before Peter Dey, the Union Pacific's chief engineer, could begin the complex analysis of engineering problems to be surmounted, the route would have to be established. Dey, expecting the route to follow that of the telegraph, located his office in Omaha— casting a thin but discernible shadow into the future.

October gave way to November and still there was no word from the White House. Senator Charles Sumner of Massachusetts, a powerful neutral whose own state would not be affected directly, had long favored the Platte route, and he was known to have conferred with Lincoln on the matter. So had many others. All of November passed, and with it the last of what could be regarded as good weather for beginning the task. Some

Lincoln and Gen'l Dodge
at Council Bluffs. Aug.1859

Abraham Lincoln saw the Platte River from a Missouri river-
boat in the summer of 1860. An artist recreated the scene at
Council Bluffs, where Lincoln met railroad builder Grenville
Dodge. *(Union Pacific Railroad Museum)*

General Sherman was responsible for preventing Indian disorders during the construction of the railroad, a position which was later taken over by General Sheridan.

Union Pacific's first engine, named after General Sherman, arrived in Omaha in July 1865. It cost $15,450, had a 14x22-inch cylinder, and 56-inch drivers. The building of the railroad through the Platte Valley to the Pacific was one of the great events in the American story. It started a transformation that within half a century made America the most powerful nation on earth. (*Union Pacific Railroad Museum*)

100th Meridian Expedition, October 22 to 26, 1866. Here, congressmen, writers, and financiers are seen landing at Omaha before boarding the Union Pacific Special into buffalo country. (*Union Pacific Railroad Museum*)

September 1867 meeting to determine the railroad's route. Front row: Mr. Van Lenep, geologist; Mr. Duff, Boston financier; Grenville Dodge, Chief Engineer; Major-General John A. Rawlins; Captain Dunn, on plains duty. Back row: Sergeant Whelan, on plains duty; Captain Mizner; H. C. Parry, M.D., U. S. Army Surgeon; Mr. Chaworth, newspaperman. (*Union Pacific Railroad Museum*)

FIGURE IN DOORWAY IS
DAN CASEMENT
(IDENTIFIED BY DAN DILLON
CASEMENT-SON OF GENL.
JACK CASEMENT-JAN. 1945)

TAKEN IN VICINITY OF ECHO, UTAH
DURING PERIOD OF CONSTRUCTION O
UNION PACIFIC RAILROAD. DONATE
BY MRS. FREDDA BAREILLE, SALT
LAKE CITY, UTAH, MAY, 1940.

The Casement brothers, John and Daniel, did most of the actual track building after General Dodge had selected and surveyed the right-of-way. Dan Casement (standing in door) with building crew supervisors at a Union Pacific work camp headquarters in 1868. (*Union Pacific Railroad Museum*)

General Jack Casement made the field decisions, leaving office work to his brother. He is shown in front of a work train car. *(Union Pacific Railroad Museum)*

In January 1867, the coldest on record, the Union Pacific built a railroad trestle on the frozen Missouri River, completing direct rail connection between Chicago and North Platte, Nebraska, the westernmost point. *(Union Pacific Railroad Museum)*

A small forest of logs was required for the largest trestle the Union Pacific had to build between Omaha and the Great Salt Lake. *(Union Pacific Railroad Museum)*

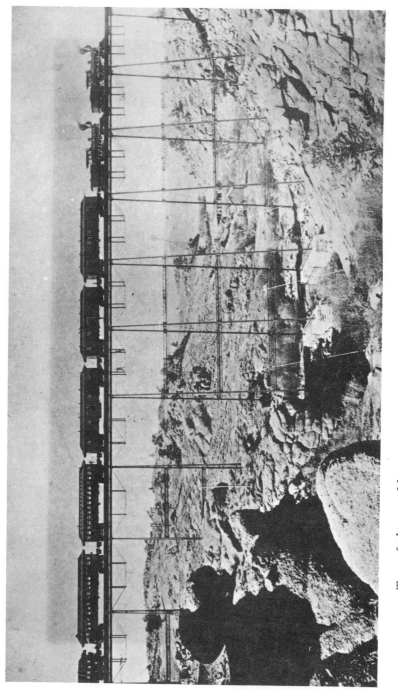

Two of the wood-burning engines pulling one of the crack trains. A 24-hour trip replaced the month's travel of a wagon train. (*Union Pacific Railroad Museum*)

General Grant, center, at conclusion of treaty with Sioux, which stopped raids against railroad. General Sheridan is the fifth person to Grant's left; General Sherman, fifth person to Grant's right. (*Union Pacific Railroad Museum*)

Union Pacific Engine 119, the first to reach the Great Salt Lake. (*Union Pacific Railroad Museum*)

Linking of the Union and Central Pacific or the north rim of the Great Salt Lake, making transcontinental railway a reality. (*Union Pacific Railroad Museum*)

The President Lincoln Car, built to honor the man who made the transcontinental railroad possible, and intended for his lifetime use. (*Union Pacific Railroad Museum*)

planners began to talk critically of the President. The telegraph, they said, was not enough to insure California's remaining in the Union. They held that every day lost was a day gained by those determined to bring California into a Confederacy of the West. Finally, late in the morning of December 2, 1862, the Western Union operatoi al Omaha began recording the historic message from President Lincoln to Peter Dey. Even before the last of the code had been transcribed, Omaha's Main Street was astir from end to end. The message read:

> Fulfilling the responsibility placed upon me by the Act of July 1, 1862, I have fixed the initial point of the Pacific Railroad on the western boundary of the State of Iowa, opposite Omaha—opposite section ten in township fifteen, north of range thirteen, east of the sixth principal meridian, in the Territory of Nebraska.

Both St. Louis and St. Joseph had been abandoned as "gateways to the West." The scratch of the President's pen had relegated St. Joseph to the role of river town in northwest Missouri, serving only the farming and ranching enterprises of the immediate area. With the same pen Omaha's future was set: foremost city of the Central Plains. President Lincoln's decision had shifted America's center of economic and political power farther north, out of reach of rebellion and the men whose loyalties to the Union were tainted. By fixing the starting point of the railroad on the western boundary of Iowa, Lincoln also made certain that the government subsidy would apply to the building of a bridge over the Missouri between Council Bluffs and Omaha, a proviso that proved highly profitable for the Union Pacific. To this day all other railroads crossing at that point pay tolls for the privilege.

The President's telegram to Dey touched off informal dedication and ground-breaking ceremonies. Governor Alvin Saunders of the Nebraska Territory put his foot to the ceremonial spade while Edward Creighton, Sterling Morton, and most of the city's civic leaders looked on. The territory's leading orator, George F. Train, delivered the major speech, stating, "The President shows good judgment in locating the railroad where the Almighty placed the signal station at the entrance of a garden seven hundred miles in length and twenty broad."

Concluding with the prediction that the great railroad would be built in not more than five years, Train was ridiculed as a visionary. Dey, the chief engineer, estimated that the job would take about ten years; newspaper editors and other second-guessers across the nation agreed. Two years later in November 1865, General William T. Sherman, then in charge of the armies from the Missouri River to the Far West, was even less optimistic. He was a guest aboard a special train that took him fifteen miles west of Omaha, to the farthest point so far constructed. Here he said, "This is a great enterprise, but I hardly expect to live to see it completed." As it turned out, George Train had considerably the better of the controversy. From the time the first rail was laid at Omaha, construction took just three years, six months, and ten days.

But the first rail was not laid for more than two years. Once the celebration in Omaha ended, in the early morning hours of December 3, 1862, a profound silence settled over the whole project. The building of the transcontinental railroad had to wait until the survival of the United States as a nation was assured. The Union cause touched bottom midway through 1863. Although it was months before its salutary effects were felt, the crisis actually was passed during the first weekend in July. General Grant had taken Vicksburg, reopening the Mississippi, Missouri, and Ohio river systems to Union shipping; and General George Meade's Army of the Potomac had repelled General Lee's attempt to capture Washington, D.C. By the end of 1863 the Union cause was secure enough so that attention could once more be focused on the construction of the railroad to the Pacific.

Early in 1864, President Lincoln approved the Pacific Railroad Act of 1864, which doubled the public land grants, raising the figure to twenty sections of land for each mile of railroad completed. In addition, the sums of $16,000 to $48,000 per mile were made available on considerably more liberal terms. By this time, however, the original Union Pacific team had dissolved. Dey and his associates were gone, Dey's place being taken by Grenville M. Dodge. Now the Union Pacific of Chicago and the Central Pacific of San Francisco set about the task.

Surveying and other engineering preliminaries and procurement and transportation of supplies occupied the remainder of 1864 and most of 1865. These efforts revealed the degree to which the project involved the entire nation. There were grave obstacles to be overcome at both ends of the line, some so formidable that only months earlier their solution would have seemed implausible. At the western end there was ample timber for ties, but there was no furnace for making an iron rail in all of California. Every piece of metal had to be fashioned in the East, from Pennsylvania to New England, and moved by ship down the Atlantic, around the Great Horn of South America, up the Pacific Coast, and through the Golden Gate into San Francisco harbor. It was a five-thousand-mile haul.

Council Bluffs and Omaha were relatively close to the iron sources and steel makers, but for nearly six hundred miles west of Omaha there were no forests. In 1864 and 1865 tie-cutting crews ranged far and wide, denuding a vast area of the Missouri Valley of every tree that could be converted into ties. Even then there were not enough—not nearly enough—to carry the railroad across the plains. Eventually ties had to be cut in New York State, Pennsylvania, and Michigan. Some were brought up the Missouri River on barges, but most had to be delivered to Council Bluffs on wagons drawn by oxen from the end of the railroad at Des Moines, 150 miles to the east. From Council Bluffs the ties were ferried across the river to the Nebraska side.

The actual work began on the California end of the line, the first track being laid in the spring of 1865. Work on the Omaha end was delayed again and again until November 5. Then workmen began laying tracks on a line directly west from Omaha toward the Platte River, thirty miles away. These thirty miles across relatively flat land were not completed until early December. By the end of 1865, when work had to be stopped because of severe weather, only forty miles of track had been laid.

Blizzards continued into March and early April. By the time work could be resumed, a month later than anticipated, responsibility for the eastern segment had been shifted to Grenville M. Dodge and General John S. Casement and his brother Daniel. Thirty-seven years old, Jack Casement had fought through the full four years of the war, attaining the rank of brigadier general. Now he directed a work force of fifteen hundred men, made up largely of toughened soldiers, Union and Confederate, whose combat skills were to stand them in good stead against the Indians.

The Casement brothers built nearly 250 miles of the Union Pacific in 1866, all the way to the point where the North and South Platte rivers meet. Jack Casement named his work camp North Platte, and one of the important towns in western Nebraska had been born. From North Platte the tracks continued along the course of the South Platte. Where the South Platte swung southwest toward the small mining town of Denver, the rails diverged from the river, continuing west by 1867 along a tributary toward work camps with such names as Chappell, Sidney, and Kimball.

The plains tribes had been slow to understand the tragic implications for them in the building of the Union Pacific. In 1866 the buffalo had already retreated, rarely moving any longer in large numbers across the lower Platte. But when the tracks reached Fort Kearny, Plum Creek, and North Platte, the leaders of the Cheyenne, Arapaho, Crow, Kiowa, and Sioux realized the desperation of their plight. By 1867 the presence of a common enemy brought about unprecedented cooperation among the tribes as they set out to challenge the might of the white man. Raiding parties struck at stagecoaches in Nebraska and the Colorado and Wyoming territories, forcing suspension of service for a time between the Platte and Salt Lake City. Even the telegraph wires were torn down by Indians suspicious that the humming sound relayed information of their actions. Construction crews were frequently decimated. The death toll included L. L. Hills and Percy Browne, the foremost engineers under Dodge.

One raid, in August of 1867, took place within sight of the town of Plum Creek. A strong force of Cheyenne ripped up the track with the intention of destroying the next train from either direction. Cutting the telegraph line, they used the wire to bind loose ties in a position perpendicular to the tracks. A six-man repair crew on a handcar crashed into the blockade, their attention having been diverted by the Indians. The men were hurled into the air, striking the ground as the Indians swooped in for the kill. Five of them were dead almost instantly. The sixth, William Thompson, a stout young Englishman with long blond hair, tried to escape into the tall grass. One of the warriors seized him, knocking him unconscious and scalping him. Thompson regained consciousness to see the Indian riding off, dropping the blond trophy in his haste. Thompson dragged himself to the spot, recovered his own scalp, and lost consciousness again.

Coming to after sunset, the cool air seeming to revive him, he saw the approaching headlight of an eastbound train. The Cheyenne warriors were attacking while the engineer and fireman, not seeing the cut track, attempted to keep up the steam and outrun the Indians.

The engine and cars left the rails, Indians swarming over the wreckage and murdering the train crew before Thompson's eyes. Falling upon the cargo of liquor destined for the work camps, the Indians got so drunk that Thompson, his wet scalp in his hand, was able to crawl and walk from the scene, making his way to the Plum Creek station where he received first aid. His skull undamaged, Thompson eventually recovered and returned to work, understandably a curiosity for having survived so harrowing an experience.

Two other events in 1867 gave the Platte country a large measure of its modern character. On March 1, Nebraska had become the thirty-seventh state of the Union, and in the same year the tracks of the Chicago and Northwestern Railroad were laid across Iowa to link Omaha with Chicago. Now passengers and freight could move over the iron trail from any point along the nearly seven hundred miles of the Platte Valley, east to Chicago and beyond to all of the important cities on the Atlantic Coast.

Of even greater importance to the infant state was the traffic that the railroad began to funnel into Nebraska and up the Platte. Before the Union Pacific introduced its immigrant car service, the population was so small that in the first gubernatorial election David Butler, the Republican, defeated Democrat J. Sterling Morton by 109 votes, a decisive number when only 8,077 votes were cast in all. Without the military installation at Fort Kearny, the number would have been smaller still. The year after the service began, twice as many settlers arrived as had come the year before, and five years later, in 1873, the number of newly arriving homesteaders swelled the population by 6,189.

President Lincoln had set the stage for this migration five years before it could become a reality, having signed both the Pacific Railroad Act of 1862 and the Homestead Act of 1862 within a period of a few weeks. Now, encouraged by the immigrant car and the orderly distribution of public lands, settlers began streaming into the Platte Valley like an army of occupation with a seemingly endless flow of fresh recruits.

By the end of 1867 Casement's men were more than halfway to Salt Lake City, the point at which the crews of the Union Pacific and Central Pacific expected to meet two years later. The mountains would present difficulties, but the outlook was good.

The fact proved even more favorable than the forecast. On May 10, 1869, Dodge and Casement and their veterans hailed the predominantly Chinese crew who had brought the Central Pacific from within sight of the Golden Gate to a spot overlooking the Great Salt Lake. Governor Leland Stanford of California was there, driving the last spike into the last tie as the transcontinental telegraph flashed the news. Factory whistles sounded jubilantly in cities all the way to the eastern seaboard. Bells rang across the nation. The breach between North and South had scarcely begun to heal, but uninterrupted ribbons of iron bound the East and the West. Though Abraham Lincoln had not lived to see the feat accomplished, his role in selecting the route is permanently memorialized in the name of Nebraska's capital city.

People along the whole length of the Platte recognized the coming of the Union Pacific for what it was—a new kind of life, a thrilling adventure in undreamed-of speed. Distances that had required ten days by wagon train could be traversed in less than a day. Existing towns, some of them well established, simply "homesteaded" themselves. They selected new locations on the open country along the railroad, moved some buildings and effects, and began a new existence as "railroad towns." Entirely new communities came into being, many of them developing from the work camps that the Union Pacific had set up every thirty-five to fifty miles along its route. When the work of the camps was done, enterprising people took over the buildings and founded towns, some as flourishing as Fremont—named for the great pathfinder—Central City, and North Platte.

The wagon trains, the stagecoaches, the Pony Express, and even the singing wires of Creighton's telegraph had followed the Platte route; but the impact of the railroad introduced a whole new dimension. The railroad transformed the Platte country from a thin line across the Great American Desert into homesites, farmsites, ranches, towns and small cities, shops, and factories. The Platte River had been a slender thread tugging men westward along its water-level route to the mountains and the Far West, few of them stopping. Now bands of iron down its valley served as a magnet to draw men and enterprises along its length, into the broader plains that were no longer isolated. The people of Nebraska could not anticipate the force of economic power already in process of being generated. Accessibility to the railroad would soon determine the course of countless lives, including those of men as far away as Texas. One of these men was Isom Prentice Olive.

PART ONE

THE OLIVES ARE COMING

[1]

THE LONGHORN MEN

CERTAIN STRATEGIC AREAS located on our earth's surface have since time immemorial provided the stages upon which man's greatest dramas have been enacted. Singapore, the Dardanelles, the Ruhr, Gibraltar, Runnymede on the Thames, Long Island at the mouth of the Hudson, and the Platte Valley on the American Plains are all examples of places which have provided the settings for history's important developments. Whoever holds and controls them has for centuries past, and will for centuries to come, command the thought, the commerce, and the power of which empires are made.

The Platte Valley has been important to the men traveling or residing on the plains since the beginning of recorded time. The Valley became vital as Americans stepped up their determination to build one nation from sea to sea. Created by the only river flowing completely across the Central Plains, the Platte Valley provided the route for the Oregon Trail wagon trains, the stagecoaches, the Pony Express, and the first telegraph and railroad to cross the United States. Of all man's special uses for the Platte Valley, the building of the first transcontinental railroad proved to be the most momentous event of all. The railroad provided vast new opportunities and exerted such powerful economic influences that the lives of Americans, not only on east and west coasts, but north and south, as far as Canada and Mexico, were profoundly affected.

33

Logically, then, the railroad, representing markets that in turn represented "Yankee gold," exerted a powerful influence in such far distant places as San Antonio, Austin, and Georgetown, all in southern Texas. The Olive family ranched just north of Georgetown, and, prompted by the building of the great railroad, the Chisholm Trail soon ran past their cattle pens. The Olives had carved out a small empire in longhorn country, an empire ruled by Jim and Julia Olive's eldest son, Isom Prentice Olive. No one called him Isom. Some called him I. P., his mother called him Prentice, but as the name was shortened to a nickname and the vowel surrendered to the soft southern tongue, his name became Print. Print Olive would be a name to reckon with in Platte country, but as yet it was not even heard there.

The James Olive family had come to Texas as part of a great movement of people out of the lower eastern and midsouthern states to the frontier on the plains. Sam Houston and Davy Crockett were among these capable and determined pioneers who traveled by wagon, horseback and on foot, intent on establishing a new home in the great country—not state—of Texas, under the Lone Star flag.

James Olive was born in North Carolina in 1804 into a family that had arrived in America more than half a century earlier. Caught up in the westward movement, he spent an important part of his youth in Mississippi where at the age of 22 he married 16-year-old Julia Ann Brashear of the land-holding Brashear family, who carried more than a trace of Cherokee blood in their veins. Julia Olive and most of her children, especially her son Prentice, had the jet black hair, tawny skin, and striking dark eyes of the Cherokee.

Although he had no formal education and could write his name only with difficulty, James Olive was a highly intelligent, perceptive man; he talked well, too. A patient man, he tended to be slow to anger, fair, and reasonable.

Julia Olive was reared on the Mississippi upland where corn and livestock often pushed cotton into a secondary role on the plantations. Having received some schooling, she could read and

34

write with ease and was good with figures. Quiet in manner, she was nevertheless decisive and direct, resourceful and courageous, well fitted to become the mother of a family on the frontier.

Julia and Jim's first child was a girl, Mary Elizabeth, usually called Betty. In 1840 their first son, Isom Prentice, was born.

For six years after their marriage Jim and Julia Olive farmed on shares and raised livestock in Mississippi, managing to end each year with a little profit. But in both his own home community on the North Carolina Piedmont and in Mississippi, Jim Olive had observed that opportunity to get ahead depended on owning land, and he was determined to get his share. By the time Prentice was three, the family had completed preparations for moving to the Republic of Texas, where land was free. Jim and Julia had saved enough money to buy a strong team of oxen, a covered wagon, and vital food supplies. They still had a reserve to meet the cost of first necessities once they were located on their own land. Pioneering took money, and Jim and Julia Olive had the cash.

The family started west early in the year in order to arrive in time to raise some food and arrange for shelter before winter. They drove the oxen west until they crossed the Mississippi River, and eventually the border, leaving behind the United States with its caste system that decreed slavery for persons of black skins, suspicion for slightly dark skins like Julia's, and poverty for whites unable to get either an education or land. Jim Olive believed that the plantation caste system that prevailed from Virginia to Louisiana would never be able to come into Texas—not in his time, anyway.

During the journey from Mississippi, the family discovered that young Prentice was able to give the commands to the oxen and horses and, more important, the animals responded to the tiny lad's commands. This affinity for livestock would grow and become increasingly important as Print grew to manhood.

The Colorado River of Texas flows in a generally southeasterly direction, passing through the capital city of Austin on its way to the Gulf of Mexico, emptying at a point midway between Corpus Christi and Galveston. The Olives' covered wagon rolled to the banks of the Colorado at a point near the present small city of Bastrop, a short distance downriver from Austin. Jim Olive decided not to continue west across the Colorado but to turn toward the San Gabriel River to the north.

Crossing the San Gabriel, Olive decided he would locate his family in this portion of the sparsely settled country. Ranging about, he finally chose a tract of land made up partly of black, open prairie soil, partly of timberland, and partly of brushy undergrowth. The prairie would serve for crops, the woods for timber to build a home, barns, and fences, and the brush area for livestock. Yegua Creek lay to the south; Brushy Creek to the north.

The most valuable feature of the landscape was also the most unexpected. The area was populated by wild longhorn cattle of a kind the Olives had never seen in Mississippi, mostly somewhat yellow in color, taller and higher off the ground than the oxen that had pulled their covered wagon into the new country. Jim and Julia Olive had been accustomed to seeing big animals, like steers, that belonged to someone; but these big longhorns belonged to no one and simply came as a part of the new land they were moving onto, like the grass and the timber.

The Olives' nearest neighbors, Sarah and Adam Lawrence, answered their questions about the strange cattle. The big animals provided very good meat, hides for clothing, rawhide for everything from string to stout ropes, and tallow for candles. Or the longhorns could be captured and driven to markets on the Gulf Coast and sold for hard money with which to buy the necessities for survival on the Texas frontier.

Jim Olive, not being a writing man, left no diary of what he saw. But Noah Smithwick, who settled near Brushy Creek in 1850, wrote that the wild longhorns were everywhere, "descendants of the Spanish cattle brought to the Mission San Gabriel away back in the eighteenth century. Some were very handsome brutes, coal black, their white horns glistening as if polished."

The story of Jim Olive and his sons is in reality the saga of the Texas longhorn. From the 1840s until the 1880s, the Olives were principals in the age of longhorn greatness—forty thundering years when the longhorns out of Texas brought a new kind of strength and nutrition to families of workingmen across a continent. These were the men who were erecting the courthouses, factories, schools, churches, and homes of a newly united America as the country moved toward the twentieth century and worldwide power.

Jim Olive had taken his family to Texas with the intention of raising crops and some livestock, farming after the fashion he had known from North Carolina to Mississippi. He had stumbled instead onto the beginning of a new era. He had been in Texas only two years when Sam Houston led the Republic into joining the United States, and in the ensuing climate of greater political stability, the longhorn men attained a prosperity that pioneer farmers rarely knew.

Olive's economic enterprise soon rested on a much broader base than the seven hundred acres of his farm. Before 1850 he was gathering the wild longhorns from an additional thousand acres or more. He used some of them for food and clothing for his own family, but there were far more than he could use—herds which he drove to Gulf port markets and sold for more hard cash on a single trip than most pioneering farmers saw in their entire lives. On one such marketing trip to New Orleans, for example, he brought home $3,000 in gold coins—the only money of worth in a country too new for banks.

Each year Prentice gave increasing signs that he was destined to be a longhorn man and a good one. When he was eight he wanted to ride his pony on the hunts just to see the excitement, but his father could not both manage the hunt and take care of a boy, so his initiation was postponed. The boy continued to press the matter, though, and when he was nine he was allowed to ride on the hunts as an extra, helping around the campsites and keeping the hunters in touch with one another.

A year later, when Print was ten, he asked to be permitted

to handle the bell mare on the hunts. The bell mare was a sort of animate chuck wagon, carrying enough food, liquor, and supplies for a day's hunt. Tin cups strung on a rope that looped her neck produced a bell-like sound, keeping the men in the bush advised of the location of the campsite. Thus the boy on the bell mare functioned as a combination water boy and office manager for the hunt—and held the cornhusk torches for the evening card games.

After talking with Julia, Jim gave in to Print's insistence that he could handle the responsible job, and Print rewarded his parents' confidence by promptly becoming an expert. By the time he was eleven, young Print was finding time to hunt and rope longhorns himself. At twelve, he could find, catch, and rope the toughest longhorns to be found in the San Gabriel country. Unlike his father, the boy enjoyed the work, and his skill entitled him to join the ranks of the men, so he turned his job over to a neighbor boy, Lee Moore. Print was now a longhorn man.

The five years between Print Olive's fifteenth and twentieth birthdays, 1855 to 1860 were years of almost uninterrupted happiness, the last carefree period of his life. His interest in the family enterprises grew, but so did his activity. He was a man doing a man's work and taking a man's responsibility. These were the golden years.

In 1854, Betty Olive had married a neighbor boy, George Wynn, leaving the family circle, but on January 9, 1855, it expanded once again. On this date the next to the last of Julia's sons was born. She named him Robert A. Olive. He would become a longhorn man too, though a very different one from Print, and his life would profoundly affect the lives of every member of the family, especially Print's.

Print had been only a little boy himself when his brothers Jay and Ira were born, and though Laura was born when Print was twelve, he had felt no particular responsibility for rearing a girl. Toward Bob his feelings were different from the start. As for little Bob, he seemed to realize very early, too, that there was a special relationship between him and his eldest brother. Each would always have a particular hold on the other, a bond that almost bordered on the mystic.

During the years when bright young fellows his age in Boston or New Orleans were "reading for a profession," Print Olive studied longhorns. He made the grade, too, gradually taking over complete direction of the hunts and branding operations from his father. By the time Print was seventeen, Jim Olive was telling his neighbors, with a quiet pride, that Print was the cattleman in their family. Jim Olive continued to handle overall management and to take an important direct role in marketing, but production, the hub of the enterprise, fell more and more to young Print.

With both the risks and the rewards so great, hunting longhorns offered individual challenge to every man engaged in the work. Cowboys were paid a share of the catch from every hunt, yet there were no firm guidelines as to the size of the shares or their distribution. When Print took over direction of the Olive hunts, he immediately instituted more liberal terms for those who worked hard and took the risks with him. His handling of the boys on the bell mare was a case in point. These boys were customarily paid little or nothing until they were at least twelve years old. Then they received only enough to keep them from demanding a chance to hunt with the men. Having slaved under this system himself for two or three years, Print promptly ruled that any boy capable of handling the bell mare should receive a full share of the catch. Then there were the longhorn handlers, the men who took over after the hunters had secured and tied the big animals. These men usually received only wages, but Print felt that their dangerous and vital contribution entitled them to proportional shares of the profits. In short, fairness and generosity came to mark all his business dealings, and it was to Jim Olive's credit that he allowed his son to set his own standards.

It was not long before Print Olive's liberal terms were the

talk of San Gabriel country cowboys. All the good men tried
to find openings on the hunting teams operating along the Yegua
and Brushy creeks. The result was that Print Olive's men roped
more and more longhorns. More longhorns went to market, and
more gold flowed to the Olives and their men.

Things were going exceedingly well for the family as the
1850s slipped away. Neighbors joined to build a new church
within sight of the elder Olives' home. Lawrence Chapel everyone agreed it should be called, since Sarah and Adam Lawrence
gave the land on which it was located. The need for community
recreation increased as families grew, and weekend socials became more frequent. The Olive family home was often the scene
of these good times that began early in the evening and often
lasted until light showed in the eastern sky. Print especially enjoyed the picnics at Gentry's Well, near present-day Taylor,
Texas. Beginning in the midafternoon of a summer's day when
the weather was too warm for hunting, the picnic would continue by the light of a campfire, well into the night. The fact
that Print was the most successful young man in his part of
San Gabriel country made him a particularly good catch, but
he was too intent upon advancing his longhorn business to single
out one girl for serious attention just now. The picnics and socials
gave him a chance to mix with all the people of his own age.

Jim Olive and his boys were never active politically, but they
always took interest in their local government. Back in 1849,
Jim had spearheaded a move to have Milam County carved into
two counties so that he and his neighbors would not have to
spend the better part of a week going to and from the county
seat to attend to necessary business. The Olive petition was
successful, and, early in 1850, Williamson County came into being with what is today Georgetown as its county seat. Jim Olive
and his neighbors could thereafter ride to and from the courthouse the same day. Still earlier, when Sam Houston led Texas
into the United States, Jim and Julia Olive were glad enough
to resume the national ties they felt they had never really lost.

Now, as the 1850s were drawing to a close, an ominous political cloud hung over Williamson County, over Texas, and over the entire nation. The issue of secession had as yet little practical meaning in cattle country, but the cotton planters along the Gulf Coast were as alarmed at the prospect of abolition as were their counterparts farther east. Olive longhorns were sold on the Gulf Coast, and every trip to market brought renewed discussion of the issue back at home. Then, in 1858, the people of Texas had a chance to express their views when Sam Houston campaigned for reelection to the United States Senate. In his campaign, the hero of San Jacinto reminded Texans that it was he who had led Texas into the United States in the first place, and he promised that if he returned to the Senate he would advocate preservation of the Union. When the ballots were counted, the Old Warrior had been defeated.

But Sam Houston was not convinced, nor was he ready to give up. The next year he offered the people of Texas an opportunity to "think this matter of secession over once more." Their state was far from the center of the main controversy between North and South, he said, and Texas would be keeping its word and serving its own best interests to stand with the Union. Texans could not find it in their hearts to vote twice in two years against the man who had called on his countrymen to "remember the Alamo" and then crushed Santa Anna and his Mexican hordes. Sam Houston was elected governor, the only man in the history of the United States to serve as a governor of two states, having been elected governor of Tennessee thirty-one years before. The war clouds over Texas receded as he took office.

Jim Olive breathed easier. He had refused to lecture his sons on secession, but James Olive had not named his second son Thomas Jefferson Olive (Jay) without reason. He and Sam Houston were of one mind; their sympathies were with the Union. Print usually agreed with his father; but when it became evident that he was willing to give up hunting longhorns for a chance to fight Yankees, Jim Olive spoke out. He did not raise his voice, but he counseled his sons to go right on hunting and let Sam Houston deal with the problems of union or secession.

But within the year the flames of secession leaped higher. The state legislature forced the issue to a referendum early in 1861. Secession was defeated in Williamson County but carried in the state as a whole. The Texas legislature voted to leave the United States on the twenty-fifth anniversary of Texas' independence from Mexico.

As he had been elected governor of two states, so Sam Houston resigned for the second time. In Tennessee, at a moment when a landslide reelection had seemed assured, Houston's beloved young wife had suddenly deserted him. Crushed by sorrow, he had withdrawn temporarily from public life. In 1861, once more people he loved had repudiated him. When the legislature moved to enter the Confederacy, his "I cannot take two oaths of allegiance" speech was tantamount to resignation. He could not join his fellow Texans in secession, but neither could he bring himself to fight them. The last two years of his life saw the dissolution of all he had fought for in the state he had served so well.

The massive wedge that split Sam Houston from his Texas also drove relentlessly through the James Olive family and a thousand others in the San Gabriel country. Jim Olive could not deter young Print from joining the Williamson County Volunteers that also included young men from nearby Milam, Lee, and Bastrop counties. They were ready to go to war in June 1861.

After his decision and enlistment, Print knew a few brief echoes of his golden years. He resolved to put the summer longhorn work in shape for his father and remain with his mother, who was expecting again, until she delivered her baby. Waiting was especially difficult because Print and his friend Frank Condron had a solemn pact that they would stay together. Frank, without family restraints, was impatient to be off to join the Texas volunteers in the rapidly forming Confederate Army.

Julia's baby, a son named Marion, was born on August 15. Now all that remained was to say goodbye.

Jim Olive found it difficult to find the words. The father feared his son's willingness to "handle the tough ones" himself might cost him more dearly in the war against Yankees than against longhorns. "Don't try to do God's work for him," he admonished, adding that Print must do his duty and not worry about things at home even if Jay, too, had to go to war. The words trailed off, ending with a firm handshake and a silent exchange of loving glances from moist eyes.

Julia said, "You have always been a good boy at home, Son. You are thoughtful and helpful to others. Now you must go among rough strangers. Keep your hopes, for without hope you will be lost. If it is written you must die, die like the great oaks, from the top down. Always keep your roots planted in God, in His Great Spirit."

Then there were the last minutes with brothers and sisters. The young people tried to keep their farewells light, but one parting was unexpectedly difficult. It came last, when Print turned to six-year-old Bobbie. The older brother picked the little boy up and held him very tight for a long, mute moment. Then the Williamson County boys climbed on their horses and rode to Lexington in Lee County northeast of Austin to join Company H, 2nd Texas Infantry Regiment, and their commanding officer, Lieutenant N. L. McGinnis.

Print Olive was twenty-one years old.

[2]
THE NIGHT THAT DID NOT END

DURING THE WINTER following their enlistment, the men of Company H learned that their mission would be to help keep the Mississippi River in Confederate hands. Thus they were spared the weary, endless policing campaigns across Louisiana, Arkansas, and the plains of the Southwest that occupied many other units. They were also cheered to have their own Albert Sidney Johnston as their general. Johnston, they were told, had resigned from the Union army to lead them. What better omen of victory could they be given? Every Texan was a little taller.

That their destiny was ultimately to rest more in the hands of a former circuit-riding lawyer from Illinois than on any other one individual the Texas volunteers could not suspect. While Olive and Condron were learning their new job, Abe Lincoln was learning his—one of the most awesome tasks ever to confront a man. A man of peaceful inclinations, Lincoln found himself finally responsible for directing the greatest war ever fought in the hemisphere and one of the most critical wars in history.

The President's destiny was thrust upon him. He had tried to avoid the fratricide; he had thought he could. Then the Confederacy fired on Fort Sumter in South Carolina on April 12, 1861.

Although Jefferson Davis was chosen president of the Confederacy because of his willingness to strike the first blow, he had no plans for launching an immediate offensive. The defensive posture of the South gave Lincoln time to plan his own strategy. He hoped it would be a short war. Most military men on both sides shared his view that by overrunning northern Virginia and capturing the Confederate capital at Richmond, the Union forces could win a quick victory. But the Army of Northern Virginia did not allow this easy resolution of the conflict.

Then President Lincoln's plan began to emerge—the plan that eventually won the war. Lincoln came to realize that the Confederacy had to be rolled up from west to east like a rug. But first the Mississippi River must be secured against Confederate control so that this artery of mid-America could provide the lifeline for operations against Nashville, Jackson, Mobile, Montgomery, and finally Atlanta, Charleston, and Richmond.

The plan, however, would need greater military genius than the Union had so far produced, and it would have to wait until such leadership could develop. More than three hundred officers of the army, most of them graduates of the military academy at West Point, had resigned as the war began in the spring of 1861. The defection of men like Robert E. Lee and Albert Sidney Johnston cost President Lincoln and the Union cause dearly, but it proved to be a greater calamity for the South in the long run, since the South might not have seceded at all had the Confederacy not been assured that it would have the heart of the federal officer corps.

Albert Sidney Johnston, born in Kentucky and a giant of a man in physique, intellect, and charm, was graduated from West Point in 1826. He fought in the Black Hawk War in 1832, during which he became acquainted with both Abraham Lincoln and Jefferson Davis.

As the war clouds darkened in the early spring of 1861, General Scott, now seventy-five years old, reported to President Lincoln that he must resign because of his advanced age. He urged Lincoln to appoint General Albert Sidney Johnston to his post. General Johnston, who had fought for Texas independence with Sam Houston, did not accept. Texas had already seceded from the Union. Unable to face the possibility of having to fight

Texans, he decided instead to follow Houston into retirement, tendering his resignation on April 10—just two days before the firing on Fort Sumter. In August, Jefferson Davis sought out his services.

Lieutenant Colonel Robert E. Lee, an army engineer who had been graduated with highest honors from the United States Military Academy in 1829, was General Scott's second choice as his successor. Lee was in Washington at the moment, and President Lincoln offered the great Virginian the command of the Union armies on April 18. Lee too resigned, offering his services instead to the Governor of Virginia.

The weeks and months of 1861 faded into memory, a year of war passed, and still no Union general appeared capable of bringing the war to a speedy conclusion.

Too, time was on the side of the South. The Confederacy was gathering strength, moving major armies into position to protect the line that extended from Austin to Vicksburg to Atlanta and north to Richmond. The Davis strategy of waiting, forcing the Yankees to come to the Confederacy to fight, looked better with each passing day.

This was the situation on the morning of Sunday, April 6, 1862. Spring was in full bloom along the Tennessee River, and the Shiloh Church community north of the Mississippi border was mantled in soft green. Around the church itself, northern forces were massing for a drive against Corinth, Mississippi, just across the state line. The federal forces were unaware that General Johnston's troops, including the 2nd Texas Volunteers, were poised south of Shiloh Church, ready to intercept the push and drive the Yankees back north. Corinth, a rail and communications hub, must be held for the Confederacy at all costs.

The Union commander, General Henry Halleck, a brilliant West Pointer, was, as usual, not to be found with his troops, despite the critical campaign about to be launched. A relatively obscure general, Ulysses S. Grant, was in command.

Print Olive had never heard of General Grant on this April

morning. This was not surprising; few persons had. Even some of those who had, including his commander, sour-faced Henry Halleck, held the forty-year-old "Sam" Grant in no particular regard.

All during the first week of April, Confederate forces from west of the mountains were converging for the attack against the Union forces massing at Pittsburg Landing. This army must be wiped out, Johnston knew, if the Union pincer fastening itself on the lower Mississippi River was to be broken.

Reveille for Johnston's forty thousand Confederates camped just south of Shiloh Church sounded early, but for thousands of the men the bugle call to action was unnecessary, so great was their excitement. A chance to "get at the Yankees," the moment they had been waiting for through long dull months of training, had arrived.

The morale of an army of the Confederacy was never higher. The idea that every Confederate was worth ten times his weight in Yankees warmed Johnston's proud, well-trained, well-equipped army like the sunshine of this April morning. There was a feeling in the ranks that the Johnston men were invincible, and they very nearly were.

Print Olive's contingent was one of the first General Johnston moved into action that historic morning. The 2nd Texas Volunteers drove against the troops of William Tecumseh Sherman, a Union general whose name Print Olive and the entire Confederacy would soon know well. Under the command of General William Hardee, Print Olive and thousands of other young southerners from farms, plantations, and ranches, never before under fire, drove north directly toward Sherman's command and around the east side of Shiloh Church. Sherman's troops were mostly green too, but he did have a core of veterans from the Union's successful Kentucky campaign. Yet, within the first two hours, the Texas volunteers had overrun Sherman's position south of Shiloh, killing the first of three mounts Sherman would lose in this battle, inflicting a painful, bloody hand wound on Sherman himself, and littering the soft grass of spring around

Shiloh Church with Union wounded and dead. In contrast, their own casualties were moderate.

The victory drive during the morning and early afternoon made a deep impression on Print Olive. Shocking as the sight of the wounded and dying must always be, fighting Yankees was exhilarating, almost like hunting longhorns in the Texas brush. Here, too, a man had to be careful or he could get badly hurt; but things moved rapidly, and the results were immediately evident. There was one important, distressing difference: in hunting longhorns the goal was to save the animals unhurt. Here the goal was to shoot to kill—men, young men just like himself, young men who bled, cried out, and died in grotesque postures, young men who had come a disturbingly long way from their homes, unaccountably, "to fight for niggers."

At nine-thirty General Grant assessed the situation and found it hard to believe that the Confederates could have attacked in such force and with such telling results in the short time since the first roar of heavy cannon reverberated at his headquarters three hours before. Impending disaster always brought out the best in U. S. Grant. As at Fort Donelson two months earlier, the usually stolid Grant became a man of quick and decisive action. He issued orders to aides for organizing fresh supplies of ammunition. He had ordered one aide to go quickly to Crump's Landing seven miles to the north, and direct General Wallace to bring his division to Shiloh at once.

The nearer to the center of action Grant rode, the more he found to do. This time, and this time only, Grant directed the battle from the front lines, disregarding his aides' frequent urging to move farther to the rear and out of such imminent danger. He rode back and forth along the fluid front lines, directing officers and men where to close this gap or blunt that Confederate charge.

His horse was shot from under him, but he continued on foot until another mount could be brought to him. A bullet tore his hat off. He took no notice, continuing to smoke his black cigar and directing the troops bareheaded. A bullet ripped the rank insignia from his shoulder. A bullet cut through the coat of his uniform, passing between his arm and body but drawing no blood.

The true military stature of Grant was showing plainly now. At the same time that he was directing the front-line defense, he was instructing his aides to make preparations for assuming the offensive. Shortly after noon an officer was dispatched to J. D. Webster, Grant's artillery chief, ordering him to ring the high ground north and west of Pittsburg Landing with heavy guns, hub to hub, preparatory to carrying on the battle all night. Grant was not only holding his battered army together; he was also planning to turn tomorrow into victory.

Print Olive, Frank Condron, and the thousands of Confederate men at Shiloh felt the impact of Grant's iron will. Though they suffered no setbacks, actual victory eluded them time after time. The Union lines would bend and crack, but they would not break beyond repair. Before noon, Union casualties had crawled and been carried to a little nameless pond to cleanse their wounds. By afternoon men of both the Blue and the Gray crowded around this small spring-fed inlet until its waters were red with blood; it acquired the name "Bloody Pond" by which it is known to this day.

General Benjamin Prentiss' division, having retreated north past the church, the peach orchard, and Bloody Pond—almost to Pittsburgh Landing itself—made its stand in a sunken roadway. The men in blue fighting from this depression, "The Hornets' Nest," were preventing a major Confederate breakthrough and protecting Grant's forces. Grant ordered Prentiss to hold onto his sunken roadway at any cost and promised him reinforcements. So desperate was the situation that Grant committed the last of his reserves, ordering General W. H. L. Wallace and his men to move into the Hornets' Nest.

Johnston, for his part, sensing that only the tenacious defense at the Hornets' Nest stood between his men and victory, decided that a few words from him, even his physical presence, could inspire the last offensive effort needed to end the battle then and there. In midafternoon he rode into the front lines, heading directly into the sagging Union right which had little more ground to lose in front of the Tennessee River.

"One more and we have them!," General Johnston called to his men at almost the same time that Grant, only a few hundred yards away, was conferring with Prentiss and Wallace. A few minutes later a rifle bullet from the Hornets' Nest struck Johnston in the thigh. Although blood filled his boot and spilled to the ground, he insisted on staying in his saddle. He was so intent on cracking the weakened Union lines that he could feel no pain. He continued to ride up and down the front with words of praise and encouragement for his tired troops.

Suddenly the General of all Confederate armies west of the Allegheny Mountains reeled and fell from his saddle. Laying him on horse blankets, aides soon discovered the terrible truth: Albert Sidney Johnston was bleeding to death, and there was nothing anyone could do to help him. Minutes later death claimed the soldier-statesman who had served under the flags of three nations, the man who stood with Sam Houston at San Jacinto to wrench independence from Mexico for the Republic of Texas, the man who served as the first Secretary of War for the Texas Republic, the man who used reason instead of bullets to end the Mormon rebellion in the Utah wilderness, the man who had been offered by Abraham Lincoln the command of all the armies of the United States. Jefferson Davis, president of the Confederacy, would speak what was in his heart and say, "He was the greatest soldier, the ablest man civil or military, Confederate or Federal," of his time—high praise from the man who also counted among his generals "Stonewall" Jackson and Robert E. Lee.

General Pierre Beauregard, the general who had first ordered Confederate cannon to fire on Sumter, was close by when Johnston went down. He took over the command so smoothly that Print Olive and Frank Condron, even in their forward positions, were not aware of the change in command until the next day. Capitalizing on the forward momentum generated by Johnston's last appeal, Beauregard continued the relentless drive against General Prentiss and his Hornets' Nest. Late in the afternoon Prentiss and the remnants of his command surrendered.

Private Print Olive and the men of the 2nd Texas Volunteers had been in the thick of the fight, first against Sherman's 1st Brigade and then against unidentified contingents all through the long day. They had driven Bluecoats steadily back north from dawn to dusk, back past the Shiloh Church and meeting house, past the peach orchard, past Lick Creek, and back through the woods where quick death lurked behind the trunk of every tree.

Following the capture of Prentiss and his men at the Hornets' Nest, the Confederate tide moved more rapidly north and crossed Little Dill Creek which ran from west to east and emptied into the river near Pittsburg Landing. The goal General Johnston had seen so clearly was at hand: compress the entire Union army against the river and force a general capitulation.

The 2nd Texas Volunteers crossed Dill Creek and moved through the wooded area beyond, into a ravine formed by a backwater from the river less than a quarter of a mile to the east. The Yankees were by now giving ground rapidly, plunging across the ravine, into the timber, and up the sharply higher ground on the other side. The bright warm weather of midday had been giving way during the afternoon to increasing cloudiness; at nightfall it began to rain.

Now as night approached, the Confederates pulled back out of the ravine and south across Dill Creek to await the morning and get as much rest as possible. They, like the Union troops, were dead tired after being under constant fire for more than twelve hours. Suddenly cannon thundered across the little ravine from the high ground west of the river, now obscured by trees and darkness. Within minutes the roar became continuous, each round of fire creating a rush of air through the trees like a sudden storm. Grant had ordered his two gunboats on the Tennessee River to pull up below Webster's cannon on the bluff, and they were providing flanking fire from their eight-inch guns.

The shower turned into a heavy thunderstorm that lasted much of the night, and the clap of thunder mingled with the roar of the Union cannon. The Texans were so far forward, so close to the heavy guns, that most of the deadly charges went overhead.

The downpour continued. There was no food—not even a campfire for warmth. Print Olive lay on the ground, his hands on his gun, attempting to get what rest he could. Whether from the cannon on the high ground to the north or the eight-inch rifles of the Union gunboats to the east he never knew, but suddenly a searing fragment ripped through the muscles of his right thigh. The metal missed the bones, inflicting a painful but not critical wound. The pain and the immediacy of his peril, however, shocked young Print into full recognition of his plight. In view of what they had seen at Bloody Pond late in the day, he and Lieutenant McGinnis, the nearest officer, agreed that such first aid as they could provide on the spot would have to suffice until morning. Then McGinnis would arrange to get him over to the field hospital for treatment.

This was a long night for the young San Gabriel longhorn hunter, a night in which fears and doubts he had never experienced before returned again and again in spite of his efforts to put them out of mind. The years with his family, their care and protection, a world in which his welfare had meant everything to those around him suddenly seemed remote and unreal. Here the individual man did not count; his very survival depended on luck—and on his fending strictly for himself. It was a night to remember.

For General Grant it was a night without pause, with little food, and without even thought of sleep. After the Hornets' Nest was surrendered late in the afternoon, Grant ordered his temporary headquarters turned over to the army doctors and their endless burden of critically wounded soldiers.

At midnight the other General Wallace—General Lew Wallace—arrived. He had been lost since noon the day before, having marched his seven thousand troops, Grant's 3rd division of the Army of Tennessee, down the wrong road out of Crump's Landing and having to retrace many a weary, time-consuming mile.

Wallace's arrival gave Grant his first opportunity to begin rebuilding his army for the second day at Shiloh. He sent Wallace's fresh troops to reinforce Sherman's badly battered western end of the line and placed General John McClernand's battle-worn 1st Division behind both Sherman and Wallace.

Shortly after midnight Grant got his first really cheering news when the 4th Division of Buell's Army of the Ohio arrived under the command of General William Nelson, a three-hundred-pound giant of a man. "Bull" Nelson greeted Grant at two A.M. good naturedly: "Here we are. If stupidity and hard fighting are what you want, we're the men."

Almost at the same time, river boats docked at Pittsburg Landing, bringing the 5th Division of the Army of the Ohio under General Thomas Crittenden. These men were rested, having traveled by boat rather than on foot. Grant assigned them to the sector right next to Nelson.

The rain diminished as Monday dawned. By five in the morning, just twenty-four hours after the battle had begun, Grant was ready.

At daybreak the Union army shifted from defense to offense.

On that second day the roles of the two armies were reversed. On Sunday the Confederate offensive had pushed the Union army back three to four miles; Monday the Union men drove the Confederates back over the same ground; Sunday the Union sustained the heaviest casualties; Monday it was the Confederates' turn.

Print Olive, his wound becoming more of a handicap with each passing hour, managed nevertheless to stay with Company H and help slow the Union advance. But by mid-morning the Texans had been forced back through what the afternoon before had been the Hornets' Nest, where they had seen the spectacle of a Union general captured with two thousand of his men. Half an hour later they were back to Bloody Pond, its shores still rimmed with torn men whose blood now dyed the water a deeper red than before. Still they had to give ground. Shortly after passing Bloody Pond, Frank Condron sustained serious wounds in the chest and had to drop out of the fighting. Print Olive did not see his friend fall, and in his own extremity, he did not notice Frank's absence until much later.

The fighting intensified as the day progressed. Yankee riflemen were everywhere north of the Texans and at times to the east and west of them as well. The ranks of the Texans were thinning. Even short sprints from tree to tree were fraught with danger, and south of them were tree trunks with two and three bodies propped against them—bodies of men who had stayed too long before moving back.

Back past the peach orchard and Shiloh Church they fled. Shortly after noon the 2nd Texas Infantry crossed Lick Creek and was back at the point from which it had launched its attack in such high spirits the morning before. Only yesterday morning, Print Olive thought—an eon ago.

In midafternoon the word came that General Beauregard had ordered the Confederate army to return to Corinth which was now safe, the general said, from Union attack. The foot soldiers were advised that Nathan Forrest's cavalry, just beginning to earn its reputation as the "shield of the Confederacy," could now contain the spent Union offensive so that the pullback could be orderly. But Corinth was twenty-five miles away, a distance that sound, rested personnel had taken a full day in good weather to traverse, Print Olive and the other Texans knew. Now there were thousands of battered men, bodies and souls lacerated by Union lead and steel; hundreds were so desperately wounded that their survival was unlikely. The weather, too, was following the pattern of the day before. Dark clouds gathered across the western sky again as evening approached. The longest night was about to begin, a night of unbelievable confusion, pain, and terror for Print Olive and most of the Confederate army pulling back toward Corinth.

Trains of baggage wagons bore men piled like cordwood, some crying out deliriously, others obviously having died since being placed on the planks. Jolting along without springs, these vehicles offered only one advantage: they were moving in the direction of Corinth. There was no food, medicine, or drinking water. And the pounding of the Union artillery continued.

The men on foot were dividing themselves into two groups—those who still had a desire to struggle toward Corinth and those past caring. Despite pain so severe he had to choke back a scream every time he put his weight on his right foot, Print Olive was determined to get to Corinth.

As darkness fell, Print came upon an artilleryman whose terrible head wounds had blinded him. He was just sitting by the road, helpless and alone. Having stopped to rest his leg, Print started to move on, but the blind man with his quiet courage haunted him. He asked the gunner if he could walk. The blind man answered that he could, but it was no use walking when he could not see. Olive found himself proposing that they become partners, Olive providing the sight for both of them, the artilleryman walking arm-in-arm on his right side to take a little weight off Olive's right leg. By now it was very dark, and a cold rain was beginning to fall.

The partnership seemed to pay dividends for both soldiers. Olive's pain was somewhat eased and the blind man was glad to be able to move again with the army. His blindness was not without some blessings; he could not see the flash of Union cannon behind them that continued to light their way, nor could he see the occasional shell that landed close and blew a hole in the mass of retreating men.

About nine o'clock the sound of cannon receded as the Union force abandoned its pursuit. In another hour only the rain broke the silence. But the worst of the night was yet to come.

About midnight the temperature suddenly dropped, and sleet began to fall, giving way to hail that continued intermittently for nearly three hours. The hailstones, some of them an inch across, pounded the Confederates like spent rifle slugs, more immediately painful, most soldiers claimed, than bullets driven through the skin.

The blind artilleryman had said little during the long night trek and had murmured not at all at his pain. At the peak of the storm, however, feeling faint, he asked if Olive could find him a tree by the side of the road where he could rest a few minutes. Others had the same idea, and it was not easy to find a sheltering tree trunk. But in time Print found an unoccupied spot and helped his blind companion to a sitting position on the side of the tree affording the most protection. Olive himself gratefully rested nearby. Almost an hour passed before the storm slackened enough so that they could again take to the road.

In the darkness it took a minute or two to find the tree where he had put the artilleryman down to rest. There he found him —dead.

Eventually the storm stopped and daylight came. Everything was quiet for the first time since the Texans had charged into battle on Sunday morning, certain that they could lick the Yankees before noon. But daylight was powerless to dispel the memory of that terrifying night on the Corinth road, a night that could never be forgotten by any southerners who survived it.

Back at Corinth the Confederate army nursed its wounds and gathered strength to fend off the Union assault expected at any time. But, strangely, the attack did not come that second week in April, nor the next week, nor the one following that. Print Olive grew restless. His wound was better, and he could move about with greater ease. Often he would go to the yards where the regimental horses were kept, helping to feed and groom the animals just to pass the time. Anyway, he preferred being with horses to "playing cards and telling lies," as he later described the waiting period in the Mississippi town.

The officers observed his willingness to take on extra work with the teams. They noticed too that he had a way with horses. In a day or two the animals he cared for were following him around almost like dogs. Since good horsemen could never be too numerous in an army that depended upon horses for transport, Print was transferred from Company H of the Texas infantry to the regimental teamsters.. Here he was assigned a team and baggage wagon to manage and drive.

Frank Condron was in the army's rest camp, recovering from chest wounds incurred the second day of battle. Print visited him almost every day. Still the attack on Corinth did not come, and Olive was free to lavish time on the horses. He led them out to graze for hours after each day's work was done. Soon the team was in better condition than any of the others attached to the company. It was a good thing too: there was a lot of traveling ahead.

At last, by the end of May General Henry Halleck, who had come from his St. Louis headquarters to take over field command from General Grant, seemed ready to attack the Confederate army at Corinth. Halleck had not moved out of Pittsburg Landing at all until early May; then he had used up twenty days to advance south about twenty miles. President Lincoln agonized over the delay in pursuing Beauregard's army. U. S. Grant was so discouraged that he decided to resign from the army, but his friend Sherman prevailed upon him to be patient and await further developments. Lincoln, Grant, and Sherman, although not in direct communication, were worrying about the most important resource at the disposal of any army: time.

Meanwhile, General Beauregard's cavalry scouts kept him well informed as to Halleck's activities. They reported that by the end of May, General Halleck had reinforced the Shiloh army until he had at least one hundred thousand men ready to throw against Corinth. Beauregard at best could count no more than sixty thousand in his defending army, about half of whom had successfully retreated from Shiloh. So on the last day of May, while appearing to be making ready for a stout defense, he skillfully pulled his army out of the railroad and communications center and retreated south down the Mobile Road, known today as U.S. Route 45, to a point near Tupelo, Mississippi, here to build up his army until he could retake Corinth. His disengaging movement was known as the first Battle of Corinth, little more than a creation in Halleck's report to headquarters when he finally occupied the city.

The summer passed. By September the army and the 2nd

Texas Volunteer Infantry with its baggage wagons were on the move back north. There were preliminary battles at Farmington and Iuka in the vicinity of Corinth. Then, during the first week in October, occurred the second Battle of Corinth, this time with the Confederates attempting to dislodge the Yankee defenders.

Print Olive "fought" this battle at a safe distance—from the seat of his baggage wagon. He had an eyewitness position on October 4, as his regiment was thrown into a tragic assault on the fortifications. Before his eyes, half the men of his 2nd Texas Volunteer Infantry regiment were mowed down by Union lead as Colonel Rogers and his officers and men hurled themselves into a brave but useless frontal attack. Having returned to active duty, Frank Condron emerged from the debacle without injury.

The Confederate forces now retreating south in the direction of Jackson, the centrally located capital of Mississippi, escaped being overrun only by astute rear-guard action by the horse soldiers of Nathan Forrest. November, and still the Confederates dragged painfully south. Of Olive's regiment, only 250 of the 1,300 who marched up to Shiloh Church in the spring remained. Hunger was becoming a more formidable foe than the Union raiding parties. At Coffeyville, where the townspeople piled food on picnic tables on the main street, the soldiers ate well for the first time in weeks.

Despite the shortage of supplies, Print somehow managed to keep his team in good condition. Constantly on the move under short rations, many of the regimental teams weakened and had to be shot. But Print always found a little special forage or grain for his horses, often secured in the evening after the team was unhitched.

By mid-December the retreating troops had reached Grenada, the most important city still in Confederate hands on the Memphis-to-Jackson road. Here Print and the troops were issued full rations again and received new clothing and supplies. Here too, a few days before Christmas of 1862, President Jefferson Davis paid the army a visit, singling out the 2nd Texas Volunteers for special commendation. "Other troops have a reputation to gain," he said, "but the soldiers of the 2nd Texas Infantry

Regiment have a reputation to sustain." The Texans responded with cheers and the songs of the hour.

By Christmas week the pattern of retreat began once more. The Texans were headed south through Jackson and on to Vicksburg, but this time they were traveling in railroad cars, leaving Grant's Yankee pursuers far behind. They were in higher spirits than they had been since that April day when they had first pushed off toward Shiloh. They could not know that throughout the long winter and the entire spring they would try to defend Vicksburg, first from its perimeter and then from within its precincts, only to lose the city at great cost. It was not until July 4, 1863, that General John C. Pemberton capitulated to General Grant, following a conference held the day before at almost the very hour that General Lee's final charge failed at Gettysburg. Grant decided that Pemberton's army should first be taken prisoner and then be offered parole as individuals. The only condition attached to their release was that they agree not to fight the Union again. Those who wanted to preserve their status as belligerents in good standing could refuse to sign the parole slips and be sent to a prisoner-of-war camp. Officers electing to sign were allowed to keep side arms and personal property; cavalry officers were permitted to take one horse. For his generosity, Grant was criticized, curiously enough, as much in the South as in the North.

Olive and Condron and thousands of other young men like them had assumed until that morning, July 4, that even should they be forced to surrender, they would be transferred to a prisoner-of-war camp: they would still be a part of the war. To be faced suddenly with the choice of going home raised all sorts of complications. Olive and Condron quickly agreed on one thing: they could not face returning to Williamson County as beaten Confederate soldiers from a war that had not yet been acknowledged lost on the home front. They would be laughed at, and it would be unfair to their families.

Their officers understood the problem. Major N. L. McGinnis of the 2nd Texas Infantry suggested a plan: take the parole and reassemble at the wharf in Galveston where there would be work to do for Texas no matter who won the war. The McGinnis plan was good enough for Olive, but Condron did not want to go back to Texas until the war was over. Then, he argued, everybody would be going home, win or lose, and all would be accepted. Condron did not sign the parole but went to the prisoner-of-war camp with more than one-fifth of the Confederates who fought at Vicksburg. This choice between parole and maintaining full status as a belligerent brought the first open split between the two boys who had vowed to see the war through together.

It was Tuesday, July 7, before the paper work and other preparations were completed. All arms carried by the Texas regulars were stacked in front of the 2nd Texas Lunette fort, and Print Olive signed the parole which read:

> Vicksburg, Mississippi
> July 7th, 1863
>
> To All Whom It May Concern, Know Ye That:
>
> I, Isom P. Olive, a Private of Company H, Regiment 2nd Texas Volunteers, C.S.A., being a Prisoner of War in the hands of the United States Forces, in virtue of the capitulation of the City of Vicksburg and its garrison, by Lieut. Gen. John C. Pemberton, C.S.A., commanding on the 4th Day of July, 1863, do in pursuance of the terms of said capitulation give this my solemn parole under oath
>
> —That I will not take up arms against the United States, . . .
>
> > Sworn and subscribed before me at Vicksburg, Mississippi, this 7th day of July, 1863—
> > Geo. W. Goddard
> > Capt., Co. C, 31st
> > Regt. Illinois Vols.
> > SIGNED—Isom P. Olive

The career of Private Isom Prentice Olive spanned what some have called the most decisive period of the long war. Privates

Olive and Condron and their 2nd Texas Volunteers were in combat for 454 historic days, from dawn on April 6, 1862, until noon on July 4, 1863. Before that April morning the Confederacy had suffered no critical defeat, and the Union had won no decisive victory. From that day forward, although the great conflict lasted almost two more years, the Confederacy won no important victory and the Union suffered no major defeat. Print Olive saw the Confederacy die. He knew its cause was lost, and with that knowledge a vital part of the boy known by his family and friends vanished forever.

From the same terrible crucible Ulysses S. Grant emerged as the general that Lincoln had waited for, General-in-Chief of the Armies of the United States. He had destroyed the Confederacy's foremost general at Shiloh and his remaining army at Vicksburg. He had opened the Mississippi River so that, as Lincoln had said, the great stream might "flow unfettered to the sea."

In defeat, Print Olive headed south and west out of Vicksburg toward Texas. Victorious, Sherman headed east toward Atlanta and the sea.

With his parole slip in his pocket and the rest of his possessions in a blanket roll on his back, Olive walked down the road toward Natchez. He stayed on the east side of the Mississippi River for a time until he came to a place where the big stream narrowed and there were logs close enough to the water's edge to make possible the floating of a small raft on which he crossed to the Louisiana side.

He elected to head west along the Vicksburg-to-Monroe railroad for easier walking. He did not know in whose hands the railroad might be, but he had not gone far when he was halted by a Confederate sentry of the outfit known as Walker's Greyhounds, little more than a large raiding party compared to the Pemberton army Olive had just left. It was the job of the Greyhounds to resist the Union occupation of Louisiana.

Print soon learned that he was almost a man without a country. The sentry took him to the captain of the Greyhounds, who had expected the collapse at Vicksburg but had not yet encountered anyone carrying a parole slip. Though Olive was no longer of any value to the Confederacy, the officer said that he could move west with the Greyhounds and eat with the rest of the soldiers. Before they reached Monroe in north central Louisiana, on July 14, the company had picked up other Vicksburg parolees, some of them from Olive's former outfit.

The Greyhounds moved on west, but, before the end of July, Print Olive and two other paroled soldiers set out for Galveston, arriving less than three weeks later, about the middle of August.

Major McGinnis was already at Galveston and expressed great pleasure upon seeing Print, who was soon back at his old job of driving a team and wagon. Although at least half of the men of the Texas Volunteers had gone straight home, there were enough left to take over responsibility for guarding the important dock area. Galveston had been in Union hands during the previous fall, but General John B. Magruder had retaken this most important of Texas ports for the Confederacy on January 1, 1863, and there were Union sympathizers in the area willing to cause the Confederate parole troops every possible trouble when they came to his aid. Magruder was woefully short of troops, his command numbering in the hundreds rather than thousands of soldiers. Major McGinnis, knowing this, offered his paroled men from Vicksburg an opportunity to serve the Confederate army as guard troops for the docks at Galveston.

If any heavy fighting had developed in the Galveston area, the 2nd Texas Volunteers would have been back shooting at the Union army in violation of their parole terms, and everyone, including Print Olive, knew it. At times he even hoped for such a development as one way to end the boredom. But the United States, relying chiefly upon a blockade to control the Gulf Coast for the remainder of the war, left "Prince John" Magruder and his Texans alone.

Boredom became a major problem within a few weeks. Print often wondered how Frank Condron was getting along; perhaps Frank had been right after all. Print could have walked away from Galveston almost any day, but he could not bring himself to go home until the war was over, one way or another.

In Galveston, Print confronted many temptations that he was ill-prepared to face. There was little alternative to visiting the taverns and houses of prostitution along the harbor front as an escape from the lethargy and depression that his situation imposed. In some ways, Print thought, the army service in Galveston was just as dangerous in the long run as fighting up front.

By the end of 1864, the South, even as far west as Galveston, was being increasingly overrun by men on the move. These were the dregs of battered and crushed army units of both North and South, roving individually or in small gangs who ran together like dog packs. Most of these renegades, who would wantonly kill a man or ravage a woman, had been respectable citizens before the catastrophic war. The brutal pillage of the South was beginning; a down payment on the price of defeat. By early 1865, every man of the old 2nd Texas Volunteers who was determined to live carried a loaded revolver and carried it all the time—on duty, to the tavern, or even when he went to see a girl. Men who did not recognize this necessity often disappeared forever or turned up floating in the water or jammed under the wharf.

In these months when depression and desperation often closed in on him completely, Print formed many of the attitudes that would govern his actions all the rest of his life. An atmosphere of guarded suspicion or outright hostility hung in the air. The only way, he concluded, to keep from being constantly victimized was never to trust anyone completely. Above all else, he must depend upon himself and never forget that in the last analysis, since right is on the side of might, he would go armed.

Only eternal watchfulness, a six-shooter, and a quick draw made it possible for Print to drive his team outside the fortified area or go on foot along the docks after hours of guard duty. Use of a gun was hardly respectable in the golden years, but the brutalizing effects of mass killing and the lesson it taught that life was cheap were not without their influence. For Print, like many another young Texan, his revolver became his boon companion.

Although the great struggle between North and South dragged on through the early months of 1865, to the Confederates in Galveston and elsewhere on the western sector, the war had receded to a relatively small area along the East Coast. The question now on both sides was little more than how long Richmond could be held. The men in Galveston would stay as long as General Lee was in Richmond, but when the Confederacy had to give up Richmond, they would go home.

The defense of their homes assumed urgent priority in the minds of men who witnessed the gradual disintegration of order in the wake of war. As the lines of authority crumbled, every man became a law unto himself, committed to the protection of his own life, property, and loved ones. The situation was most difficult for the Texans who had families in the coastal areas more exposed to the ravages of war. On the Texas frontier in the longhorn country, the practice was long established that each family and each community must look after its own. Even so, Olive wondered what he might find when he got home.

On Sunday and Monday, the 2nd and 3rd of April, General Lee pulled his army out of Richmond; by the middle of the week the word had reached the Texas waterfront. Some of the officers and men who had no families would stay on to maintain what order they could and guard the army warehouses until the federal troops arrived to take charge of everything. The others were free to go home.

Print Olive turned in his team and wagon, loaded a haversack with as much food as he could carry, made room in it for an extra six-shooter, and began the walk west toward Austin and the longhorn country. Evidence of the war was everywhere, but after he turned north from the Galveston-Austin road toward the San Gabriel River he saw fewer stragglers and less devastation. Two weeks later Print Olive was home.

Four long years had worked many changes at home that the returning soldier could not anticipate. His mother and father looked much older. When he had gone into the army his sister Betty had been a young mother with two small children;

there had been two teen-age brothers at home, Jay and Ira; two small children, Alice and Bobby; and one infant, Marion. When he returned, Print somehow expected them to be unchanged. Instead, Betty was a war widow. She seemed middle-aged. With her two now half-grown children, she had come back to live with her parents. The two teen-age brothers at the war's beginning were now grown men. Jay, soon to be married to a neighbor's daughter, was twenty-two, and handling many of the jobs that had been Print's.

Bob was no longer a little boy but a big fellow ten years old whose head nearly came up to Print's shoulder. Even Marion, an infant in the cradle in 1861, was now an active lad of nearly four. Finally there was an additional sister, whom Print had never seen. Isabella had been born while Print was away and was still an infant in Julia's arms.

Everything was awkward, the more so since no one wanted to talk about the war, least of all Print. Even when soldiers come home victorious, discussion of the war experience is often too difficult to provide a conversational bridge between the long parted. Returning from a war that had been lost made it an even more difficult matter to discuss. In the first days at home Print wondered if there really was any place for him at all, Jay and Ira having grown up and become so capable in all phases of the family business.

Julia wisely insisted that everyone leave Print alone for a few days. He was tired, she knew, not only from his trip back from Galveston, but from being so long without hope. He found it hard to meet her eyes. His first need was for rest and food. Julia saw how much of her son's confidence in himself and others had been destroyed. How much of it he would regain she could not know. He must be led back into the family circle, but the means by which this could be done were not immediately clear to her.

Finally, it was Betty who provided the key. As the days passed she found that she could talk to her brother. She of all the family had suffered most from the war. Her young husband had died in a Union prison camp. Seeing the collapse of her dreams, she still had to rebuild a life for herself and her children. In their talks, short at first, Betty always emphasized how proud the family was of Print for having stuck it out and how fortunate they were to have been spared the actual devastation of the war itself. They had no burned buildings to restore, and their herds were not only intact but actually had increased during the war years.

Most of all, she impressed Print by her realistic approach to the present and the future. Not trying to cover up or gloss over things that were true and could not be changed, she talked freely of the adjustment they all had to make; their great personal sacrifice was only part of a greater price paid by the entire South. She explained how their parents had aged under the strain and how important it was for Print to be back and take over some of the responsibility for maintaining the big family. "How important it was for Print to be back." Those were the magic words that got through to him.

In time Print began talking more freely to her, and slowly his communication with everyone in the family began to return. Soon he was the idol of the younger children, especially of his brother Bob, who followed him everywhere. The children even got him to talking about the lighter side of his experiences in the war.

Bob, particularly, was at an age to be fascinated with Print's two army revolvers, asking again and again to be allowed to handle them. It was natural that his young brother would notice the six-shooters; Print always had one of them within reach.

[3]

HOOFBEATS ALONG THE PLATTE

THE DAY CAME when Jim Olive suggested that Print and he spend a day just riding through the San Gabriel brush to have Print appraise the longhorn situation. Leaving before noon, the two men headed south to Yegua Creek, turning west upstream, finally swinging north to Brushy Creek and back home.

Jay and Ira had told Print that the herds had increased during the war years, but the Confederate veteran found it hard to believe what his father showed him. During the day's ride over a route where they would have been lucky to see fifteen hundred or two thousand head before Print left for the army, they saw at least four thousand longhorns. Only a few were branded, and most of those bore Olive markings. Print pronounced them the best longhorns he had ever seen. They were in good condition, some of them even fat. Most of the full-grown animals he estimated at a thousand pounds or more, and some he thought might top fifteen hundred. Some had horn spreads of six feet.

The war had isolated the longhorn breeding grounds. Hunters had gone to war in search of human quarry, and the westward movement had been suspended. Behind an invisible barrier the wild cattle had increased until the San Gabriel country was literally an inland sea of longhorns, millions on millions of tons of beef for which a great demand would exist for years to come. All that remained to be done was to hunt the cattle and get them to markets that would be bigger than ever before, now that the great rivers to the north were open again to traffic. But hunting and shipping the large volume of cattle was more than old Jim felt he could handle any longer. He wanted Print to see the size of the herds and prepare himself for handling the business once again—this time on a far grander basis.

That evening seemed more like old times around the Olive supper table. The sight of all those longhorns had for the first time blurred Print Olive's memories of the war. His confidence and even a little of his old humor had been restored, and his mother was happier with her family than she had been for years.

Shortly after the trip through the brush and across the prairie, Jim Olive called Print, Jay, and Ira together. He reminded them that before Print left for the army he had been promised that there would be a full share of the Olive herd for him when he returned. Jim asked Jay for a report on the number of animals they had under brand. Jay estimated that the total had to be close to four thousand head, including cows, young stock, and old bulls that would go to the tallow dealers.

Jim Olive told his sons that since he was now more than sixty years old, he had no business hunting longhorns, and he was anxious for Print to resume his management of the production end of the business. He called his sons' attention to a hazard: the brush was almost as full of longhorn thieves as it was of longhorns. Not only would the thieves steal branded cattle, but many of them were gun-happy drifters and army deserters who made it dangerous even to be in the brush. Jay and Ira confirmed what their father reported. Print said he had learned that a six-shooter could solve a lot of problems; they would have to take steps to protect their own herds. They would need to build a new hunting organization, Print said, and they would have to get loyal men who were experts with guns so that the word could be passed along that Olive longhorns were not fair game.

One of the first men Print hired was Jim Whitehead, like himself a Confederate veteran, though he had served with the horse soldiers. Whitehead was a level-headed man. He knew the long-horn business, and he was also an expert with a six-shooter. Olive soon made Whitehead herd foreman.

Within a few days Print hired another man who would be extremely important to his business and to him personally for years to come. He was James Kelly, the son of "Uncle" Amos and "Aunt" Phoebe Kelly, the free Negroes who had worked for Print's parent shortly after they came to the San Gabriel country and had named their only son James in recognition of the fine things Jim and Julia Olive had done for them. Young Jim Kelly had spent the war years in west Texas but had recently come back to Williamson County. He was a few years younger than Print, a powerful, muscular man, thoroughly skilled with long-horns, mustangs, and six-shooters. He would need all three of his specialties in his years with Print Olive, and he would come to know Olive better than did any other man.

Late in the summer Print drove his first postwar herd of longhorns south to the Gulf Coast, where he was sure there would be a market for the beef. In September, during his absence, his brother Jay married Elmira Gardner. Print was sorry to have missed the wedding, but he called on the young couple as soon as he returned, and throughout his life felt a warm, brotherly affection for Elmira.

The marketing trip had turned out well, and Print was deter-mined to increase the size of the Olive herd rapidly. One day shortly after his return, while hunting in the Yegua Creek bottom south of their ranch, he came upon a couple of cowboys driv-ing about a hundred head of cattle downstream in a south-easterly direction. Perhaps a third of the longhorns carried the Olive brand. Print rode around the cattle in order to have a chance to talk to the cowboy leading the herd. He inquired of the cowboy where he was taking the cattle and whether he had evidence of purchase of the animals with the Olive brand. Just as one of Olive's own cowboys rode up, the stranger reached for his gun, firing point-blank at Print, who returned the fire. The cowboy fell from his horse with one slug in his chest and another in the shoulder. Print was unhurt, but he had fired on another man for the first time as a civilian.

While Olive stopped the stranger's bleeding, he sent his man to get a spring wagon. Questioning the cowboy, Print learned that his name was Rob Murday, and that he was driving the cattle to Hogeye, a point farther south on the road to the Gulf ports, for the Turners of the Yegua Creek area. Olive drove the injured man to the doctor's office in Lexington. The doctor removed the bullets and kept the patient in his home until Murday was able to travel. Once able to get about, Murday came to the Olive ranch, convinced Print Olive that he had nothing to do with the actual theft by the Turners, and was hired as a cowhand. This proved to be the beginning of a long association.

The Murday incident was a harbinger of many events to come. Although Murday filed no charges against Print Olive and refused to testify against his employer, the authorities in Georgetown, the county seat, secured a grand jury indictment against the Confederate war veteran on charges of assault with intent to commit murder. Williamson County had voted against secession, and some of its officials still had strong feelings against the young men who had fought for the Confederacy. Jim Olive, whose sympathy was known to be with the Union, always had open channels in the county seat and on several occasions had to go personally to extricate Print and his other sons from difficulties.

The indictment, with the threat of early trial, nearly caused Print to miss his own wedding. The summer after his return from the army, Print had met Louisa Reno, orphaned when her father lost his life in the war, and living with her grandfather north of the Olive community. They had become engaged in the fall, and Louisa had set the date of their wedding for February 4, 1866. After the gun battle with Murday, the same date was selected for the trial. The trial date was set ahead, however, and the wedding took place as originally planned. Eventually the charges against Print were dropped, since neither Murday nor anyone else wished to press the case.

Louisa Reno Olive was a strong but sensitive woman. Their marriage was a happy one, although Print's longhorn business seldom permitted him to be home for any extended period. Louisa Olive was a capable homemaker, and the wife of a longhorn man was never at a loss for creative tasks. She was a gracious hostess with a remarkable capacity for thinking of the comfort and welfare of those around her. Whenever illness befell a neighbor, Louisa Reno Olive was likely to be the first to arrive and the last to leave.

Only one major difference ever arose between Print and Louisa. She tried again and again to get him to cease the practice of always wearing his six-shooters, even when he was not on the longhorn hunts. She discussed the matter even before they were married, pursuing it many times while they lived in Texas and afterward when they lived in Nebraska and at Dodge City. But always Print would argue that he could not afford to be without his gun. So he continued to wear Colt six-shooters jammed into his wartime holster with its CSA monogram—Confederate States of America—showing plainly.

By the summer of 1867 rumors were stirring in longhorn country of a market more lucrative than those on the Gulf Coast. The new Union Pacific Railroad being built up the Platte Valley in Nebraska, with a second line across northern Kansas, spelled opportunity all the way south to Texas. One of the most attentive listeners to these reports was Print Olive. Cattle fattened on the plains might now be sold in Kansas City or Chicago. The growing demand for longhorn meat in populous sections of the North was little short of fantastic. As a result animals that were worth no more than $5.00 to $7.00 in Texas could be sold at the sidings along the Union Pacific or Kansas Pacific for $15.00, $20.00—even $25.00 per head. For longhorn men already in operation, the cost of driving herds up the Chisholm or Texas trails was inconsequential when the number of animals involved was two thousand or more. Many enterprising cattlemen had begun a yearly northward drive. Herds of three thousand were considered ideal, and when a greater number were being moved, they were usually divided into independent herds of three or four thousand each. Some of these moved up the Chisholm Trail within sight of the Olive pens at Thrall, and Print and his brothers were eager to join the procession.

In the summer of 1868, Print sent the first Olive herd north. It was not large, but the undertaking proved profitable. Print came back from Kansas with visions of wealth the family had never dreamed of. Longhorns out of the San Gabriel country had moved south to the ports on the Gulf of Mexico—New Orleans, Galveston, Mobile—ever since white men had come to the area. By 1868, the stream of longhorns was reversed; it now flowed north.

In the spring of 1869, Print Olive had his first chance to join in a drive all the way up to the Platte Valley and the Union Pacific. Organized by Captain E. L. Price, the trail herd of two thousand included eight hundred head of Olive cattle. The drive terminated at Fort Kearny, Nebraska.

After the longhorns had been delivered, Print Olive and Jim Kelly, who had accompanied him, rode on north of the Platte River into what are today Buffalo, Custer, Valley, and Sherman counties. The Texans were amazed at what they saw. In the creek and river bottoms the bluestem grass reached to the shoulders of their horses. On the hills, hock deep, grew buffalo grass which even Texans knew had wintered a larger number of buffalo per square mile than any other grass on the continent. Jim Kelly described what they saw as the "Jordan range for sure 'nough." They had ridden a hundred miles without seeing many cattle or one single settler. And all this open range was within one day's drive of the Union Pacific.

Print reasoned that the Platte country with its grass, its water, and its more moderate summers was the answer to his dreams of expansion. He could start a herd out of Williamson County early in the Texas spring while the Platte was still snowbound. The trip north would be easier then, with the fresh green grass coming up all along the route. By the time the longhorns reached the Platte Valley, the bluestem would be hip deep. The cattle could be summered on this bounty and then shipped to Omaha,

Kansas City, or Chicago via the Union Pacific late in the summer or early in the fall. The figures running through Print's mind told him that good young longhorns on the Platte would be safe from Texas cattle thieves. Free of summer heat, they could gain up to a hundred pounds, at least double the rate of gain for the same period in Texas. They would be worth an additional $3.00 to $4.00 a head. Even one ordinary herd of two or three thousand animals, after a summer on the Platte could easily bring an additional $5,000 to $7,000 at the end of the season—more profit than the entire Olive operation had been making in a year.

Returning to Kearney from their explorations, Print and Kelly checked out the money, mostly in gold coins, for the eight hundred cattle they had driven north with Captain Price. Even after their trail expenses were deducted, they had something more than $15,000 to store away in their saddlebags. "And they start banks with $10,000!" Print Olive told Kelly. Without question they had found the Jordan range.

PART TWO

THE GOLD TRAIL

[4]
THE CHISHOLM TRAIL

IT WOULD BE NATURAL to assume that the Chisholm Trail took its name from some cattleman or legendary cowboy who led the first great herds up the trail, but nothing could be further from the truth. Jesse Chisholm was neither cattleman nor cowboy; he never owned more than a few horses or cattle, and then only as an expedient. He was an Indian trader, operating primarily in the territory, between Texas and Kansas, that later became Oklahoma. He traveled a regular route north and south for several years between two important Indian trading posts located roughly where Oklahoma City, Oklahoma, and Wichita, Kansas, are found today. Chisholm sold to the Indians the "white man's things" which Indians wanted and needed, exchanging these items mainly for furs, hides, and occasionally a horse or cow, sometimes even a small herd of horses or cattle to be sold at the first place he could find a buyer.

As the longhorn drives to the north began in 1867, the Texas cowboys were glad, when they reached northern Texas and the Oklahoma Territory, to use the route taken by Jesse Chisholm to Kansas. The trail took them where they needed to go, and there was no other north-south trail in existence. When the presence of the Union Pacific in the Platte Valley and its branch across northern Kansas began attracting cattle from all over south Texas, the route became a thousand miles long, with scores of little feeder branches coming into the main trail, especially toward its southern extremity.

The cowboys called their route "Chisholm's Trail," despite the fact that Jesse Chisholm himself traveled over scarcely more than one hundred and fifty miles of the trail that finally touched three nations, bisecting the United States and reaching from Mexico on the south and into Canada on the north.

For a few years the original trail bearing the Chisholm name was fairly well defined and constant. Starting at the Rio Grande on the Texas boundary with Mexico, it ran north past Austin, Georgetown, and the Olive cattle pens, past Fort Worth, through the Indian territory, and on to Abilene, Kansas. Then, as settlers began pushing in from the east, taking over the land and building across the original route, the trail had to be relocated to the west—always to the west—although the southern, or supply, end remained fairly stable for a much longer time. This explains how it was that the Chisholm Trail continued for a decade to run past the Olive pens east of Georgetown in the San Gabriel country while its northern end curved constantly to the west. At first each important westward variation of the great trail had a name of its own: the Texas Trail, Goodnight-Loving Trail, Dodge Trail, Western Trail, and many others. But in the end they all became the Chisholm Trail in cowboy parlance. By 1885 the Longhorn Trail south of the Platte was virtually nonexistent, and the pressure always from the east had forced Ogallala, Nebraska, to be closed down as a hub of cattle operations in favor of Cheyenne to the west in Wyoming Territory. Thus Abilene, Ellsworth, and Dodge City in Kansas, Trail City and Julesburg in Colorado, North Platte and Ogallala in Nebraska, Cheyenne and Sheridan in Wyoming, Miles City and Crow Agency in the Montana Territory, even Moose Jaw and Milestone in Saskatchewan, successively took on the attributes of "cow towns," and successively became established in the lore of the Old West.

Cowpunchers soon learned that the announcement "I came up

the Chisholm Trail" instantly gave them a place apart from other men, almost like being presented as a member of a Mayflower family.

On the trail there were usually eight cowboys against thousands of longhorns in a herd. Two of the men, called pointers, rode ahead of the animals. Each of these two had two others, called swing men, working behind him alongside the cattle. Then came the drag drivers, two cowboys bringing up the rear. These eight were supported by the boss, a cook, and a horse wrangler —eleven in all, specks on the perimeter of a solid mass of cattle.

E. C. "Teddy Blue" Abbott, a great cowboy reared in the Platte Valley near Lincoln, who came up the Texas Trail with one herd of Olive longhorns, used to talk of the perils of the trail. Of one tragic stampede that he witnessed, he said,

> Look at the chances they took and the kind of riding they done, all the time, over rough country. . . . It was [often] riding at a dead run in the dark, with cut banks and prairie dog holes all around you, not knowing if the next jump would land you in a shallow grave.
>
> We were camped close to the Blue River one night, near a big prairie dog town. And that night it come up an awful storm. It took all of us to hold the cattle and we didn't hold them, and when morning come there was one man missing. We went back to look for him, and we found him among the prairie dog holes, beside his horse. The horse's ribs was scraped bare of hide, and all the rest of the horse and man was mashed into the ground as flat as a pancake. The only thing you could recognize was the handle of his six-shooter.

As if the handling the longhorns did not pose enough problems, cowboys on the trail had to fight a wide range of natural conditions—dust, winds, drought, floods, and lightning. Of these Teddy Blue Abbott said,

> They used to have terrible storms on the North and South Platte . . . in '82 I was in one that killed fourteen head of cattle and six or seven horses and two men.
>
> One man was so scared he threw his six-shooter away, for fear it would draw lightning; and I remember old Matt Winter, with the rain apouring down and the lightning flashing, taking off his hat and yelling at God Almighty: "All right, you old bald-headed son-of-a-bitch up there, if you want to kill me, come on and do it." It scared the daylights out of the rest of us too.

[5]

ONLY QUICK GUNS COUNT

By the time Print Olive and Jim Kelly returned to Williamson County from their trip to the Platte country, their saddlebags bulging with Yankee gold, young Bob had become a great concern to his parents and brothers. Having turned fourteen, he was big for his age, and he was carrying a six-shooter everywhere he went. Jim and Julia feared their young son was becoming a gun-carrying tough, but they knew that it was Print to whom Bob would look for the final cut of the sails. Bob was quick to point out that Print always wore his gun, a practice to which few persons other than Julia and Louisa objected, since he had always shown restraint in its use and he bore heavy responsibilities. The matter had to be settled, but the showdown had been delayed until Print returned.

While he could be firm with Bob on occasion, Print had more sympathy for his younger brother than he cared to express openly. Bob was doing a man's work on the hunts now, and he needed his gun. Before the war, the men had carried guns, but then they were used to kill lobo wolves, put a steer with a broken leg out of its misery, or bring down some small game for supper. Now to be without a gun in the brush was to invite theft of the catch or an attack on one's person.

Print felt, however, that young Bob made too much show of his gun around home and at socials, and he said so. It was against the law to carry a gun in Texas now, a stricture viewed by legitimate longhorn men as some of the "eastern justice" imported by Union carpetbaggers.

The real reason, then, that Print did not take Bob's gun away from him was that he knew it was needed. Looting and killing continued in the war's aftermath. The situation, Print found, was worse than it had been in Galveston. The human wolf packs, made up of wrecked men from both North and South, were better organized now. Most were a pitiful lot, but they became deadly when ruthless ringleaders got hold of them and directed their activities. They had more power in certain areas than the county authorities or the Texas Rangers.

Gangs of these lawless men were operating in the wooded areas along both Yegua and Brushy creeks. Williamson County authorities were too few, too divided, too weak, and too far away to provide any law and order in these creek bottoms that were alive with wild longhorns worth up to five dollars apiece in gold. Only a few weeks before Print Olive and Jim Kelly had left for the Platte country, the Yegua rustlers had ridden into the big Olive pens north of the Olive community and turned the cattle loose. These animals had even been road branded, making it unlikely that anyone but an Olive would be handling them again in Texas. It took days of hard riding to round up the cattle, and after the roundup twenty or thirty of the big animals were still missing. It was then that Print called his men together and issued orders for them each to carry a six-shooter and a repeating rifle whenever they were hunting cattle or driving them in from the pasture for the night. This danger of night raiding was so widespread in southern Texas that Texans who had gone north and settled permanently in places like Colorado, Nebraska, or Montana continued to drive their stock in each night even though non-Texans trustingly let their herds graze in the open.

Sheriff Sam Strayhorn at Georgetown did the best he could, but, like Sheriff Jim Brown in Lee County, to the south, he was powerless to give protection to the Olives or any other ranchers in the vicinity. There were twenty or more farmer-cattlemen in eastern Williamson County, but the Olives were the only ones in the longhorn business on a large scale. Conspicuous for the size and number of their herds, the Olive operations were therefore most vulnerable. Only guns, constantly available and expertly used, could insure their safety. Bob kept his gun.

Among their neighbors, Print's family counted many friends. Fred Smith, a bachelor, had waited until he could build a log house before bringing his mother and two half-brothers to Williamson County. Print and his brothers led in organizing a house raising for Fred, and soon the Smith family was all together in their new home in the northwest part of the Olive community. Smith got into the longhorn business in a modest way, went on hunts with the Olives, and was soon doing well for one who had so recently begun.

Then there was Henry Hoyle, who was more of a farmer than a longhorn man. The relationship between Hoyles and the Olives was close. Henry was a man to get around to the parties and the house raisings. He heard the community gossip, reporting promptly anything unfavorable to the Olives' interests and relaying any useful intelligence as he heard it. In return, Henry Hoyle's few longhorns always went to market right along with the Olive cattle, and Henry always got the full price, with no deduction for market services.

The Olives were remarkably well regarded by their neighbors, considering they were the rich family in the community and that many of the new families were of modest means. Jim and Julia were looked upon as the real pioneers of the area by this time and as the hub of the community.

In 1870, several of the herds belonging to the Olives and their neighbors moved up the Chisholm Trail and on to Kansas and the Platte country. These herds were not large compared to some that would move north later in the 1870s; but, each time, the men returned with saddlebags stretched tight around Yankee gold coins too numerous to count. They were weighed by the pound. By now Isabella was going on seven, and the children of the Olive neighborhood often came to play in the spacious Olive home. On one occasion when they became bored and needed a new game, Julia went into her bedroom and dragged out a sack full of twenty-dollar gold pieces, telling the children that they might play they were in Paris and could buy anything they wanted.

The longhorn men were bringing so much gold back to Texas that it was quickening the pace of recovery from the war. A new sense of independence rode down the trail with that gold, an independence which the carpetbaggers were compelled to respect. Nevertheless, there were problems connected with owning so much gold, both in bringing it down the trail and in storing it. In an area where there were no banks closer than Austin, resourceful longhorn men devised a practice for cutting down the risk of losing their gold. They would sack up sizable amounts and take them to trusted neighbors for safekeeping. Often the neighbor would refuse to assume responsibility for more than a given quantity; hence it was common practice to approach a neighbor by saying, "Can I borrow you a hundred double eagles [$2,000] for sixty days?" The neighbor might use the gold in the meantime, but his honor required that he have it available for his friend to reclaim on the exact day stipulated.

The Olive brothers made extensive use of this device. Fred Smith and Print Olive often "borrowed" gold to one another. Being called upon to render this service came to have an important bearing on a family's credit and status. "The Olives wanted to borrow to him a thousand double eagles" was a report which could open up the way to buy land or cattle. The Lawrences, Morrows, Abbotts, Smiths, Kuykendalls, Littins, and Lanes borrowed gold back and forth to one another on a more or less permanent basis.

The Olives, like the other longhorn men, found it unwise to bring back anything but gold coins in payment for their cattle. On the 1869 trip, Print and Jim Kelly had brought back some bank notes drawn on Kountze Brothers Bank in Omaha, notes that were as good as gold anywhere in Iowa, Nebraska, or Kansas, and in money centers like Chicago, New York, or Boston. With worthless bills of the Confederacy still around, the Olives found Texans reluctant to accept the paper money except in the capital at Austin. After that experience, they generally insisted on payment in gold.

As the size of their herds increased, transporting the gold became increasingly troublesome. Not that the Olive brothers did not trust their cowboys; they did. But there simply were limits to the amount of gold their saddle pouches could hold. Finally Print arranged with Aaron Williams, the blacksmith in Georgetown who produced chuck wagons, to build one for the Olives with a false bottom in which could be transported up to 1,500 twenty-dollar gold pieces, or $30,000

The influx of gold tempted the roving outlaws, and as the summer of 1870 turned to fall there was more trouble than usual. First, two of Jim Olive's favorite driving horses were caught at night, tied up, and left with deep wounds on the hips and backs as though they had been hacked with a machete. The horses survived, but they were never the same. Then a few days later, Bob Olive, now nearly sixteen, was fired on from a distance in the Yegua area by assailants who remained hidden.

Jim Whitehead and Print were riding through the general area where Bob had been fired upon when they came upon a herd of longhorns being driven in a southeasterly direction. Perhaps a third of the cattle bore Olive brands. Two men were driving the herd, one of whom Print recognized as Dave Fream, rumored to be linked with the Yegua outlaws. Olive rode up to within twenty feet of Fream and asked him about the ownership of the cattle with Olive brands. Fream reached for his revolver and fired point-blank at Olive. Like Murday before and many a man after, he got but one shot. Olive's response put one bullet in Fream's chest and a second through his throat. The outlaw dropped off his horse, killed instantly by the first shot, the second merely making it a bloody affair.

Unlike Murday's, Fream's slug had crashed into Olive's chest.

However, it was deflected from the heart and lodged in the shoulder. Fream's last shot was a bull's eye, but his .36-caliber six-shooter was just a shade too light to produce the instant death he had intended for Print Olive.

Whitehead got Print home, but not without considerable loss of blood. Dr. Doak, a Confederate doctor during the war, worked long into the night before Jim Olive could ask the big question.

"He'll be dead tonight, Jim, or he'll survive. If he had been hit with a forty-four, it would have pierced his heart; but I've taken these little thirty-sixes out of a lot of men still livin' today. So have faith."

Jim Olive and Louisa sat beside the bed all the rest of the night. When the sun came up Print turned to his wife and inquired in an unsteady voice when breakfast would be ready.

The following spring, nearly eight months later, the Williamson County authorities indicted Print Olive for the murder of Dave Fream. Law enforcement was not strong enough to anticipate or prevent cattle stealing on Yegua Creek, but months later it charged those with murder who defended themselves and their property. When the full story was told, it developed that Fream had indeed been a leader of the Yegua Creek outlaws, but he had been run out of the clan and his place taken by one Cal Nutt. Deciding to go into business on his own, Fream had run into Print Olive and Jim Whitehead while driving off with the first herd he had put together. After a hearing the judge dismissed the case entirely.

The winter of 1870–71 had been severe, so the drive was delayed to let the weakened animals have another couple of weeks on spring grass before facing the rigors of the trail. Finally, at the end of March, the two herds were ready to go, Print acting as trail boss on the first herd, Jim Whitehead on the second. They took the cattle directly into Abilene, Kansas. The trail was beginning to lean to the west, now that new railroad sidings had been built at Ellsworth, so although more than 600,000 head of longhorns came up the trail in 1871 (most of them marketed at Abilene), that was the last big year for the original Kansas cow town.

The Olive steers were sold to processors who took them directly into Kansas City for slaughtering, whereas the cows were sold to Nebraska ranchers, primarily for breeding. The total income from the two herds came to more than $50,000, all paid in gold. Thirty thousand dollars in gold coins filled to capacity the compartment under the floor of the chuck wagon. The remaining $20,000 was divided up among the saddlebags of the cowboys.

When the longhorn men reached home, everyone was elated over the unexpectedly large return—everyone, that is, except Jim Olive. He wondered how his family would adjust to such riches. "Great wealth brings greater responsibility," he told Julia and his sons.

[6]

JIM KELLY FROM THE HIP

—◄◦●◦►—

IN MAY 1872, Print Olive, by now one of the real cattle kings
of the plains, moved out of the Olive pens at Thrall with 3,000
longhorns. They were almost entirely Olive cattle, although
neighbors like Fred Smith and Henry Hoyle had put in enough
steers to bring them cash for living expenses during the coming
winter. In all the Olives had invested in this trail herd something more than $15,000. The animals could have been sold in
the Olive pens for $18,000 to $20,000, but if the markets in
Kansas sustained the trend of the previous summer, these same
animals would command $60,000 to $70,000. The cost of taking
them up the Chisholm Trail would not be more than one
dollar a head. Like the gold miners in California, the longhorn
men were harvesting a precious natural resource for which the
demand was unlimited. So long as both the "mother lode" and
the markets held at existing levels, lasting fortunes could be
created in a single big year. Four dollars return for every one
dollar invested soon turned longhorn men into cattle kings.

Barney Armstrong and Gene Lyons, who had been with the
Olives almost from the beginning, were Print's right-hand men
on this trip. Jim Whitehead stayed in the San Gabriel country
to work with Ira, Jay, and Bob to bring together the herd that
would go to market the following year. The key swing man
was Gene Lyons, a soft-spoken Texan whose company Print
especially enjoyed. Handling the horses for Print was the Negro

Jim Kelly, now acknowledged to have few equals as a horse wrangler on the big trail.

Print added a few additional men for two reasons. First, he wanted to get to Kansas early enough to sound out the market before having to sell; yet he wanted to get back to Texas before the summer was over to supervise preparations for the 1873 herd drives. Therefore, the herd would have to be closely held and kept moving. Secondly, these animals were not as gentle as Olive and his trail men would have liked.

As Print expected, the extra hands were needed. There was more trouble holding the herd than they had heretofore experienced. The steers ran night after night during the early part of the trip, which meant that the men were getting no regular rest, and the animals were tired and troublesome. In the course of one stampede in northern Texas, the herd charged into a dead-end canyon, crushing two dozen of the lead steers to death. The men, suspecting that the troublemakers in the big herd were the ones that had been crushed against the canyon wall, saw their loss not as a calamity but as a boon.

The trouble with the cattle made the men touchy. One of the new cowpunchers, Bushy McGuire, provoked a fight with Jim Kelly, and the Negro would have killed McGuire on the spot had not Print arrived to intervene. A few days later, McGuire, serving as a point men, took issue with veteran swing man Gene Lyons at a moment when the herd was causing particular difficulty. McGuire swore viciously at Lyons and reached for his gun. The usually placid Lyons killed him instantly. Print called off the drive for the day, found a gravedigger, and, reading some verses from the Bible, conducted as formal a burial as circumstances would permit.

The Olive herd eventually moved out of Indian Territory into Kansas at the point where C. H. Stone operated a supply store, variously called Cox's Crossing or Caldwell, and finally known as Caldwell, Kansas. Soon after, Print elected to leave the Old Chisholm Trail from Cox's Crossing to Abilene—almost exactly today's U.S. Route 81—for an alternate route. He turned slightly

northwest, helping to trample a new branch for the big trail
through or near what is now Hutchinson, Kansas, and on north
to the new cow town of Ellsworth.

Having reached the Smoky Hill River within sight of Ellsworth and the vast network of new cattle pens along the railroad being laid from Kansas City to Denver, Print left the
herd in charge of Armstrong and Lyons and went to town to
size up the marketing situation. Grass around the herd was
in good condition, and Olive thought the market would get
stronger as the season advanced. He waited one week, two
weeks, a couple of days more, and finally sold the herd, on
July 19, for something more than $71,000. Payment was in gold.
Much of the coin was put in the floor of the chuck wagon, the
rest, as usual, being divided among the saddlebags of the crew.

Print hoped to get started back quickly, but the trail crew,
he realized, had to be given at least two or three days' rest.
It was July 20 and the middle of the week. He told his men
to have a little fun and be ready to leave by the weekend. Then
he and Gene Lyons went to Nick's Place on Ellsworth's one
main street for a game of cards.

After a drink at the bar, Olive and Lyons got into a card
game with two men from Ellsworth and Jim Kennedy, the son
of Miflin Kennedy, a cattleman near Corpus Christi whom Print
knew.

Lyons and Olive learned that Kennedy had brought no cattle
to Ellsworth but had been around town for some time, just
playing cards with Texans who had marketed their cattle. There
were reports that he had been a little too fast with some of the
cards, too. But the Ellsworth men were friendly, so Olive stayed
in the game despite some misgivings.

After several hands had been played, Kennedy questioned
Olive's dealing of the cards. Olive's eyes blazed with anger,
and the air became charged. Print made it plain that he regarded Kennedy as a no-good saloon cowman who let the
other Texans do the work and risk their lives on the trail while
he devised means of taking their money away from them after

payday. Fearing a violent outcome, Gene Lyons and the Ellsworth men hustled Kennedy out of the building. Olive told his friends that had Kennedy worn a gun and made a move to use it, he, Olive, would have killed him on the spot. Even with Kennedy gone, the mood of the game had gone sour, and Lyons convinced Olive that they should get back to the modest room they shared in the new Drover's Cottage.

Olive and Lyons soon had unexpected callers. Marshal J. L. Councell of Ellsworth and Sheriff Chauncey Whitney of Ellsworth County explained that they just wanted to know what had gone on at Nick's Place during the morning. They told Olive that they had not had a killing in Ellsworth yet in 1872 and they hoped to get through the entire year without one.

Print Olive explained why he had told Kennedy to cash in his chips and leave. The officers conceded that they had been worried about Kennedy for some time. He had been lounging about Ellsworth ever since the first herds of longhorns had arrived from Texas, always playing cards with men who had just been paid off in substantial sums of money. Some of his other games, too, had ended in hostilities, but up to now there had been no shooting. The officers exacted a promise from Olive —one he readily gave—to refrain from playing with Kennedy and to leave him alone. They promised him, in return, they would personally deliver the same message to Kennedy.

After the noon meal at the Drover's Cottage, Olive and Lyons visited at the hotel with other cattlemen, some of them from the Platte country. Later in the afternoon they walked down the main street to the Ellsworth Billiard Saloon for a drink and perhaps another round of cards, since the game had turned out badly in the morning. The entire front of the building housing the Billiard Saloon was made up of large windows which could be opened wide in warm weather. The sidewalk was wide enough not to be obstructed by the row of chairs placed back against the building, facing out on the main street of Ellsworth. A man sitting on one of the chairs when the big front windows were open could, by turning slightly, com-

mand a view of the entire interior of the saloon. Above the bar
a spread of massive horns from a Texas longhorn testified to the
role Texas cattle had played in bringing Ellsworth into being.
The legend on the shield supporting the horns read "Allegiance
to the Union." Carved on the same shield were likenesses of
Abraham Lincoln and U. S. Grant.

The proprietors of the Ellsworth Billiard Saloon were prepared to prevent gunplay and remove customers who let their
liquor get the best of them. Everyone except officers of the law
were required to place their six-shooters and knives on a backbar upon entering. Farther back was a stout wire cage where
those who became drunk could be confined until they sobered
up. As they entered, Print Olive and Gene Lyons went to the
backbar and hung up their six-shooters. Print could not suppress a twinge of uneasiness. For ten hectic years now his gun
had almost never been out of reach, day or night. At least ten
times, this vigilance had saved his life. Times without number,
he knew, the mere presence of his six-shooter had prevented
violence.

After laying aside their guns, the Texans ordered drinks at
the bar. A few minutes later, when two men left one of the
card games, Olive and Lyons were invited to take their places.
The game had been resumed only a short while when Jim Kelly
and one of the Mexicans on the Olive trail crew came down the
main street. Seeing their trail bosses inside playing cards, the
two settled down in the chairs on the walk.

At about four o'clock, after Olive and Lyons had been in the
card game an hour or more, Jim Kennedy stepped inside the
saloon door, looking around as though he were seeking someone. Spotting Print Olive, he started in the direction of the table
where the cattle king was playing cards. The card players,
intent upon their game, were unaware of his approach. He
paused near Print Olive as though he were sizing up the card
game. Then, springing to Print's left side and standing almost
directly over him, Kennedy shouted, "Now, you son of a bitch,

you can cash in your chips!" As he screamed, he reached inside his shirt, pulled out a concealed six-shooter, and began firing. In his haste, the first shot was fired before the gun had entirely cleared his shirt front, the bullet striking the hand in which Print held his cards. Lyons, seated almost directly opposite Olive, shoved the table hard enough to knock Print to the floor, forcing Kennedy to shift his stance. Thus his second and third bullets struck Olive in the groin area, entering the left hip close to the shrapnel wound received at Shiloh.

Outside the saloon, Jim Kelly hardly heard the first shot. At the sound of the table scraping, he turned his head. Seeing Olive on the floor with a man firing down at him, Jim whipped out his six-shooter and fired through the open window, fusing the sweep of his arm and the flight of the bullet into a single movement over his shoulder, never leaving his chair. His .44-caliber slug hit Kennedy in the hip with such force that it knocked him off balance momentarily. Before the gambler could get back in position to fire again at the now completely helpless Olive, Gene Lyons slugged Kennedy with his fist on the side of the head, knocking him to the floor.

Print Olive was laid out on the card table while two doctors worked over him to stop the bleeding. His life hung in the balance a second time. For six days his trail crew would not leave. After a week, the crisis past, Barney Armstrong and Gene Lyons took charge of the trail crew and started back down the Chisholm Trail to Texas, taking with them Print's horse "White Flanks" and Kelly's "Chowder," and the chuck wagon with its cargo of gold.

Jim Kelly stayed with Print at the Drover's Cottage to see that he got everything he needed. The three slugs were removed, but in the groin was a length of the cattle king's gold watch chain, embedded too deeply for its safe removal without the facilities of a clinic or hospital. Neither was available closer than Kansas City, Fort Worth, or Denver. In time the wound healed over the chain, leaving it as a permanent reminder of the episode—especially when he rode in the saddle for long hours. Ever afterward he unconsciously favored his left hip and thigh when riding.

While confined to his room, Print Olive asked for a Bible and read most of the Old Testament for the first time in his life. He was particularly interested in the account of Jacob and called Jim's attention to a certain similarity he thought he detected between Jacob's life and his own. He even speculated as to whether he might live to attain a similar old age. Jim responded that if he insisted on taking off his gun, his chances of reaching three score and ten were not good. Print agreed; he vowed he would never be without his six-shooter again.

While his body mended, his mind was more active than ever, and he took advantage of an opportunity he had never experienced before. For several weeks his room at the Drover's Cottage became a gathering place for the plains cattlemen. Trail bosses, cowboys, and cattle buyers from Kansas City and even from Chicago came to visit the Texas cattle king. He would talk during the day and far into the night with these leaders, men who ranched in Platte country all the way from Lincoln near the Missouri River to the Colorado and Wyoming mountains, men who were proving it was possible to raise cattle up north in large numbers and to heavy weights in no more time than it required in Texas, men who shipped their cattle on the Union Pacific directly to the greatest market of them all, Chicago.

Print became convinced that although Texas with its milder winters was a good place to drop the calves, the buffalo grass and bluestem range in the Platte Valley, with its endless supply of fresh water, with its cooler summers, and with its short drives to the Union Pacific, could produce more pounds of meat per animal than could the more arid range in Texas. Even more important, Olive was convinced that there were fewer cattle rustlers in the North.

Summer was gone before Olive was able to travel, even by train. This was the longest train trip either he or Jim Kelly ever took. From Ellsworth they rode into Kansas City, caught another train to Fort Worth, and then a third from Fort Worth to Austin. Print was so weak that Jim carried him off one train and onto another. They got off at the McDade station near Thrall where Jay, Print's brother, met them.

During his long absence, Print's third son, Harvey, had been born, on July 20, the very day that Print had been gunned down. Louisa had now given birth to all three of their children while Print was absent from home.

The family and neighbors were quick to sense that Print Olive had come back from his Ellsworth experience a changed man. Though he had been practically without pain for weeks, he was too weak to do any work before Christmas.

But he was not too weak to plan. The talks begun during his long stay in Ellsworth continued to occupy his thoughts through the fall and winter at home. Print often pointed out to his brothers that changes were coming. The hunting of wild cattle in Texas could not go on forever. The transfer of longhorns to northern grazing lands would eventually clean them out of the Texas brush. Marketing was already beginning to show signs of change. Print used their own experience as an example. He had been able to hold the Olive herd outside Ellsworth and wait out a period of soft prices offered by the packing houses, but holding a big herd at the railroad siding without sure access to grass and water had its limitations. The cattle business, Print insisted, would eventually belong to the ranchers who maintained a permanent range near the railroad. It was the railroad that was changing everything.

The family was split in its reaction to Print's ideas. The split was almost as deep as the one caused years before when Print insisted on volunteering for the Confederate army. Jay, who was becoming the image of his father in attitudes as well as in appearance, could not picture himself in the cattle business anywhere but in Williamson County, Texas. He did not even want to be away from his family for the time it took to get a herd to market; the thought of trips up the trail to manage a business on northern range held no appeal for him. Print's proposals interested Ira, however. Bob was sitting in on the family councils for the first time, and he wanted to do what Print wanted to do. It would never be any other way. As for eleven-year-old Marion, he had been wanting to ride up the Chisholm Trail for a year or two already. Thus Jay was clearly out-numbered.

Jay, Ira, Bob, and Jim Whitehead had kept the longhorn hunts on schedule during the summer and fall when Print was unable to work. Cattle stealing and shooting incidents had continued, but the Olive pens steadily filled, so that, early in 1873, there were once again enough longhorns to send a small herd to market. The Olive brothers also had an opportunity to sell a cow herd to a rancher in Colorado. It was decided that this time Ira should take the cows up the trail so that he could see for himself the range possibilities along the South Platte and Republican rivers. He returned with a glowing account of the grass and water he found.

Cattle prices had declined, but the Olive herds got onto the trail early and were sold before the prices dropped drastically, as they often did in midsummer. Then in September the first major panic since the Civil War gripped the entire nation. The market for longhorns stopped falling: it simply ceased to exist. Small cattlemen who had their entire assets tied up in long-horns and who had sent herds up the trail late in the summer went bankrupt. The Olives still had gold, but much of it was "borrowed out" to neighbors, most of whom were unable to return it on the contract date.

There came a time, in January 1874, when a decision had to be made whether the Olives, pooling their resources, could out-fit a trail crew to take a herd up to the Platte country. Jay and Ira had complicated the situation two years earlier by insisting that they separate their interests and establish their own brands. They had taken the action over the objections of their father and Print. Their young families had lapped up the high in-come, and now they lacked the cash to stake the trail herd. Print had money but not enough to stake them all. This was the kind of problem Jim Olive had anticipated when he had wondered aloud whether he and Julia had reared their sons to withstand the dangers of great wealth. He was speaking to the women his sons had married, too; especially to Ira's wife, Lou, who had been reared in town and found it difficult not to look down her nose at the rest of the Olive family. In the end the brothers had to admit that they could send no herds up the Chisholm Trail in the spring—perhaps none at all in 1874.

Jim Olive had little to say until his sons had faced up to the fact that their greed for larger herds and extravagant living had left them without the reserves necessary to weather the hardships that had come to everyone in some measure. Then, and only then, Jim Olive taught his sons a lesson they would never forget, and he did it by deeds rather than preaching. He invited his sons, including seventeen-year-old Bob—who now looked as much a man as any of them—and twelve-year-old Marion, to take a walk with him. The five were so surprised at their father's resuming his role of head of the clan that they got right up and followed him out into the yard without a word.

Jim walked directly to the deep cistern he had dug at Julia's request when they had built the house long years before. He directed Bob to bring up the bucket that Julia used for keeping foods cool in hot weather, a bucket made of iron so that it would stay under water and remain upright.

Bob had brought the old bucket up many times at his mother's bidding; it was a slow but reasonably easy task. When finally the bucket rested on the solid cistern rim, Bob lifted the lid and the Olive sons stared in disbelief. It was filled almost to the brim with gold. Jim and Julia had saved most of their share from the herds sent up the trail for just such a moment as this.

With Jim Olive's cache and what funds his sons could put up, Olive herds moved up the trail on schedule in 1874. Their longhorns were more in demand than they had been the year before, because so many operators were unable to function. During 1874 and 1875, Olive longhorns went to Kansas cow towns and to the Platte country in Nebraska, Colorado, and Wyoming where many ranchers came to depend on the Olives for brood cows because the quality was excellent, the price was fair, and the Olive word was good. When a deal was made with an Olive and hands shaken, the cattle were delivered on time.

Once the trail drives were over in 1875, Print and Ira reviewed developments on the northern range, and the results clearly supported the conclusions Print had reached during his long convalescence at Ellsworth three summers before. Longhorn cows would drop calves as freely in the North as they did in Texas, although the calves came a month or two later. The calves started more slowly in the northern springs, but by the end of the first year they could be as big as Texas calves.

The advantages of having longhorns raised close to the railroads were becoming obvious. Whereas the system of driving herds up the trail each year played into the hands of cattle buyers because the ranchers could not hold a herd long at the rail sidings, raising them up north meant the cattle could be held until market conditions were favorable to the cattleman. In addition, there were no organized bands of cattle rustlers in the North; an occasional cattle and horse thief, of course, but no gangs with leaders strong enough to coerce county and state governments as they often did in Texas.

Finally, and perhaps most important of all, in 1875 homesteading was not a problem in the Platte country of Nebraska, Colorado, and Wyoming. There were a few farmers trying to plant crops, to be sure, but most of them would almost certainly be starved off the dry land in a short time. Those who were left could be converted into small cattlemen working with the Olives on the shares. In fact, some of these farmers would be needed to replace most of the Negro and Mexican help who would not go north to face the cold winters.

Print had been up north so often and by now had his hands on cattle operations in so many different places from Texas to Wyoming that he had discovered one more advantage not obvious to men who did not travel. The weather varied widely up and down the plains in any given season. When it was dry in Texas, there was almost certain to be rain elsewhere on the plains. When it was cold during the winter in one place, the weather might be moderate a surprisingly short distance away. For the cattleman who had operations in several different areas up and down the plains, this variety was a great advantage, and Print Olive understood this fact perhaps better than any of the other cattle kings.

The Christmas season of 1875 was a happy time for the Olive families, but Julia was uneasy. It was evident that the family interests were shifting far to the north. No one had yet proposed moving their families, but the alternative was to have the men away even more of the time. The violence that continued all around them also made the thought of living in the North more attractive to the younger generation. Julia was sure that Louisa, for one, would be only too glad to leave all the killing in the longhorn brush behind. Julia and Jim recognized, too, that their youngest sons were taking on the responsibilities of men and their wishes would have to be considered. Bob was now twenty years old, married, and newly settled in a house raised for him and his bride near his parents' home. But Bob would go with Print. There never had been any question about that. Even Julia's baby boy, Marion, was fourteen and smitten with a full blown case of Chisholm Trail fever, pleading for his parents' permission to ride north with each new Olive herd. Jay alone seemed loath to go.

[7]
DEATH OF AN OLIVE

THE TEMPO OF VIOLENCE in the San Gabriel brush accelerated in 1874 and 1875. The *Austin Statesman,* the nearest daily newspaper, reported that deaths in the Texas cattle country in 1875 exceeded the number of Texas men killed in the Civil War. The newspaper reported that the more than twenty known deaths in Williamson County represented without question only a fraction of the actual number. The men who made their living stealing cattle had become so numerous and so brazen that several unorthodox attempts at control were seriously proposed, including castration upon conviction. The threat, it was judged, would serve as a strong deterrent; the punishment as a cure.

The frequency of attack and the powerlessness of law enforcement officials prompted Print, Jay, and Ira to post guards at night during particularly troublesome times to protect their families and those of the neighbors close by. Bob Olive and his buddy, Sam Carr, always ready for a little excitement, volunteered for patrol duty. There were occasional disturbances but no arrests.

During Reconstruction years, from 1865 to 1870, no Olives served on Williamson County juries because Print's Confederate war record clouded the family's loyalty to the Union. But between 1871 and 1876 Print and Jay often served on juries, both the petit jury and the grand jury in Georgetown. A sort of oligarchy of cattlemen was establishing itself, and as community leaders and affluent businessmen the Olives, of course, wielded considerable influence. From 1875 on, one or another of the brothers sat in on a majority of the cases before Williamson County grand juries. Their neighbors regarded them as well informed and capable of being objective, despite their personal involvement.

Cool heads in Williamson County government recognized that inevitably the rustlers would get some of their sympathizers on the grand jury; hence it was important to have the cattlemen represented too; and Print Olive, as the foremost cattleman in the San Gabriel country, was their logical spokesman.

Jay had also attained a reputation for leadership in Williamson County, the mantle of Jim Olive having fallen more and more upon his shoulders. Ira was respected too, but his tendency to stutter made him reluctant to seek public attention of any kind. Bob was not yet old enough to hold positions of responsibility. Even had he been, he had disqualified himself by his administration of gun whippings and other breaches of the peace. He was gaining a reputation as a hothead.

By the mid-seventies the stock of wild longhorns was beginning to decline as the result of years of hunting and exporting. From 400,000 to 700,000 animals had gone up the Chisholm Trail each year. With the shortage, the boom market in the North made the longhorns more valuable, presenting the rustlers with a constantly growing incentive to steal. County and state justice seemed inadequate to cope with the problem. Only private guns could preserve a semblance of law and order. Since this responsibility fell most heavily on those longhorn men with operations extensive enough to include effective gun power, the rustlers knew their enemies. In eastern Williamson County and northern Lee County, the Olives were high on the list of the Yegua and Brushy creek gangs.

Of the two, the Yegua Creek crowd to the south and east was by far the more dangerous. They were strong enough in certain areas to boast that neither county authorities, Olives, nor anyone else could touch them with impunity. The identity of their leaders was obscure, but it was generally understood that one of them was the flashily dressed Cal Nutt, often attired in a costume complete with yellow waistcoat when he visited the bars. That Nutt had contacts in Austin few in Williamson County doubted. The Texas Rangers, for example, never took an interest in the Williamson County longhorn war until much later, when Cal Nutt was gunned down, not on Yegua Creek, but in Austin.

The fifteen months between July 1875 and October 1876 brought matters to a head. The rustlers' arrogance increased as their actions went unpunished. It was during this period that the Yegua gang publicly proclaimed that it would execute the offending members of a Williamson County grand jury unless an indictment was obtained against cattle kings involved in one range killing.

One day early in the summer of 1875, Print and Jay and some of their men came upon three strangers brazenly driving a small herd of Olive branded longhorns away from the Olive pens and out of the community. The Olive party, screened by the brush, rode up ahead of the herd and secreted themselves on the path along which the herd was moving. When the longhorns pulled up even with them, it was Jay who demanded that they halt and prove ownership. All three of the rustlers reached for their guns and fired, but they got off only one shot before two of them dropped off their horses, killed instantly by a hail of Olive bullets. The third man had his gun shot from his hand before he could fire a second time, and he was wounded more painfully than seriously. Like most legmen for the rustlers, they were poor shots, and none of the Olives was hit.

The Olive cowboys drove the longhorns back to the Olive pens. The two dead men they left untouched where they fell; the rustlers would come and get them rather than permit their bodies to be seen by other cattlemen—and other rustlers. Once more, a wounded man was carried off, this time to Jay's home.

The injured man said that his name was W. H. McDonald and that he had just been hired by one of the dead men to help drive the longhorns that he supposed belong to his employers. It was the usual story, but Jay Olive kept the man in his home until he was well enough to travel. Then he returned his horse to him and ordered him to get out of Williamson County and stay out. Instead, McDonald went back to the Yegua men, and within a few days he was in Georgetown filing charges of assault against Jay and Print Olive. That there was some legal chicanery involved is indicated by the fact that no mention was made of the two men who had been killed in the encounter.

The Williamson County grand jury returned an indictment against the Olives in the McDonald case. However, the records of the case against Print Olive were "lost," according to the prosecution, and when Jay paid a one-dollar fine for disturbing the peace, the case against him was closed. Olive prestige counted for something, it seemed. Weeks later, however, after the affair had quieted down, District Attorney Thomas P. Hughes "found" the records of the case against Print. Hughes was determined to replace six-shooter law with statutory law as he understood it, and he was not convinced that right was always on the side of the cattlemen in these altercations. Moreover, he thought he had found a split within the Olive community that he could exploit. But when the witnesses, Allen Wynn, a nephew of Print, and James Williams, a longtime friend, failed to show up, the case was dismissed for lack of evidence. Once more the family had been spared any serious consequences, but their position was weakening.

Print called his father and brothers to a meeting in the old store building whose main function now was to provide a quiet place where the men could meet to make decisions about serious matters. Print pointed out that they were gradually losing the struggle to the rustlers, particularly the Yegua mob. Matters had taken on a new and a much more serious aspect. Their families were no longer safe, and the Yegua crowd was moving in on the county seat to the point where they might muster a majority on a grand jury. The cattle king put the choice squarely up to his brothers and his father: "Let's either pull up stakes and move the Olive families and Olive holdings up the trail, leaving the Yegua thieves to take over, or let's make it an open war and shoot it out."

The talk lasted all afternoon and most of the night. The decision was to stand and fight. Now, instead of giving the rustler the benefit of the doubt, instead of giving him the chance to shoot first, the policy would be to shoot on sight, and in any manner, persons caught with livestock in their possession bearing only the Olive brand. What little livestock was sold to neighbors would be branded with the new owner's brand before the animal left the Olive pens.

Jim Olive would not permit the decision to be final until his sons had agreed to act openly and at least talk with Sheriff Sam Strayhorn in Georgetown and Sheriff Jim Brown of Lee County. Accordingly, Print and Jay drew up a public statement putting everyone on notice that any person having in his possession horses or cattle bearing only the Olive brands would be shot on sight. All of the numerous Olive brands for horses and longhorns were listed, displayed, and explained on the same notice.

The *Georgetown Record* was the most widely circulated newspaper in Williamson and Lee counties. The Olive brothers decided to reproduce their public notice in a large ad, at least half a page in size. First, however, Print and Jay must talk to Sheriff Sam Strayhorn, an Odd Fellows brother of Print's and a more than casual friend.

Sheriff Strayhorn was immediately sympathetic to the Olives' position in the matter, but he was opposed to their placing the notice in the newspaper. He was afraid that such an act might touch off a full-blown reign of terror—a renewal of the Union-Confederate animosities which could get completely out of control.

Strayhorn asked Print not to publish the notice but to allow him instead to post it on his bulletin board in the courthouse. The Olive brothers agreed, and the sheriff posted the notice, with the Olives helping him tack it up. The language was as uncompromising as any ever used in the West. It read:

PUBLIC NOTICE

All horse thieves and cattle thieves pay attention. Anyone caught riding an Olive horse or driving an Olive cow will be shot on sight. Our brands, legally registered in Williamson County, Texas, are as follows: . . .

Print and his brothers felt that in having given the rustlers a public warning, they were not under any compulsion to report details of consequences. The Olives went to their graves with no one ever knowing the number of lives their guns claimed in their efforts to stamp out cattle and horse stealing in the San Gabriel country. Stories that they stuffed abandoned wells with bodies of their victims were fabricated, but it is true that the bodies of many persons who were known to have been murdered were either never found or were not conclusively identified. It is true also that the Olives finally broke the power of the Yegua gang, though the cost was so great that the family felt neither satisfaction nor a sense of victory.

The first step had yet to be taken, however, once the notice was posted. One night, raiders rode into the Olive pens and wantonly cut the tongues out of several of the best horses. The horses the raiders were after, "White Flanks" and "Chowder," were spared only because they were not in the pens at the time. Bob Olive established to Print's satisfaction that the perpetrators of the crime were the Kelley brothers who had drifted up from father south in Texas and attached themselves to the Yegua rustlers. Bob Olive declared he would murder one or both of the Kelleys.

At about the same time, the night-alert man making his rounds through the Olive community reported seeing two members of the Yegua band lurking near Print Olive's home. One was Turk Turner, and the other, Grip Crow. The pair slipped away quickly and were not seen in the area again, but this kind of harassment produced the fear under which the cattlemen's families lived constantly. Print and his brothers tried to keep reports of these incidents from their parents, wives, and children; but usually Louisa found out from her house servants, who were devoted to her and felt they should keep her posted. Louisa in turn shared her information with Julia, to whom she was always close; so Jim Olive always knew, although he and his family rarely discussed the incidents.

Two weeks later occurred the "green hide" incident whose report swept the length of the plains and made the columns of newspapers on both the East and West coasts. Since neither the Olives nor Lee County authorities ever gave any account of the matter, the newspaper stories stood without contradiction. They related that the Olives had come upon two settlers driving a small herd of Olive-branded longhorns out of the area. Print Olive and his gunmen were accused of having stopped the rustlers, forcing them to kill two of the longhorns and skin them. Then the two are said to have been wrapped, mummy-like, in the green hides with the Olive brands plainly showing on the outside, whereupon their captors rode away, leaving their victims to suffocate in the Texas sun.

Since apparently Print Olive and Sheriff Jim Brown of Lee County agreed that neither of them would even acknowledge that the incident happened, only hearsay contradicts the published accounts. From the families of the murdered men it became clear that two Olive longhorns were killed, skinned, and butchered just south of the Yegua Creek area in northern Lee County. Olive men came on the butchered carcasses with the hides folded up and still warm. Obviously someone had gone for a wagon to pick up the meat and hides. The Olives waited. When the same Turk Turner who had been seen with Grip Crow near the Print Olive home several days earlier returned with James H. Crow, Grip's father, the cattlemen waited until Turner and Crow had loaded the meat and the hides in the wagon. Then they did exactly what the public notice stuck to Sheriff Strayhorn's bulletin board said they would do. They shot the men—a single bullet through the brain for each. There was no other mark on either body. Crow and Turner were not tortured as the newspaper accounts reported. From all indications death was instant and painless, albeit without warning. Probably neither man was even aware that he was being attacked. It was then that the Olives wrapped the bodies up in the hides, leaving the Olive brands showing to drive home the message: Those who stole Olive livestock after the public notice went up in Georgetown could expect a swift and deadly vengeance.

The Olive campaign of extermination moved relentlessly on, quietly for the most part, except for Bob's activities. Bob was given to dramatics, often forcing a showdown with rustlers in front of witnesses when his brothers thought he could have been more effective settling accounts more privately. His killing of Lawson Kelley late in 1875 was a case in point.

Lawson Kelley and his brother, Dock, were probably as tough a pair of gunmen as any in San Gabriel country. Dock Kelley, known to have connections with Johnny Ringo's outlaws, the Jesse James outfit of Texas, was reported to have killed at least twenty-five men, possibly as many as fifty. Lawson Kelley worked more constantly with the Yegua rustlers than did Dock, and his own six shooter was notched a dozen times or more.

The Olives were convinced that the Kelley brothers were two of the nightriders, if not the only ones, responsible for mutilating the horses during the summer of 1875. Bob resolved to hunt them down. Weeks passed. Then one day he came upon Lawson Kelley in a Williamson County bar. Olive openly accused the outlaw of having cut up the Olive horses. Kelley reached for his gun, but he was no match for Bob's premeditation. He never got a chance to fire. A slug from "Lulabelle," Bob's favorite six-shooter, killed him instantly. Since there were witnesses, Sheriff Strayhorn had no choice but to issue a warrant for Bob's arrest. However, witnesses reported that Bob had simply beaten Kelley to the draw, firing in self-defense, and the charge against Bob was dismissed. But the episode contributed to Bob's reputation as a rash and dangerous gunman.

Print Olive, now alarmed for Bob's safety, organized a body-guard of four men to ride with his younger brother for several weeks. One of these guards was Sam Carr, who had ridden patrol with Bob. He was about Bob's own age and an expert with the six-shooter. Instead of protecting Bob, Carr apparently goaded him into further provocative actions. The names of both were soon linked to several shootings and other acts of violence, some against men who were clearly not cattle rustlers.

From 1872 on, a new group of settlers began coming into eastern Williamson and northern Lee counties. They were first- and second-generation immigrants from western and northern Europe, including many Germans. They spoke English with difficulty or not at all. Some of them were taking out homestead claims on land over which the cattle traveled from the Olive pens to the Chisholm Trail, a development which signaled the beginning of the end of the longhorn era in the San Gabriel country. Bob contended that these settlers were taking up some of the land just to force the Olives to pay tolls for the right to cross territory that had heretofore been open to them. For a year or more Bob had been trading tough language with Pete Zieschang, one of the newcomers, and even occasional shots that each was careful to keep harmless. But there was always the chance something serious would occur.

For years Print and Ira had seen the settlers move in from the east, especially in Kansas. They tried to convince Bob that nothing could be done about this trend toward farming opera-tions where previously the land had been totally available to cattle. Yet Bob's aggressiveness toward the small farmers con-tinued. After one sharp exchange, Zieschang swore out a war-rant for Bob Olive, charging him with carrying a gun, and the affair cost Bob a twenty-five-dollar fine.

By February and March of 1876 the Olive brothers were pre-paring their herds for the northward trips that Print hoped could get started in mid-April. This year an additional herd of cows owned jointly by the brothers would be sent up to be located on good range near either the Union Pacific or the

Kansas Railroad. The herds were trail branded by the end of April. By the first week in May they were ready to go. Despite all of the difficulties Bob was having with the authorities, Print declined to take him up the Chisholm Trail with the spring herds. His fast, accurate gun was needed to protect Olive homes from attack by the Yegua renegades.

This drive of 1876 saw many of the Olive regulars on the trail again: Jim Whitehead, Barney Armstrong, Gene Lyons, and Jim Kelly, the Negro wrangler. Those men would help Print handle the steers that were destined for the markets. In addition, several cowboys went along to handle the cows and stay north with Ira all winter, if need be, to locate the stock herd on permanent range where, for the first time, Olive long-horn calves would be produced the next spring. These cowboys included Rob Murday, the first man Print shot down after his return from the Confederate army, Will Steers, Oscar Lowden, a Mexican *vaquero* who was known only as Leon, and another Mexican, Sanchez. Sanchez was in charge of the wagons that would carry the calves born along the trail, protecting them for a few days until they got strong enough to follow the mother cows on the trail. A second Negro, Will Teabolt, was the cook.

Print led the uneventful trek up the most recent version of the Chisholm Trail and into the latest Kansas longhorn mecca, Dodge City, on the new Santa Fe Railroad. Arriving there the last week in June, they heard the news of the massacre the week before of General Custer and his Seventh Cavalry at the Battle of the Little Bighorn up in Montana Territory.

The heavy steers were cut out of the big herd and sold at Dodge City. Two days later the balance of the herd was on the move again, headed across the Kansas prairie toward a winter range in Nebraska. Though both grass and water in the Saw-log Creek area just west and north of Dodge City were ade-quate for a herd of five or six thousand cows, Print and Ira decided to push on to a range that could support ten to fifteen thousand head with room for expansion. Maintaining twenty to thirty thousand animals on year-round range close to a railroad over which the beef could be shipped to market—this became Print Olive's goal. There was no such ranching operation on the North American continent yet, Print knew, but he was sure he could succeed, given sufficient grazing land.

As the Olive herd moved across northwestern Kansas on July 14, 1876, a courier rode up from the direction of Dodge City. Galloping past the herd until he found the trail boss, he handed Print a telegram. Written on the outside of the envelope was this message:

> DELIVER TO I. P. OLIVE—Mr. Olive: This message came to you through the city marshal's office last night. I thought you would want to see it so am sending it with Tom Wray, a friend of mine who is going north to Nebraska. H. B. Bell.

Tearing open the envelope, Print read the telegram:

> July 11, 1876
> Taylorsville Station, Texas
> Via: I&GNRR
> City Marshal,
> Dodge City, Kansas
> Can you get word to I. P. Olive, Texas drover with herd road-brand H4 en route to Nebraska, that he is badly needed in Williamson County, Texas, by his brother. Need I. P. Olive presence if he can return at once. Suggest Ira Olive remain with cattle if not sold, to Ogallala or where winter range is found. My respects to brothers Print, Ira, and trail men. Louisa, Lou, and babies all well—Thos. J. Olive.

Print and Ira wished that Jay had been more specific about the crisis he faced in Williamson County. They narrowed the possibilities down to two: Bob must be in trouble of the worst kind, or the battle with the Yegua gang must be completely out of hand. In either case, they agreed the need was real and urgent, or Jay would not have asked Print to return immediately.

Ira did not like being one man short in strange territory. The cowboy who had ridden out from Dodge City said he knew the Platte country from Fort Kearny to Colorado and Wyoming, so Print suggested that Ira invite him to sign on. As for Print, he started for Texas immediately, stepping off the train at the Taylorsville Station exactly one week later.

Print went directly to his home from the railroad station, and his first look at Louisa told him that the crisis, whatever it was, was real. She had the appearance of the women he remembered at Vicksburg after forty days and nights of unbroken Union shelling. She explained that for weeks now the Yegua outlaws had been threatening to kill every Olive in Williamson County. The servants were afraid to come to the Olive homes, and it was no longer possible to keep the children ignorant of the danger. It had been, she told her husband, like the war, when one could never really get a night's sleep because of constant rumors of impending raids. Print declared grimly that not only was it just like the war, it *was* war. They would have to mount an offensive.

Print saddled a horse and went to see Jay and his father. Bob, as usual, was away—not even his wife knew where—over at Georgetown, perhaps, or out seeing some of the neighbors who were still friendly, such as Henry Hoyle.

Jay told Print that reports had been circulating for a month or two, some of them obviously planted by the rustlers, that a massive raid was planned against the Olives. He had been concerned about the reports from the first, he went on, but about three weeks ago the Yegua began openly to advertise in the Georgetown bars that a reward of $500 awaited anyone who would kill "any Olive male." This terror tactic struck at the boys and their father. The situation called for action.

Jay explained his reluctance to summon Print back from Kansas. He was sure that was exactly what the Yegua crowd wanted him to do. The rustlers would want to attack while Jim Kelly, Barney Armstrong, Jim Whitehead, and the other cowboys were too far away to help, of course. But they could not fail to realize that as long as Print was alive they would never be safe; bringing Print back alone would fit into their plans splendidly. In the end, however, Jay and his father had concluded that the fate of the whole family was too great a responsibility for Jay to bear alone. They had sent for Print.

Even the offer of such a large reward had not seemed so deadly serious, Jay said, until a Negro boy came to Bob Olive and asked for a job—just any kind of job. Bob, who frequented the bars more than did his brothers, had of course heard about the reward for killing Olives. Bob suspected from the first that the young Negro had been sent to kill as many Olives as he might find together at a time when it was possible for him to use his gun. Bob was convinced that the boy carried a six-shooter concealed inside his summer shirt. Within a day or two he had his conjectures confirmed. Determined to head off what he regarded as an imminent attempt on their lives, Bob had sent the boy to the corn crib, ostensibly to get feed for the horses. While the boy was filling the sack, Bob had killed him instantly with a bullet through the head. He then called in the neighbors and told them that he found the boy stealing corn, and that after shooting the culprit, he had discovered him to be carrying a concealed six-shooter. Jay thought that Sheriff Strayhorn had taken no notice of Bob's killing of the young Negro, probably because the sheriff shared Jay's belief that the boy had posed a real threat.

Following this incident, Jay had stepped up the night watch. He had divided it into two shifts of two or three men each. At least twice a week, he said, the watchmen would report hearing suspicious sounds or seeing vague shapes in the darkness which they felt sure were spies for the rustlers. On occasion they had fired in the direction of the commotion, and once the fire was returned.

Jim Olive observed that the first thing to do before tackling a major problem was to get a full night's sleep. Print suggested that they meet the next afternoon after he had had a chance to talk to Henry Hoyle and some of the other neighbors. By then, too, Bob would probably be back.

When they came together the next day on the big veranda at Jim and Julia's place, Print reported that Henry Hoyle had heard the Yegua rustlers' plan to attack confirmed only the day before, and that it could come any night. Henry said that from what he could learn, the outlaws planned to stake everything on a single night raid against the Olive homes, using twenty or more gunmen, perhaps dividing them up into two or three raiding parties so that they could strike in several places at the same time.

Print visited two or three other neighbors and heard pretty much the same thing. The outlaws were describing the proposed raid as retaliation against the Olives' "will be shot on sight" notice and the implementation of the policy which had followed. Bob next reported that Cal Nutt was openly boasting that not only would the reward be paid immediately, but the Yegua men would assure the killers that there would be no grand jury indictment coming out of Georgetown. Bob Olive therefore wanted to strike directly at Cal Nutt and the others known to be directing the buildup for the raid, but Print had other plans. He pointed out that battles were not often won by frontal assault; that by concentrating Olive strength at one point and forcing the thugs to attack them there, the Olives could give the Yegua crowd such a whipping that the brush war would be brought to an end.

Print proposed that they increase the night guard immediately to prevent a surprise attack. This proposal was made on a Saturday. Figuring that it would take a day or two for Cal Nutt to get his gunmen over the observance of the weekend in the saloons, Print thought that the raid would likely come on Tuesday or Wednesday night. By Tuesday evening, he, Bob, and Jay along with a full complement of men, could be moved into the log ranch house at the Olive pens, making it appear that Print had come back from Kansas to help prepare another herd of longhorns to go up the trail with the fall drives. The cowboys could pass this word along, Print suggested, reducing the likelihood of attack on their homes.

Jim Olive would not go to the pens with his sons. The men

hoped that his age and standing made him immune, even though the $500 reward applied to every male in Williamson County whose name was Olive. Besides, Jim no longer took an active part in getting the herds ready. His going up to the pens now might arouse the suspicions of the outlaws that a trap was being laid for them.

During the weekend, Print went to Georgetown and talked over the plans with Sheriff Sam Strayhorn, who conceded that he was powerless to assure protection to the Olives and their families. He did deputize Milt Tucker of Taylorsville, instructing him to watch the situation closely and be ready to make arrests quickly, getting information which would be useful before a grand jury.

By the afternoon of Monday, July 24, Jay, Bob, Print, and their men were at work around the pens. They would begin living in the ranch house that evening. While some of their best men were up north with Ira—men like Barney Armstrong, Gene Lyons, and Jim Kelly—the Olives were far from shorthanded. They had Henry Strain, possibly not only the best cook but also the best shot in the San Gabriel country; Bill Wells, no great shakes with a six-shooter, but a magician with a Winchester rifle; and a ranchhand known only as Bumpus, who had been up the trail with several Olive herds. All three men had been with the cattle kings for years. They would stand and fight. Several others were less experienced, but they could at least stand guard. Every man in the compound had come because he wanted to be in the fight.

Sam Carr wanted to join Bob for the showdown, but he was asked instead to stay in the Olive community and supervise the night guard there. Some of the neighbors wanted to come too—the Abbott boys, the Kuykendalls, young Tom Smith, even Frank Condron. But Print and Jay explained that the presence of all that additional help would scare off the Yegua gang entirely. Some of the neighbors did, however, swell the night watch in the Olive community.

One offer Print did accept came from Lee Moore, the boy

who had once handled the bell mare. He was now a veteran longhorn handler. He usually worked at the Olive pens when Snyder-branded cattle were to be sent up the trail with the Olives'. Thus Moore's presence at the pens would seem perfectly natural at the same time that it would provide one more capable gunman. In future years, Lee Moore would write the best single account of the episode, but only after he had gone up the big trail himself and become a great cattleman in the Wyoming Platte country.

That evening, when Henry Strain served one of his finest suppers, the ranch house had been organized for an effective defense. "Fort Olive," the cowboys called it at supper. The ranch house was a sturdy log building that could be defended, in the daytime anyway, by as few as two or three men. The big yard around the log house was completely enclosed by poles set tightly together stockade-fashion to keep out grazing cattle and horses.

After supper, while it was still light, Print assigned each man a position for his sleeping pallet. The pallets were placed so as to afford maximum protection behind the few trees in the ranch house yard and the post fence. There were only two points of access to the pens for men coming on horseback. One was from the east, the road over which the longhorns moved as they started up the Chisholm Trail. The other was a less used path in from the west. Print placed two men on guard to the east, but with so few men at his disposal, he put but one guard in the grove of trees on the west approach. Everyone else would get as much sleep as possible.

Monday night passed uneventfully, both in the Olive neighborhood and at the longhorn pens. So did Tuesday night. Print's strategy of drawing the Yegua rustlers' attention away from the homes by moving the Olive men to the longhorn pens had apparently worked. Sam Carr's night watch reported meeting strangers on their rounds on Sunday night, but they never encountered another night prowler. Communications through to the Yegua gang were remarkable—and alarmingly responsive.

A long week passed during which life in the log house became routine, if not boring. The men inside the fort—for that is what it was—maintained a constant vigil. The watches both east and west of the ranch house were maintained with precision. The final days of July passed.

Nothing seemed different on August 1 until dusk, when a lone horseman rode in from the west. Bob Olive was on the west watch and stopped the visitor at the grove. Seeing that it was Fred Smith, Bob waved him on without even firing the signal shot to announce an arrival to the men at the ranch house.

The bed rolls were already in place for the night when Fred Smith rode up and announced himself at the gate. Print and Jay both went to the gate to meet him. Smith explained that he was on his way to see some cattle a considerable distance to the east and that he was already late, having intended to arrive there before nightfall. Print urged him to bed down with them until daylight, but Smith said he would ride during the night so as to be at his destination by breakfast time. He then explained that he had $750 in gold that he did not want to leave at his home while he was away overnight, and he asked Print to keep it for him a day or two. He handed the money bag to Print, who turned it over to one of the men and directed him to take it inside the house and put it in the front-room dresser. A moment later Fred Smith was off, disappearing in the thickening darkness down the road east toward the Chisholm Trail. Only the glow from the embers of the fire where Henry Strain had cooked supper lighted the yard as the men prepared to bed down for the night. Henry Strain and Bill Wells lay down on the veranda. The others took their usual places in the front yard, Jay and two of the cowboys sleeping fairly close together.

Shortly before midnight, Print and some of the other men were aroused by the loud braying of the big donkey in the breeding pens. Seconds later Print thought he heard someone walking just outside the fence. He listened. Thinking Bob might be coming in from the grove, he called out, "Bob?" A shotgun blast raked the area where he had been lying moments before. An instant later firing began in force from each corner of the ranch house; by the light of the gun flashes men could be seen coming through the gate. Jay Olive and the two men nearest him did not rise after the first volley. Clearly the attackers knew where to fire, even in pitch darkness. Except for the jack's warning, every man in the Olive yard could have been slain before any of them had a chance to reach for a gun.

Print Olive, Lee Moore, W. P. Butler, and Bumpus were not hurt in the exchange. Guns in hand, they began returning the fire. Moments later Print was hit in the left thigh hard enough to knock him to the ground and numb his leg for a few minutes, but the cattle king got to his knees and continued firing. At least one outlaw cried out and dropped his gun. Two of the invaders ran to the veranda, shooting one of the cowboys stationed there and forcing the other, Henry Strain, into the ranch house to surrender the $750 that Fred Smith had brought only a few hours before. Then they set fire to the inside of the house.

Bob Olive, and the two guards on the east exit road, had been adroitly skirted by the horsemen, who obviously knew their positions. These three now joined in the firing, but the rustlers had gunmen in reserve outside the fence to hold the road guards at bay. Consequently, with four men wounded inside the stockade, seven Olive guns were out of the fight. Lee Moore called to Print that he was out of ammunition. Print was too busy firing to pay any attention, and when he called for young Moore minutes later he got no response.

Now flames from the burning ranch house illuminated the shapes of the attackers. Presenting clear targets, they scurried from the yard before any of them could be identified, dragging the bodies of some of their comrades through the gate. Except for bloodstains on the ground, the attackers had made a clean escape, leaving no immediate clues. The fire soon leveled the ranch house.

As Bob Olive started for help, he met the Stiles brothers and their team pulling a wagon half full of hay coming to the aid of the wounded. Lee Moore, when he ran out of ammunition, had dashed to the Stiles' nearby ranch, directing them to take their team and wagon for the wounded while he borrowed a horse and galloped to town to bring Dr. Doak.

Jay, Print, and three of their men were wounded, Jay most seriously. His entire left side had been ripped by shotgun slugs, and he was losing a lot of blood. He was already delirious. All of the wounded men were placed in the Stiles wagon and driven to Print's home. It was daylight by the time they arrived.

Dr. Doak and Lee Moore got to the Print Olive place soon after. The doctor confirmed what Print feared. Lingering between life and death, Jay could not be moved, and it would be some time before the doctor could say whether he would recover. As for the other men, they would all be well within a month. The former Confederate army doctor told Print to keep his weight off his injured leg and predicted that the pain would be gone in a few days.

Bob rode back to the scene of the battle to look for some mark that would tell who had carried out the raid against them. Near the ashes of the veranda, he picked up a gold watch attached to a broken length of chain. An inscription identified the watch as belonging to Fred Smith, who for years had lived close to the Olives and posed as a trustworthy friend. Little wonder that the raiders knew where to aim, how to storm the ranch house yard, and where to retrieve the gold Smith had "borrowed" to Print so short a time before.

Jay Olive seemed improved after a week, but Dr. Doak guardedly refused to predict his recovery as the anxious family awaited the crisis still ahead. Nor would the doctor allow Jay to be moved to his own home.

The August 12 issue of the *Austin Statesman,* by this time one of the foremost newspapers in the South, carried an account of the pitched battle between the Olives and the outlaws, concluding with an appeal to the newly elected governor, Richard Coke, for the establishment of order under which the lives of Texans might be safe. The account read in part:

On the night of August 1, a party of fifteen or twenty
men attacked the Olive brothers on their ranch. . . .
Jay Olive was shot in the body in twenty-two places,
and it is thought he will die. Prentice Olive was shot
in the hip; and a man named Butler several times in
the leg and hip. Bill Wells, one of the Negroes, was
shot twice in the head. The raiders got $750 from the
house. . . .

   . . . the Olives are engaged largely in the raising of
stock and have suffered severely for a long time at
the hands of horse and cattle thieves. Several months
ago they gave out that they would kill anyone they
found skinning their cattle or riding their horses. Not
long after that, Old Man Crow and a suspicious character named Turk Turner were killed in the woods
near McDade while skinning a beef with the Olive
brand.

   Crow had a son who served one or two terms in
the penitentiary, and he accused the Olives of killing
his father, and threatened to avenge his death. Since
that time, it is said that he was been at the head
of a band of desperadoes and toughs and this crowd
is suspected of committing the horrible tragedy pre-
petrated on the Olive brothers and their employees
on the night of August 1.

   The Olive brothers are said to be upright men and
they have many warm friends in the vicinity of where
they live, and that further trouble and bloodshed
will follow is probable.

   What action the Governor and the authorities will
take we cannot say, but certainly the affair calls for
rigid and hearty work. Life and property are not safe
in Texas, and there is no use of anyone asserting that
it is.

Although Texas law enforcement agencies had found nothing

in the San Gabriel butchery to interest them for a decade, suddenly the state, on August 10, launched an investigation—not of the "Battle of Fort Olive," but into the death of the Negro youth in the Olive corn crib in July.

When the Texas officials remanded the matter to Williamson County authorities, Sheriff Sam Strayhorn still declined to take any action, but the name of Bob Olive for the first time appeared on the records of the Texas Rangers.

A few days after the battle at the Olive pens, Bob and Sam Carr caught up with Sam Malone and Charles Haskell, two men they believed to be associated with the rustlers. They held them at gun point for two hours on August 10, questioning them about their knowledge of the night raid. The men were released unhurt, but within a week the Texas Rangers issued a warrant for Olive and Carr for kidnapping.

Neither Williamson County officials nor the Texas Rangers had done anything to prevent the raid, though it had been widely discussed in every popular bar in Austin and Georgetown for weeks; nor were these agencies actively looking for the outlaws after the move to wipe out the Olive family. But in about the time it took a man to ride from the San Gabriel River to Austin, the Rangers issued a warrant for Robert Oliver, as they always listed him. Bob Olive was a marked man.

Meanwhile, Dr. Doak, calling to see Jay Olive on Saturday the nineteenth of August, found what he had feared: the damaged left lung and intestines had become infected. The doctor said little as he left some medicine to reduce the pain and fever, but Julia, who had maintained a constant watch over her son for eighteen days and nights, understood what Dr. Doak could not bring himself to say. She gave way to the only tears her family had seen during the long ordeal. At thirty-three, the first Olive to be born in Texas, the son who never went up the Chisholm Trail, was waging his final battle. The next day, surrounded by his parents, his brothers and sisters, and his beloved "Mira" and their children, Jay Olive died. It was ironic that death claimed first among the Olives the son who had seldom found occasion to draw his gun. Like his father whom he so admired and resembled, there is no record of Jay's ever having killed a man.

The next day, Monday, the little Lawrence Chapel and the surrounding yard were filled with friends who had come to pay their last respects. Men in little groups around the open grave expressed the opinion that Print and Bob Olive would exact a high price from Jay's murderers.

Jay's grave was still a fresh mound when Sheriff Sam Strayhorn and his East Williamson County deputies, Milt Tucker and Jim Myers, called at Print's home one evening. Strayhorn handed Print the Texas Rangers' warrant for the arrest of Bob Olive on charges of having kidnaped Malone and Haskell. As Strayhorn and his men started to walk out into the twilight, Print Olive called them back, ordering supper for them and beds for the night.

After supper the cattle king explained to the county sheriffs that while he understood what they were up against, the warrant for Bob Olive established the futility of any efforts to check the marauders. He reminded them that Williamson County officials had known that the Olive family faced annihilation in the summer of 1876; yet, beyond appointing another deputy, Strayhorn had been unable to do anything to help. The San Gabriel outlaws' threats still hung over the Olives' heads, but Strayhorn could not get an indictment against Jay's killers.

Print was growing more and more desperate as the law grew less and less capable of handling a worsening situation. Forgetting the men he and his brothers had killed along the way without having been called to account, Print saw the whole Olive family as being under attack and vulnerable without the protection of the law. He saw his enemies as Union sympathizers, carpetbaggers from Austin, and outlaws who were determined to kill off the Olives. He gave no evidence of understanding that the law was as helpless in these troubled times to protect his victims as it was to protect his family. Further, Print was enraged by the thought that others seemed to be trying to gain control of what he and his family had worked so hard to attain.

Print told Strayhorn that he had fought one war through to the finish, and he had no intention of doing so again. Instead, he announced, the sheriffs from now on could fight the San Gabriel outlaws alone; the Olive brothers, Bob, Ira, Print, and their families and herds, were leaving Texas as soon as the grass was green again in the spring, going north to the peaceful Platte country. Even the longhorns belonging to Jay's widow would go north with them.

Yes, they had some unfinished business to take care of first, Print told the sheriffs, that came under the heading of settling up Jay's "accounts." But within the year, the Olive guns that had maintained order for the cattlemen along the Chisholm Trail in Williamson County would be gone from Texas.

The Olive brothers' decision to leave Texas, far from quieting the turmoil, was followed by increased violence. The outlaws did not believe the cattle kings would ever give up their hold on the longhorns in the San Gabriel prairie and brush. Print and Bob Olive, for their part, resolved that the three men whom they held most responsible for the murder of their brother must die, certainly before the grass of another spring turned green. Dock Kelley, Cal Nutt, and Fred Smith had conspired to bring about the death of an Olive. Which of the brothers found Kelley or Nutt first did not matter. But Print would deal with Fred Smith.

Before Jay had been in his grave a week, Print took $750 in gold from his own funds, placing the coins in a money pouch along with Smith's gold watch with its broken chain. Accompanied by Bob, who insisted that he go along "just in case," Print took the money and the watch to the Smith home. Although the brothers were convinced that he was at his ranch, Fred's mother said that he was away. Print explained that he had come to return the $750 in gold that Fred had "borrowed him" on the evening of the trouble that killed Jay. He handed her the pouch, then the gold watch. Fred must have dropped his watch the same evening, he told her, since it had been found on the ground near the burned ranch house the next morning.

Olive's men watched Fred Smith's comings and goings, keeping Print informed. For a week Smith managed to evade his stalker. Then came the afternoon when he had piled his wagon high with personal belongings in an effort to get out of the country for a while. Ricardo Moreno, shadowing Smith, allowed him to get started from his home before reporting to the cattle king.

Smith had just eased his heavily loaded wagon into the bed of a small stream. As his team strained up the bank on the other side, Smith looked up. There, completely calm, motionless, appearing almost friendly, sat Print Olive on his horse, "White Flanks." Smith did not see the cowboy Moreno, who had slipped behind some brush, sensing that the cattle king wanted to be alone with his quarry.

Smith urged his team up onto high ground so that his horses passed Olive. Then he stopped. Olive was to Smith's right, gun to gun, no more than ten feet away.

Smith made one or two futile efforts to talk, but Olive cut him short, ordering him to "draw." Finally, Smith's nerves could stand the strain no longer. He reached for his gun and fired, but his shot went wild as a single slug from Olive's six-shooter crashed into his forehead, ripping away a part of his skull, leaving his brain exposed to the Texas sun.

Without a backward glance, Olive swung "White Flanks" toward home, calling to Moreno to take care of the body in a manner previously agreed upon. Moreno turned Smith's team around and sent it home without a driver. The Smith family told the neighbors that Fred was "away."

Fred Smith's body was never found. Only Moreno knew for certain what became of it, but through the years, to every inquiry he merely responded with a little, friendly, almost shy smile. Even after Print Olive was in his own grave, the Mexican cowboy gave the same response.

So the price of Jay Olive's murder was one-third paid by the end of August. On the third of September, a Sunday, Bob Olive and Sam Carr were riding into Georgetown when they unexpectedly met Dock Kelley and two of his companions. Bob told Carr to keep an eye on Kelley's companions while he asked Kelley about his part in the killing of Jay Olive.

Kelley was wearing both of his multi-notched six-shooters. Bob swung his horse across Kelley's path, careful to keep his right side next to Kelley's gun hand, and demanded to know what part Kelley had taken in the fatal raid. As soon as Bob put the question to Kelley, the big tough threw his horse forward in Olive's direction, reaching for his gun. Bob Olive crumpled Kelley's hand and forearm before Kelley could fire. Olive's second shot drove squarely through Kelley's heart. The butt of the gun with which Kelley made his last draw was completely covered with notches. Eight more notches decorated an attached ornamental piece. Olive handed Kelley's guns to Sam Carr and never asked for either of them again.

Despite his calm exterior as he faced Kelley—and many other adversaries—courage did not come any more easily to Bob Olive than it does to most men. Over the past year, constantly on the lookout for dangerous outlaws and defending the Olive homes from attack, the young Texan had developed what for lack of a better term old Dr. Doak called a "weak stomach" (actually ulcers). He suffered a particularly severe attack after the encounter with Dock Kelley.

Bob and Sam Carr left Kelley's body and his horse for his companions to dispose of. They rode directly into Georgetown, told Sheriff Strayhorn what had happened, and asked for a hearing on whatever charges would be placed against them. Sheriff Strayhorn, recalling his visit with Print two weeks before, kept the Texas Rangers' summons in his pocket and did not place Bob under arrest since he had come in voluntarily.

Cal Nutt had lost two of his top men in ten days to the Olives, and he was determined to conclude his own purge of the Olives before he, too, became their victim. Late in the same week that Kelley was shot down, Nutt bought drinks and pushed a gold coin into the outstretched hands of a redheaded Negro drifter and a Williamson County half-wit, promising them a handful of gold and all they could drink if they would go to Thrall and kill a man by the name of Print Olive.

The Negro's last name was said to be Banks, and perhaps because his hair was so red, no one ever bothered to ask about his first name. He was just "Red" Banks. The other man, known only as "the Donaldson Boy," was a mentally retarded resident of the community where he had lived since before the war.

The attack on Print Olive was a pitiful affair. The two hirelings rode up to the Print Olive ranch house shortly after mealtime when Print was at home. Banks, neglecting to carry even the rifle he had strapped to his saddle, pushed past Louisa when she came to the door, and looked for Print. When Print came to Louisa's aid, having picked up his rifle on the way to the door, Banks broke and ran.

Olive held his fire, watching to see whether the Negro was going for his gun or merely trying to get away. When Banks reached his horse, he did grab his rifle, wheeling on Louisa and Print, who were standing on the veranda. Print killed the man with a single shot. Meanwhile, Donaldson raised his gun to shoot, and Print, knowing the boy's mental condition, shot him in the leg, knocking him down. Donaldson artlessly told Olive that Red Banks and he had been sent to kill Print Olive and they were each to get a handful of money and all they could drink for doing the job.

Print called some of his men, and, loading Bank's body onto a wagon, took it to Deputy Sheriff Tucker at Taylorsville. Meanwhile, he sent Donaldson in his buggy first to be treated by Dr. Doak and then on to his home.

Donaldson, with Cal Nutt's aid, filed charges of murder and attempted murder against Print Olive. The grand jury was scheduled to hear the case September 22. With Smith and Kelley both dead, Nutt was beginning to sense that he was marked for execution by the Olives; he was desperate to get Print into prison as quickly as possible. He openly threatened the grand jury with violence unless there was an indictment against Print Olive for the murder of Red Banks and the attack on Donaldson. The same neighbors who had attended the funeral of Jay Olive only a month before were thoroughly aroused. They went to Georgetown in a body on the day of the grand jury hearing to signify their outrage that a man defending his own home and family should be liable for prosecution while state and county law was unable—or unwilling—to protect him. The Yegua gang had nearly twenty men massed on the street jeering and threatening Olive, his neighbors, and members of the grand jury. To make certain there would be no violence in front of the courthouse, Sheriff Sam Strayhorn finally deputized the ranchers from the Olive community and ordered them to stay in front of the courthouse and shoot if necessary to keep down trouble.

Cal Nutt got his way with the grand jury, notwithstanding. The indictment was returned against Print and a heavy bond set for his freedom. The cattle king put up the bond money and went home. His trial was held the following March, in 1877, just before the Olive herds started up the Chisholm Trail. When court actually convened, yet another case against Olive was dismissed, and his bond money was ordered returned.

Bob claimed Cal Nutt as his game, just as Print had asserted his right to catch Fred Smith. Nutt was not easy to corner. He never rode for longhorns in the brush or on raids; he dealt chiefly in useful contacts at Austin and Georgetown. Bob's opportunity came unexpectedly. He and Print had gone to Austin to recruit the trail crews for their biggest drive up the trail. Print wanted the best men available, and he knew that during the winter, when the trail's northern reaches were locked in ice and snow, Austin probably had the largest pool of unemployed cowboys to be found anywhere in America.

The brothers had finished hiring the men they needed on Saturday afternoon. It was just one week before Christmas. Print had been working hard, talking and bargaining with trail men all week, and enjoying poker games at night. He was tired, and although he and Bob could have reached home by midnight or a little later, they decided to stay overnight and get a good start early in the morning. They went to their hotel on Congress Avenue for supper. After a leisurely meal, Print went to bed.

Bob, who did not enjoy card games as much as Print and who consequently had not been up so late the evening before, decided to take a walk down the street from their hotel to the Iron Front Saloon, a fashionable place in the 1870s. Upon entering the saloon, he was startled to encounter Cal Nutt, who stood out among the cowboys in work clothes, attired as he was in a natty gray felt hat, fancy yellow brocade vest, highly polished black boots, and a pair of large-rowled Mexican-type spurs worn for decorative effect only. Olive noted especially that Nutt was wearing a gun. He was apparently alone and had been drinking. He was not drunk; his voice was crisp, and his eyes were alert; but his face was more flushed than usual, and he leaned rather than stood at the bar. The two men spoke, Nutt offering Olive a drink. Bob, who rarely drank since his stomach had become a problem, knew that he was master of the situation. He accepted Nutt's offer of a drink, standing close to the rustler's right side to keep him from reaching for his gun, exchanging pleasant small talk in a low voice.

Nutt gulped his drink and said he had to be on his way. As he stepped back from the bar and started toward the saloon door, Olive set down his own unfinished drink, starting toward the door with the man in the fancy vest, walking now on Nutt's left, purposely leaving the gang leader's right hand free. Halfway to the door Olive put the question: "Cal, were you there the night you sons of bitches killed my brother Jay?"

Nutt reached for his gun and fired, but Olive threw his body against the leader of the outlaws as the six-shooter discharged, ruining his aim. The bullet cut harmlessly through the left shoulder of Olive's heavy coat. In less time than it would have taken for the startled men at the bar to count three, Olive's six-shooter had pumped that many slugs into Nutt's chest. The leader of the San Gabriel longhorn rustlers was dead before his body hit the corner of the bar, turning over a shiny brass spittoon whose rich

127

brown contents splashed over the face and vest of the man who had planned the raid on the Olive pens.

Bob slipped out of the saloon before anyone had a chance to ask his identity. He took a side street back to his hotel. Arousing Print, Bob told him what had happened. It was one thing to shoot an outlaw in the brush in Williamson County, but it was something entirely different to shoot down a friend of the carpet-baggers in the Iron Front Saloon on Congress Avenue in Austin. Print lost no time in throwing on his clothes, and the brothers left at once for Thrall.

On the ride home, Print insisted that Bob must get out of Texas before the Rangers could discover who had murdered Cal Nutt and go into action. Two days was about as much time as Print figured they could depend on. Bob must start north immediately, though it was winter, and hide out until the spring. Print advised Bob to use an assumed name for a few months after reaching the Platte, in case the Rangers carried their search that far. They agreed upon "Stevens," and Bob's true identity remained a secret from many people up north until the time of his death.

They were home in time for Sunday breakfast. They gave Louisa an account of their successful recruiting, but they did not mention that Bob had gunned down Cal Nutt. Instead, Print proposed that since they already had their trail crew, they could advance their departure date by as much as a month, and it would be necessary for Bob to start north even before Christmas to have range ready by the time the herds arrived. This explanation seemed to satisfy the family, and Bob made preparations to leave Texas forever.

When he reached the Platte Valley, Bob would explore both the North and South Platte rivers for a range capable of sustaining Print's dream herd of twenty to thirty thousand head. Print doubted that Bob would find a suitable site on the South Platte. Previous exploration in eastern Colorado and in western Kansas had disclosed excellent ranges but also indicated that, for the most part, the ranges would feed no more than four or five thousand cattle. Therefore Print thought their prospects were better north of the Platte, from the Wyoming Territory eastward through the panhandle of Nebraska and into the central part of that state as far as Kearney, Grand Island, and Central City.

Print instructed Bob to go first to Colorado and see Ira. He warned Bob that Ira might be in a difficult mood after so many months away from home working day and night, and told Bob to persuade Ira to leave the Colorado herd in charge of Tom Wray and come home for the remainder of the winter. The old-guard cowboys, Armstrong, Lyons, Whitehead, and the others, must also come back to Texas to help with the spring drive— all except Jim Kelly. Since Ira could be quite overbearing with Negroes and Mexicans, Print thought it best that Jim should go on with Bob to explore the Platte country rather than accompany Ira home. If Ira wanted to discuss these arrangements further, he could ride into Ogallala and communicate with Print by tele-graph. After receiving his brother's instructions, Bob headed up the Chisholm Trail to Dodge City.

[8]

PLUM CREEK ON THE PLATTE

BOB FOUND THE RIDE north exciting and educational. He would have preferred to make his first trip up the Chisholm Trail with one of the Olive herds, making camp and meeting people, but his overnight stops at such places as Belton, Fort Worth, Caldwell, and Ellsworth, gave him a sense of exhilaration. He had been on the way only two or three days when he discovered that his stomach distress had almost disappeared.

The long rides each day seemed even longer because Bob seldom encountered anyone on the winter-stilled trail. His solitude gave him time to muse about the role he had just played in avenging Jay's death and about the effects of the event on the entire family. He had noticed particularly a distinct change in Print. Print seemed frequently lost in his own thoughts. His temper was nearer the surface. He kept his guns closer at hand. He drank a little longer and a little more often. Bob had the feeling that when Jay died something of Print had died too.

Jay had been a family man and a real leader in the Olive community. People had come long distances just to talk over their problems with him. Yet Jay had lived, Bob thought, behind the protective shield of Print's aggressiveness. When there was real trouble, Jay had known he could count on Print for help.

Ira was more like Print than Jay had been, a little younger and less experienced, but as good with cattle and better with horses; and that was high praise. Like Print, he could work long hours;

like Print, he had a quick temper. However, his stuttering when he was angry or excited was a handicap that he shared with no one else in the family. Nor was Ira ever as close to the rest of the family as Jay and Print were. Perhaps because of his wife's "town ways," he found it hard to relax with his family. Ira also found it more difficult to make friends. He preferred to work with white cowboys rather than Negroes or Mexicans and made a sharper distinction between white and dark skins than did other members of the Olive family.

Such were the thoughts Bob had as he rode north. He decided to ride through Ellsworth, Kansas, to see the town and the saloon where Jim Kelly had saved Print's life. Besides, Ellsworth was probably the most direct route to the Olive camp on the eastern Colorado line.

It was nearly the middle of January when Bob reached the winter camp. He was tremendously impressed with what Ira and Tom Wray had accomplished since their arrival the summer before. These were no temporary winter quarters, as he had expected, but a luxuriant range with water and other facilities for permanent operations, extending across the border into Nebraska and on east for several miles.

Just east of the Colorado-Nebraska line, Ira had devised a pen-and-corral complex that in some ways was more efficient than the big pens in Texas. Taking advantage of a small canyon which had sheer walls eight to ten feet high and a hard, flat floor, his men had built the corral and pens by erecting sod walls and installing gates across two narrow corridors within the canyon. This shelter would be equally useful summer and winter. The men had named it Corral Canyon.

The headquarters for the operation were located in Colorado near the main water supply at a point just east of present-day Wray, Colorado, named for the cowboy, Tom Wray. The little spring-fed stream coming out of the hills to the west had already been named Olive Creek. More important, Ira and his men had already built an effective sod dam across the little stream, creating Olive Lake, a reliable source of water. Just north of the little lake they had built two sod structures, a bunk house and a combination kitchen and mess hall. There was even a sod windbreak for the saddle horses. Jim Kelly had seen to that.

Print's misgivings however, about Ira's ability to withstand prolonged separation from Lou and the rest of the family had been justified. Bob learned from Tom Wray and Jim Kelly that the strain had combined with Ira's prejudice and short temper to cost a man his life. It seemed that, in the movement of the longhorns out of the corral each morning, Ira always insisted that a cowboy and his horse be stationed in the center of the gate to see that the cattle moved out slowly so that none was injured. On one particular morning the chore had been assigned to Leon, a trusted Mexican cowboy who had been with the Olives for several years. He was slow getting into position, and some of the animals became involved in a small stampede at the corral gate, resulting in a few broken horns and other minor injuries. Ira became so insulting and abusive that Leon reached for his only weapon, a knife. Ira pulled his gun and shot the Mexican, killing him instantly. The other cowboys had dug a grave high above the canyon wall where the water even at flood stage could not reach it. (Three-quarters of a century later when some heavy grading was being done at this point east of Wray, the bulldozer unearthed Leon's skeleton, his Mexican shoes, and his spurs.)

Ira had realized that he had gone too far and that another incident of any kind could touch off a full-blown mutiny. He had turned the camp over to Tom Wray and gone to Ogallala for winter supplies to let things cool off.

Such word traveled fast, even during winter on the long trail. By the time Ira got back to Thrall in accordance with Print's instructions, Print and Leon's widow had already learned of the incident. Ira went to see the widow and paid her an amount equal to several years' wages Leon would have been sending home to her. This was no altruistic gesture on Olive's part. Unless he made a satisfactory settlement, he knew that he would be finished as a boss on the Chisholm Trail. No cowboys would work for a cattle king who murdered unarmed cowhands, whatever their nationality or color.

But before Ira's return to Texas, Bob acquainted him and Tom Wray with Print's determination to move the Olives' entire holdings from Texas just as soon as spring conditions were right. Even the longhorns belonging to Jay's widow would come up the trail so that she might have the additional income that came from fattening them on northern pasture and shipping them over the Union Pacific into the Chicago markets.

No open range remained on either side of the trail from Fort Dodge to Ogallala, Tom and Ira agreed, that could take fifteen thousand head. All along the trail Texans were moving in quickly. There were small range areas such as the one they had claimed here in Colorado for the herd of cows, but they were few in number and far apart. It was agreed that Bob should ride farther north in search of less crowded grasslands for their purposes.

Bob spent the last days of January and all of February in the Platte country of the Wyoming Territory and western Nebraska. His trip took him northwest to Cheyenne, where he saw the Union Pacific Railroad for the first time. He followed the general route of the railroad to Fort Laramie, talking to ranchers and cowboys along the way. He was using the name of Robert Stevens, the alias he and Print had agreed on, and this had some advantages. Wyoming ranchers expressed themselves more freely about many things than they might have had their visitor introduced himself as Bob Olive.

From Fort Laramie, Bob rode north and east until he came to the North Platte River west of the present Wyoming town of Torrington. By this time he was convinced that the new Wyoming Stock Growers' Association had control of the range in the Wyoming Territory. The founders, mostly longhorn men who had left Texas for many of the same reasons that the Olives were coming north, had found that as a territory, Wyoming was still relatively free of laws affecting the operations of cattlemen. The longhorn men were in effect forming their own government, making their own law, and backing that law with their guns, just as they had in Texas. They encouraged only those men it suited their purposes to accept and allotted land only to them. To others

—and to Bob Olive—they explained firmly and unequivocally that "the range was closed." The Wyoming Stock Growers' Association was in the process of establishing a regime on the Wyoming range reminiscent of the land oligarchy of the prewar South that Jim and Julia Olive had sought to escape when they left Mississippi for the Republic of Texas.

Bob turned his horse east at Laramie and rode down the North Platte River, following the old Oregon Trail, which was still used by wagon trains even though the Union Pacific Railroad had taken over the long-haul freight to the West Coast. In the big Nebraska panhandle region, cattlemen had already pretty well taken over the range, just as they had in Wyoming. Here and there he found limited grass available, but nowhere was there enough for the big Olive herds that would be heading north in another forty-five to sixty days. From Ogallala Bob turned south to Corral Canyon, arriving somewhat dispirited at the end of the first week in March.

Ira had by this time returned to Texas. Tom Wray had moved the herd of cows a few miles west into Colorado for better winter feed. Jim Kelly had stayed behind at Corral Canyon waiting for Bob with fresh instructions from Print, again urging him to locate free range for their herds by the end of July at the latest. But Bob knew there was no important range available along the Chisholm Trail, either in Wyoming or western Nebraska. If any open range existed, it had to be in central Nebraska, probably north of the river—perhaps far north.

Olive and Jim Kelly rode north to Ogallala and bought supplies. Then they headed north and east along the South Platte until they reached the town of North Platte, now a rapidly growing, bustling community. One of North Platte's enterprising businessmen, Henry Clarke, had built the first non-railroad bridge to span the Platte in that area, and it was often choked with traffic headed toward the Black Hills in South Dakota, where gold had just been discovered. Major Frank North had already joined Buffalo Bill Cody in a large ranching operation north of town that extended into the valley of the Dismal River.

The Dismal River flowed southeast out of Nebraska's famous sandhills through counties that were just being laid out, bearing the names of Union heroes: Grant, Hooker, Thomas, McPherson, and Logan. The Middle and North Loup rivers north of the Dismal also flowed out of the sandhills and in the same southeasterly direction, the South Loup draining the land immediately north of the larger Platte River.

All of these river valleys and the sandhills north of them had been promised to the Sioux Indians, and as a result there was relatively little farming or cattle raising in the region. But ever since the coming of the railroad the Indians had been driven farther north. Though a few Sioux families still hunted in the area, ranchmen were beginning to move in.

For the first time since his search began late in January, Bob looked upon unclaimed range when he and Jim rode to the edge of the North-Cody operations near the headwaters of the Dismal River's south fork. This was also the best grass they had found in their ride through the Platte Valley. Jim was not entirely surprised, since he had been with Print Olive in 1869 on the trip north of the Platte River from Kearney. Still, what the Olive advance men saw for two days, they found hard to believe: lush grass relatively untouched—the kind of grass that could support a thousand cattle on every ridge. They saw some buffalo, entire herds of antelope, and a goodly number of elk and deer; but they saw not a single homesteader or settler. The only human activity they encountered was a solitary band of Sioux moving northwest to the spring hunting grounds in the sandhills.

When Olive and Kelly reached the point near the present-day town of Dunning, Nebraska, where the Dismal and Middle Loup rivers join, they met the first cowboys they had seen since leaving the newly built headquarters of the North-Cody ranch.

The men, line riders for the Dryden Ranch farther east, confirmed what the Olive men had observed: the range was unclaimed from the Dryden grass west to the North-Cody operations. In fact, there were only minor ranching operations all the way south to the Platte River and Union Pacific, through the new

135

Custer County and the older counties of Dawson and Buffalo, a distance roughly equal to the area they had found open to the west. However, still farther east and south, the Dryden cowboys said, there was extensive homesteading. Already enough fences were up to spoil the open range for cattle.

Plum Creek on the Platte, after the railroad was built to this point in 1866. *(Union Pacific Railroad Museum)*

Olive and Kelly did indeed find only a few small herds of cattle and an occasional homesteader as they rode south toward the Platte. The brands were generally familiar on the few long-horns they saw. About halfway to the Platte, they stopped at the new ranch of Texans Dan Haskell and Ed Hollaway. Haskell confirmed what Print Olive had guessed: longhorns and horses did grow heavier and develop better bones on the Nebraska range than they ever did in Texas. (Soil scientists half a century

136

later would discover the superior mineral content of the Platte country soil responsible.) Mustangs, Haskell said, grew several inches taller and up to three hundred pounds heavier.

The Olive men moved on south and found the valley of the South Loup practically unclaimed. Here Bob picked out a site that he judged to be ideal for the Olive headquarters. It was located on the north side of the stream, almost due north of the little town of Plum Creek on the Platte, and four miles from a place named Devil's Canyon. Bob admitted to Jim that after traveling across the Wyoming range and through western Nebraska without success, he had come to the conclusion that Print's dream of a range on the Platte was just that—a dream. But here in the Dismal and Loup valleys of Custer County, Print's dream could come true.

The two men moved on south to Plum Creek. This little town on the California-Oregon Trail, the Pony Express route, and now on the route of the transcontinental telegraph and the Union Pacific Railroad immediately appealed to Bob. Here the Olive families might live in town, yet be close enough to their longhorn operations for the men to be home most of the time. Triumphantly, Bob sent his report back to Print.

The weeks since Bob had hastily departed from Texas had been a period of furious preparation in Thrall. Plans had to be made not only to move the herds but also the families. Jim and Julia would stay in Texas and so would Jay's widow, but everyone else would come north in the fall. If Plum Creek looked as good as Bob reported, that would be where they would establish their new home.

The livestock had to be started up the Chisholm Trail in several herds. Ira was the trail boss on the first drive to leave, turning his herd out on the trail May 12. By the end of May he was past Fort Worth, and Print's herd was only eight days behind. A third, led by John Gatlin, left the Olive pens on May 29.

Print and Ira were as enthusiastic about Plum Creek as Bob had been. The word went back to Texas for their families to be prepared to spend Christmas 1877 in Plum Creek.

PART THREE

DUG IN
NORTH OF THE PLATTE

[9]

ANDERSONVILLE AND BLUESTEM

Just as the luxuriant grasslands and accessibility of the railroad drew Texas cattlemen to the Platte country, so the lure of free land and the Union Pacific immigrant cars brought farmers to the same area after the Civil War. Vigorous young couples came, eager to strike out on their own; and young men whose family holdings could not support several children; curious men who wanted to know what life was like beyond the Mississippi; and Union veterans, some unwilling or unable to resume a routine life back home.

Johnny Bryan had planned to get started right after breakfast this first Monday in September of 1876. He had assured his friend Charlie Baker that he would be ready to ride up the Springfield road not later than nine o'clock. By eight-thirty, completing his own farewells, he mounted his horse and turned north out of the Bryan farmyard toward the Baker place two miles away over the rolling Illinois prairie and woodland.

At ten o'clock Johnny had not yet arrived, and the Bakers watched anxiously lest Charlie become upset. He had never been the same since the war, ten years ago and more, and this trip west was in truth the first thing that had aroused his real interest in all that time. Finally, when Charlie could stand the waiting no longer, his family urged him to ride down the road and see what was holding Johnny. On turning the bend past the woodlot, Charlie saw Johnny's horse tied at the cemetery gate. A few steps farther, and he saw Johnny just where the Bakers knew he would be: sitting beside the grave in which his youthful hopes lay buried. The inscription on the marker read, "Sarah Ingraham, wife of John Bryan, departed this life. . ."

Sarah and Johnny had been sweethearts since school days, when Johnny had come to live with his aunt and uncle after the death of his father, William H. Bryan, killed that terrible first day at Shiloh. Johnny's aunt, a gentle, resourceful woman, had cared for him from then on, teaching by her own example the compassion and kindness that marked his character.

By the time he was fifteen, Johnny had developed a fine tenor voice and was singing in the choir of the little Methodist church. At twenty, he had begun to lead the singing and he was teaching music in their rural community near Taylorville in south-central Illinois.

Encouraged by Johnny, Sarah had also developed a love of music. The two had sat together regularly in church and attended socials together. When they became engaged, everyone said they were a perfect match, and when they were married in December 1874, the church was filled to capacity.

Soon after the young couple had started farming on rented land, Sarah began to show the first symptoms of tuberculosis, declining steadily until her death early in the summer of 1876.

Johnny had continued to tend his corn and cattle through the summer, but the joy was gone. Then, in late summer, his aunt, who had been reading the Union Pacific advertisements describing the fertile land available to homesteaders in the Platte Valley, had suggested that Johnny go out to visit his brother Joe in Lincoln, Nebraska, and investigate the possibility of becoming a landowner. Johnny had shown little interest at first, but gradually the idea had taken hold. He had never been farther away from home than the state capital at Springfield, about thirty miles northwest. He had broached the subject to Charlie Baker, whose sister Mary was Joe's wife, and Charlie had consented to accompany him.

Charlie Baker, tying his horse at the cemetery gate, had approached within a few feet of Johnny before the grieving young man was even aware that his friend was there. Johnny thanked him for coming and, after a last long look at the recent grave, joined Charlie at the gate, untied his horse, mounted, and rode off. Late that evening they arrived in Springfield.

Travel from central Illinois to the Platte country had become commonplace enough so that livery-stable men were familiar with the various routes and their advantages. Since Bryan and Baker were on horseback and since this late in the summer they would not be likely to encounter any high water, the men they consulted in Springfield assured them they could go the most direct route—could easily make the trip in two weeks. They were advised to take the main road west out of Springfield, through Jacksonville, and onward slightly northwest to Quincy, Illinois, where they would find frequent ferry service across the Mississippi River. They should continue northwest to Kirksville, Missouri, and then across the state to Maryville. Out of Maryville they would find a road west to the Missouri River. Crossing north of St. Joseph and entering Nebraska at the little town of Brownsville, they would have a good road north into Nebraska City and over the last thirty-five miles into Lincoln.

So the two young Illinois farmers rode west from Lincoln's Springfield to the town named for him in Nebraska. They soon found that they were part of a larger migration. Their route was almost one continuous campsite, dotted by evening fires around which gathered people like themselves, uprooted for one reason or another and seeking a new life on the free land in the West.

Johnny Bryan at twenty-six was well educated by the standards of the Middle West farm country from which he sprang. And like most successful farmers, he combined the talents of carpenter, mechanic, and engineer. Unassuming in appearance and manner, he nevertheless attracted people to him by his sincerity and integrity.

Charlie Baker was more typical, perhaps, of the men around the campfires. A veteran of the Civil War, he was already thirty-five years old, having been old enough in 1861 to enlist in the

Union army. He had moved south with Grant's forces through Kentucky and Tennessee. Captured by Confederate troops, he had spent most of the war years in one prison camp after another, having been evacuated repeatedly as more and more of the states west of the Appalachians came under Union control.

Johnny Bryan of Taylorville, the second homesteader in Clear Creek Valley, invited the Mitchell and Ketchum families to live with him.

Finally, in 1864, he had found himself about a hundred miles south of Atlanta, in southwestern Georgia's Camp Sumter, a stockade-enclosed tract of about fifteen acres along a small stream

144

just outside of Andersonville. It had been opened only a few months before Baker's contingent arrived, but already the facilities were overtaxed and food was scarce. It was impossible to get clean water to drink, and thousands of the Union prisoners had to live in the open, without shelter of any kind. Although ten additional acres were added to the campsite before the end of 1864, prisoners continued to be herded in until at one time the official count stood at over thirty thousand. Baker and his companions always believed that the actual figure was thousands higher. They kept their own records, and they counted far more dead than the 12,912 graves, preserved today as part of the national cemetery, indicated. Many of the trenches, the prisoners said, held several unlisted bodies.

The Confederacy itself was dying almost from the time Andersonville was established. Consequently many of the physical horrors suffered by the prisoners resulted from sheer inability on the part of their captors to cope with an overwhelming situation. Understandably, Charlie Baker and his companions believed the torture was deliberate. Some men lost their minds. Others, among them Charlie Baker, desperately tried every conceivable method of escape.

Some did escape—or so the inhabitants thought—despite the guards and their bloodhounds. Yet half a century later, men who had married, reared families, and achieved success in farming or business would shriek at night when visited in their dreams by the bloodhounds of Andersonville. Charlie Baker was one of those men.

Early in 1865, unable to endure the hunger and the sight of bodies piled high on carts and hauled to trenches that had been dug earlier in anticipation of the "harvest," he and two companions managed to get away one night and cover half a mile or more from the stockade before daylight, when they went into low brush to hide. Guards did not come upon them immediately, but they were close enough to pin the fugitives down for a long while. Hours passed. Then, just when the men began to think it was safe to move on, the Andersonville bloodhound pack picked up their scent and descended upon them in a ferocious rush. Flushed from their cover, the men ran for the closest trees —little more than saplings they were—several hundred yards away. In their weakened condition they were hardly able to reach the trees at all, the hounds lunging at them as they frantically struggled up the slender trunks, pulling one man down and killing him before the horrified gaze of Baker and the third man. The victim's cries for help and shrieks of agony still rang in Baker's ears.

Fortunately the third man was high enough to be safe and strong enough to hold on. Baker, whose weight did not allow him to climb any higher into the young boughs, was beyond reach of most of the bloodhounds in the pack, although they flung themselves at him again and again. But occasionally two of the largest beasts would leap high enough to tear his pants legs, their fangs ripping the skin on his lower legs as the big animals fell back to the ground.

This gruesome siege continued all the rest of the day. With darkness the hounds ceased their jumping, but some of them remained menacingly below all night, resuming their efforts the next day. By midmorning Baker's pants legs were ripped away below the knees, and his lower legs were masses of bloody welts and cuts. He and his companion were certain that this torture was deliberate—that the Confederate prison guards knew what was happening to them but wanted the bloodhounds to finish them off. The din could hardly have failed to carry as far as the ears of their hunters.

At last, however, the nightmare was over. Guards appeared before noon, subduing the bloodhounds and chaining them together to be led away—and starved, Baker thought, before being loosed to hunt down the next escapees. Then the men were ordered down from the trees. Baker's arms, hooked over two small limbs, had long since become too numb to manipulate. Prodded by guards' whips, the one thing even the Andersonville bloodhounds feared, Baker wrenched himself loose and fell, an uncontrollable dead weight, to the ground. He was taken back and paraded through the camp as an object lesson for thousands of fellow prisoners.

Charlie Baker never fully recovered from the effects of his ordeal. He never overcame his fear of the dark; and even twenty years after his journey to the Platte, the unexpected loud barking of a dog would cause him to run wildly into the barn to hide

Charles Baker of Taylorville, Illinois, the first homesteader in upper Clear Creek Valley, north of the Platte River. Photo taken two months after release from Andersonville prison.

under the hay, or to rush into the house and hide in a closet—
even a dark closet. The shredded trousers took on a special
meaning. He had had his picture taken in them after his release,
and he carried the picture with him as he rode west. He seemed
to need evidence that he was not mad—that the night that so
drastically altered him had really happened.

Johnny Bryan's brother Joseph and his family arrived after the
war between the cattle kings and the homesteaders. Mrs. Bryan
was a sister of Charles Baker.

Charlie and Johnny rode into Lincoln on the twenty-fourth of
September after nearly three weeks in the saddle. They found the
ten-year-old capital of Nebraska to be more of a frontier town
than they had somehow expected, consisting of only two main
roads and a few short cross streets, laid out on land as level as
any in Illinois. Lancaster County, outside the town limits, was on
the crest of the wave of homesteaders washing over the prairie,
transforming the open range into farmsteads. West of town the

process was only partially complete, but to the east the settlers had pretty well taken over.

Joseph and Mary Bryan had come to Lincoln three years earlier, in 1873. Here Joseph had taken a job in the salt mine, hoping to save enough money to equip a homestead. Meanwhile, as their family grew to include three children and saving became more difficult, all the good land close to Lincoln had been claimed, and homesteaded land available for purchase had become too expensive. So if Joseph and Mary were ever to homestead, they would have to depend on Johnny and Charlie to find a location for them while prospecting for their own.

According to many of the cattlemen who came to buy salt, and judging from accounts in the *Lincoln Journal,* Lincoln had been the northern end of the Chisholm Trail from 1871 to about 1873. At that time longhorns were everywhere in the vicinity, and, during the winter, especially on weekends, the town attracted the cowboys, a rough lot who took over the bars and visited the "soiled doves" in their boarding houses. This element had hardly contributed to the stability of the town, and most of the townspeople viewed them with distaste. Now, at least, Lincoln had become a suitable place to live and rear children.

Not that all dissension had ceased between the cattlemen and their neighbors: on the contrary, a more basic source of friction seemed to be developing. According to Joseph, the cattlemen wanted to keep the land in free range and objected to the encroachment of homesteaders intent on fencing the land and growing crops. Cattlemen had shot or hanged some men, accusing them of having stolen horses or longhorns when in fact it looked to the settlers as if the dead men had been guilty of nothing more than placing a fence around their land. The fledgling state of Nebraska had only recently passed laws to cope with the situation, and the Bryans felt confident that when these laws were understood, the troubles would cease.

Joseph told his brother and brother-in-law that, just as the Union Pacific advertised, good farmland was plentiful for hundreds of miles up the Platte River Valley, despite the shortage of rainfall. The men decided that Johnny and Charlie should start their search as soon as possible, while the mild weather held, because the condition of the grass in early fall was one of the best indicators of the prevailing weather and the condition of the soil underneath. Once they had found suitable homesteads, they should go to the nearest government land office and file. Then they should come back to Lincoln for the winter, and next year when they returned to break the soil, Joseph would go with them and file in the same area.

After studying the Union Pacific maps, Johnny and Charlie decided to explore the land south of the railroad and the Platte— land directly west of Lincoln. They reasoned that since the railroad lay north of the river, in the center of a swath of land twenty miles wide on either side of its right-of-way, they would be going too far north if they tried to settle north of that barrier. So on October 1, they saddled their horses and started west along the old road established by the wagon train company of Russell, Majors, and Waddell and still used by some covered wagons and freight wagons heading for points in southern Nebraska and northern Kansas not served by the railroad.

Fall could be dry in central Illinois, and perhaps this was an unusually dry year; but Johnny and Charlie had never seen so much dry grass before. Traveling twenty-five to thirty discouraging miles a day through short-grass country alive with longhorns, both men agreed that this land seemed suitable only for grazing. Along the streams where crops would grow, other homesteaders had already laid claim to the best locations. They talked with everyone they met and followed every lead that was offered. One traveler told them that their chances were best down toward the Kansas line in the valley of the Republican River, so they turned southwest across the Little Blue River and the old Oregon Trail, arriving in Arapahoe in the afternoon of October 4. Still they had seen nothing to change their minds: this looked like a good place to raise cattle, but not to farm.

Knowing that the saloon functioned as a reliable communications center in any town on the plains, young Bryan and Baker inquired there about the likelihood of finding suitable land thereabouts. The proprietor told them that if they were interested in raising crops, they were on the wrong side of the Platte. The alluvial plain formed by the river lay mainly to the north of the channel, watered by several small tributaries, while on this side there was only a narrow band of fertile soil edging the south bank, giving way rapidly to the semi-arid prairie. If they went due north about thirty miles to the little town of Plum Creek on the northern bank of the Platte, and then continued north and a little east to one of several small streams—the Loups—running southeast out of Nebraska's mysterious sandhills, they would find the finest cropland anywhere between Texas and the Dakotas. "If the grass isn't up to your horses' bellies, and so thick you can't see the ground," their informant concluded, "you haven't reached the Loups yet. Just keep going 'til you do."

Bill Green, the saloonkeeper in Plum Creek, painted an even more glowing picture of prospects in the Loups. He suggested that Johnny and Charlie go down to the railroad station and see the new Rand McNally map of Nebraska. It showed the territory clearly, and they would get a good idea of how to reach "the best farmland in the West." In response to questions about the Indians, Green said that the Nebraska Sioux had been promised the Loups as hunting grounds, but since the Indians had been driven north of the Platte, they had moved well beyond the entire area and rarely appeared in the area, and certainly not menacingly.

Some trouble had broken out between cattlemen and homesteaders, however, Green admitted. He explained that there were two kinds of cattlemen in the area. The smaller operators, most of them from the East, tried to own as much of their grazing land as possible, even fencing some of it. A number of these were to be found on the South Loup. They were friendly, and he suggested the newcomers stop to get acquainted with them.

But the cattlemen found west along the Platte and on into Wyoming Territory were quite different. They paid no taxes and no rent. They held that the grass was free like the water in the river. Most of them had come up from Texas, their herds sometimes numbering 10,000 head and more, and they carried guns and used them—sometimes a little too soon, maybe. "But you can't blame them too much for dealing pretty rough with men who steal their cattle and horses," Green added. He wished his visitors well as they took their leave and started north.

[10]

A COUNTY FOR CUSTER

NEAR THE POINT where Johnny and Charlie crossed the South
Loup River, they visited several of the small ranchers: the Frank
Youngs from Boston, Henry Stuckey and his wife, and Mrs.
Stuckey's brother, Eugene Boblits and his wife. The young Bob-
lits couple had been married two years earlier in West Virginia,
Harriet's home. Eugene had come west in 1872 and established
his holdings before returning for his bride, the former Harriet
Eliza Duling. Young Boblits would subsequently become the first
county judge of Custer County; and though he held that office
but one term as against twenty-two years as postmaster of
Tuckerville and half a century as a rancher and farmer, he would
be called Judge Boblits for the rest of his life. But at this time
he and Harriet were just getting a start.

According to Boblits, there was little farming on any of the
Loups this far west. The only kinds of crops he had known in
Maryland and Pennsylvania would not thrive in country so dry.
Moreover, the growing season was too short and the land too
hilly to make farming feasible, he thought. Cattle, though, could
flourish here. The streams provided ample water the year round,
the bluestem in the bottoms supplied abundant summer and fall
feed, and the shorter grass on the hills—buffalo grass, deriving
its very name from the animals—had long sustained the greatest
concentration of buffalo found anywhere on the plains and allowed the cattle to continue to gain right through the winter.

153

By midsummer the area was so dry that it was subject to prairie fires. Sometimes, Boblits said, a fire could be seen coming for a day or two, and when it arrived it could be a wall of flame higher than a two-story house, with smoke enough to darken the sun. Dreadful by day, the sight was even more terrifying at night.

The Custer County ranch home of Judge E. J. Boblits. Most of the notables in Nebraska public life visited Judge Boblits here. Judge Boblits experimented with many "firsts" in the ranch country. The house had running water years before such conveniences were available on Nebraska farms. Judge Boblits was using irrigation on limited areas of his ranch a quarter of a century before irrigated farming became commonplace. He introduced new plant varieties, especially fruit trees, to the Custer County area.

Boblits' parents had come west with them and settled in Plum Creek. They could afford something better than a sod house, so they had built a frame house like the one they had back in Pennsylvania. Before they could move in, a vicious prairie fire swept through Plum Creek, destroying the new home so quickly that they could not even rescue the new table and chairs, still crated. The house was a total loss.

These prairie fires were the greatest hazard in this country, the Boblits believed, but some defenses were already being improvised. Though their sod ranch buildings were less combustible than lumber, the homesteaders were planting small cottonwood trees close together to keep the grass down. As the trees grew and crowded one another, the stunted ones could be taken out for firewood. Meanwhile, a plowed-ground fire belt had to be maintained on the west and north, the directions from which the fires usually roared in. Johnny Bryan would remember this advice.

Although Boblits was convinced the area would never support a large population, he believed the time had come to begin establishing such vital county functions as voting procedures, law enforcement, schools, and roads. Custer County was, in fact, laid out and organized within the year, embracing an area larger than Delaware and twice the size of Rhode Island.

Talk turned, as it almost always did, to the great war, the one experience that had touched everyone. Johnny and Charlie were surprised that a man as young as Boblits seemed to be could have served through four years in the Army of the Potomac. Their host admitted he had enlisted only a few weeks after his fifteenth birthday, and he had almost lost his life in the bloodiest single day of the war. The Battle of Antietam, fought only fifteen miles south of Boblits' Maryland birthplace, had cost the Union twelve thousand casualties and the Confederacy more than thirteen thousand within one twelve-hour period.

Young Boblits had distinguished himself before noon on the first day of the great battle. A gunner in Company H, he had seen the regimental flagbearer go down under a volley of Confederate rifle fire. The five color guards having been shot down too, Boblits had rushed in, picked up the flag, and carried the colors as the regiment advanced. But early in the afternoon he had fallen with a rifle slug in his hip. Managing to get back to his feet, he had held the flag until Sergeant Walter Greenland from Company C had taken it from him to carry through the remainder of the battle, the Union's first important victory east of the Appalachian Mountains. In time young Boblits had recovered and returned to combat, but the wound would bother him the rest of his life.

Bryan and Baker liked the young families they found here on the South Loup, but these people had more capital than the Illinois men had. Perhaps their stake was not large enough to launch them successfully. The land was clearly the best they had seen in Nebraska, but they were dubious about trying to farm in an area apparently given over to raising these strange longhorn cattle. So after a few days of pleasant visiting—and eating more good beef than they had ever eaten in their lives—the two rode north and east to the Middle Loup River to look for Charles Dowse, a settler about whom the saloonkeeper in Plum Creek had told them.

The men from Taylorville spent three leisurely days riding across the trackless expanse that would soon become Custer County. They saw little evidence of either homesteaders or cattlemen, and the countryside astonished them more the farther east they went. For one thing, in the last miles before they reached the Middle Loup the grass in the small creek valleys reached heights nearly up to their saddle horns and became so dense their horses often attempted to go around it. This area between the South and Middle Loup rivers also abounded with wildlife. Herds of elk and antelope appeared, especially in late afternoon and early evening, when they were feeding. Bryan and Baker came across an occasional bear with cubs, the first bears either of them had ever seen. On the evening of the third day, they rode within fifty yards of a small buffalo herd that continued to graze undisturbed. "This is closer to the Garden of Eden than I ever expected to get," Johnny Bryan called to his companion. "I almost feel that we ought to go back to Illinois and leave it this way forever."

Just at sundown on the twenty-sixth of September, Bryan and Baker reached the sod house of Charles Dowse. Dowse and his wife invited the men to tie up their horses and come in for supper. Johnny explained their mission and recounted how, after riding across southern Nebraska, they had been advised to turn north into the Loup valleys if they wanted to find good farmsites. The Dowses shared the view that the Loups were certain to be homesteaded as soon as farmers had taken up the good land to the east, but at present settlers were too few even to warrant forming a county. Dowse had helped with the federal government survey of the area between the Middle and South Loup rivers, and he thought the finest land he had ever seen lay in some bluestem bottoms a few miles south of his soddy. He would move down there himself, he told them, if he had not already erected his buildings. He agreed to show them the area he was talking about and help them select the best 160 acres of land available, 160 acres being the maximum area that could be claimed by one man.

In the evening Johnny and Charlie asked the Dowses about Indians, cattle running in the area, and the year-round weather. They learned that in the North Loup River Valley, ten miles to the northeast, over in Valley County near Ord, there had been some Indian trouble two years before, but the settlers had built a sod fort as a precaution and there had been no trouble since.

The Dowse family thought the weather on the Middle Loup was ideal. The springs were pleasant, with plenty of rain to get the garden and crops started, there was usually plenty of summer moisture until the "dog days" in August, and then it could get hot and dry for a month or more.

"The fall is long and pleasant," Dowse told his guests, "usually dry like it is now, a good time to get work done for winter and the next spring. More likely than not, the weather will be moderate until Thanksgiving. May have a little snow in December, but it stays only a day or two. December can be either cold or mild. We've had them both ways. About the first of the year we usually get a good snow cover that lasts for five or six weeks and keeps the cold out of the ground."

As for cattle, Dowse said, "We have never seen a longhorn over here. There is a cattle operation over on Ash Creek south of Broken Bow that you fellows probably didn't see because you came across a little farther south. Captain Street, a Union war veteran up that way, put in cattle before we came. I think he told me that he put eight hundred head of longhorns on Ash Creek about fifteen miles west and south of here, in the summer of 1869.

"The farther west toward Ogallala you go, the more cattle you'll see. They tell me there are a hundred thousand head within ten or fifteen miles of the Union Pacific loading docks at Ogallala this fall, but that's nearly a hundred and fifty miles from here; I don't look for us to have any longhorns this far east," Dowse concluded.

[11]

STRANGER, COME HOME

NEXT MORNING, after a breakfast of pancakes and some of Mrs. Dowse's wild plum sauce, Charlie, Johnny, and Charlie Dowse rode south some ten miles to the banks of a sparkling little stream that Dowse called Clear Creek. The bluestem, four or five feet high, rippling like a calm, green-flecked yellow sea in the light breeze, stretched away to the horizon. Johnny would tell friends in later years that the whole little valley seemed to whisper, "Stranger, come home."

Dowse located a surveyor's stake indicating that the three men were standing on the 160-acre northeast corner of Section Five. Turning to Dowse, Johnny said, "This is the place I would like to live; if you'll give me the information I need for filing, I'll take this quarter section for my homestead."

Baker had said little since breakfast, but now he objected. "Johnny," he began, "I'm older, and I'm a veteran. This is the land I want." There was a finality in his voice.

"All right, Charlie," responded Johnny, "go ahead and take it, and I'll look a little further. There's plenty of good land here for all of us." And while Charlie Baker circled his homestead for a closer look, Bryan explained his friend's temperament and the reasons for it to Dowse, adding that it might be advisable for him to select a homestead a little further down the valley to make sure that he would not get in Baker's way.

When Charlie returned, they all rode on down the valley to

159

another site Dowse had recommended. Bryan noted that close to the south edge of the property, facing Clear Creek, the ground rose sharply in a sort of bluff, almost perpendicular, to a height of eight or ten feet, an ideal place for a good-sized dugout. Yes, he would file on this land. The corner marker showed these acres to comprise the southeast corner of Section Nine.

Settling with Charlie Dowse for their food and lodging, Bryan and Baker rode off toward Grand Island, arriving the next afternoon before the land office closed for the day. Thus Charlie Baker became the first homesteader on upper Clear Creek and Johnny Bryan, the second. The date was October 29, 1876.

Back in Lincoln, Charlie decided to go back to Taylorville for the winter, traveling alone this time, and confident that he could make the trip. Johnny, however, let it be known around town that he would be available for music lessons, and soon he had all the pupils he could handle. In the spring of 1878, he would go out to his homestead early, plant a good garden for a winter food supply, and break enough ground for a small stand of corn. But this first year there was no hurry. He would teach until May, because about all he could hope to accomplish on his land the first season would be to fix the locations of the buildings, plant cottonwood trees, and build his dugout house. He set off the first week in May.

The first part of his 135-mile journey was uneventful. Just outside of Seward, however, his horse threw a shoe. Inquiring about a blacksmith at Central City, Johnny was told there was a good one on a farm just north of town. To the young woman who greeted him in the farmyard he explained why he had come. The brown-haired, blue-eyed young woman invited him to come indoors and wait for the two blacksmiths who had gone to a neighbor's farm to do some repair work. Introducing herself as Tamar Snow, she next introduced him to her mother, Mrs. Mitchell, and her sister, Lydia Snow. A younger sister, Elizabeth, was at home, too, but Tamar explained that young Henry had gone to the Gagle home with his father, Luther Mitchell, and Ami Ketchum. They would be through soon, she was sure, and meanwhile the women set about preparing a meal for their guest.

While they waited, Johnny exchanged stories of the past with Jane Mitchell and her daughters. He learned that Lydia and Tamar, like himself, had lost their father, Peter Snow, in the Civil War, they were not sure where. Their stepfather, Luther

The Joseph Bryan homestead on Clear Creek in the mid-1880s. The sod house is in the background.

Mitchell, had also been with the Union forces, all the way down to Vicksburg and across the South with General Sherman. "Because he was a blacksmith, he was never in the fighting, though, except at Shiloh," she told Johnny. "I guess everyone knows how it was there."

After the war Jane Snow had married Luther and they had moved to Iowa, where Elizabeth and Henry were born. Then two years later they had come to Nebraska.

Just before dark the men came home—Luther Mitchell, a man in his early sixties, and his partner, Ami Ketchum, in his early twenties. Luther urged Johnny to stay at the farm overnight, promising to shoe his horse right after daylight so he could be on his way. Johnny was only too happy to break his journey in such pleasant company, and he settled down for the evening.

Johnny explained that he was homesteading between the Loups on the other side of Sherman County, beyond Loup City. Mitchell said that he and Ketchum had been planning for some time to look for better land than what they were presently farming, and from Johnny's description, they might come out and visit him and see that country. When Johnny left the next morning, it was with the understanding that Luther and Ami would come out to Clear Creek the first of September with a view to becoming neighbors.

Johnny spent most of the summer alone on Clear Creek. He rode into Arcadia about once a week for supplies, and twice he visited the Dowses. But during one period of more than a month he did not see another person. Time passed quickly, however, with so much to do. First he put down stakes to indicate where each building would eventually stand. Next he dug up hundreds of little cottonwood trees from the banks of the creek, transplanting some of them into a combination woodlot and windbreak and surrounding the site of each future building with the rest. By mid-June he was ready to begin work on his house.

Johnny had seen some of the dugouts used by pioneers in Illinois a generation earlier, many of which still served as cyclone cellars or winter storehouses for fruits and vegetables. Most of these were small, dark, and often damp. He would build a better dugout than any he had seen.

He planned his dugout with care, even sketching its front on the steep earthen bank with his spade. The inside, twenty-four feet long, twelve feet wide, and six and a half feet high, would require the removal of more than eighteen thousand cubic feet of earth.

He went south to Kearney, on the Platte, a distance of about fifty miles, and bought lumber for the front. Two windows, a door, corner posts, a stove, and the necessary hardware completed his stock of materials, and he hired a carter to haul them up to Clear Creek in his wagon. They arrived about the first of August, and Johnny fell to work installing the refinements.

When the house was completed, three or four feet of earth remained in the bank above the ceiling through which he cleared a channel for a stovepipe. There was a lock for the door, and a key. By the time Mitchell and Ketchum arrived late in August, a little ahead of schedule, the dugout was almost finished.

Johnny was surprised to see that Mrs. Mitchell and the entire family had accompanied the men—on an outing, Luther said. During the summer, Tamar and Ami had become engaged, and they intended to take a homestead adjoining the Mitchells', so they had all come prospecting together. The two families planned to build one large sod house, half on the Mitchell property, the other half on the Ketchums', and they would combine their farming enterprise.

When they had been on Clear Creek scarcely an hour, Luther Mitchell asserted that this was certainly the best land he had seen north of the Platte River. The difficulty, he thought, would lie in deciding on one parcel out of a seemingly limitless choice. Johnny took time from his work to help in the search, and finally the two families decided upon a location about half a mile north of Johnny's place.

Johnny enjoyed the three days his visitors spent with him. They all took their meals together, meals that included fresh meat every day since Ami, unlike Johnny and most other homesteaders, carried a six-shooter and used it with great skill. He could bag small game at impressive distances.

Evenings Ami entertained them all by shooting at various targets. One of his favorites was a silver dollar inserted into the split end of a stick which Tamar would stand in the ground at a distance of twenty-five yards, setting it back farther and farther each time Ami hit it. Often they would continue this way until the small silver target stood a hundred yards or more away.

Ami Ketchum was by all odds the best marksman Johnny had ever seen.

On the morning of the fourth day, the Mitchells and Ketchum left for Grand Island to file on their homesteads. Johnny completed his dugout a few days later, in time to receive still more callers, the Herringtons and the Murphys. Impressed by Johnny's house, the Herringtons decided to build the same kind into the bank about half a mile downstream. The Murphys favored higher ground, choosing a site to the south and a little west of Johnny's land. Next year Johnny would have several neighbors.

In mid-September, as the time approached for Johnny to go back to Lincoln for the second time, he set out one evening on a leisurely ride that took him west about two miles. Here he came upon a few Texas longhorns grazing on the bluestem. He had not seen any cattle in this vicinity before, and for some reason, he felt vaguely apprehensive. The sensation was new to him.

On the way back to Lincoln, Johnny stopped at the Mitchell farm once more. He proposed that the next spring when the Mitchell-Snow family and Ami came to Clear Creek they should all, with the exception of Ami, move into his dugout while their sod house was being built. He and Ami could sleep in the Mitchells' covered wagon when it rained, and the rest of the time they could just throw their bedrolls on the ground. They were a pair of healthy young men. His offer was eagerly accepted, and they all agreed to meet when the bluestem turned green in the spring. They set April 15 as the date to be back on Clear Creek.

PART FOUR

LONGHORNS IN THE TALL CORN

[12]

SIT UP TO OUR TABLE, MR. BRYAN

JOHNNY BRYAN met with his voice students in Lincoln through the final week in March. An early spring had hastened his preparations to leave for his homestead up the Platte, so he was ready days earlier. He finished his lessons on Friday, March 29, 1878. By the following Monday, the first of April, he was on his way to Clear Creek, anxious to see how his dugout house had fared during the winter. Would there be water inside, or had some Indians, hunters, or would-be homesteaders broken down the door and used it since he had turned the key in the lock late in the September before?

Joseph and Mary Bryan had decided that they would not leave Lincoln and Joseph's job this year. They would let Johnny get his place started, and they would plan to go to Clear Creek and homestead the following year. Actually, a second year passed before they came to live in Johnny's dugout house.

Johnny rode the direct route from Lincoln to Clear Creek, through Seward, Central City, and Loup City. At Central City he stopped to see whether the Mitchells and Ami Ketchum were still planning to arrive at Clear Creek by the fifteenth of April. Bryan arrived late Tuesday, and, at the insistence of Tamar and Mrs. Mitchell, he stayed overnight.

Things were packed, ready for the trip to Custer County, and Luther and Ami were working from dawn until dark to complete the blacksmith jobs they had promised to do for neighbors in the area before leaving Merrick County.

"Really no different now than it has been most of the winter," Mrs. Mitchell told Johnny Bryan. "The men have been working as though life itself depended on it, every day the weather would permit, since Christmas. They want to go to Custer County with as much money for fencing as possible, and they hate to leave the neighbors here without their blacksmith work done, just ahead of the spring season."

Ami and Luther came back shortly after dark. At supper they talked of homesteading, and Johnny Bryan asked if the Mitchells had gotten any news from Custer County since fall. He had seen a few items in the *Lincoln Journal* from places up the Platte like Grand Island and Kearney, but no news about Custer County, he reported.

Luther Mitchell said that some of the neighbors had bought longhorn cattle over at Ogallala and driven them back to Merrick County during the winter while the ground was still frozen and the Loup rivers easy to ford. They had reported that a new outfit from Texas, the Olive brothers, had brought one of the largest herds of longhorns ever to come up the Chisholm Trail and put them north of the Platte, mostly on the Custer County range and up in the Dismal River Valley farther northwest.

"Remember, Mr. Bryan, you told us of seeing longhorn steers grazing to the west of your homestead just before you came by here on your way to Lincoln last fall? Those probably were cattle right out of Texas, and they probably had the Olive brand. These Olive cattle began coming through Plum Creek in July. At least that's what the Merrick County men who were over that way told us when they came back this winter."

Bryan said he thought this was possible, since the longhorns certainly were like all the other Texas cattle he had seen over in south Custer County earlier last year; and they were thin, as though they might have just come up the trail.

"This is one reason why Ami and I have been working so hard at blacksmithing this winter," said Mitchell. "We are going to have to fence our corn ground. That fence wire has to be hauled all the way from Illinois, they tell me, and it sure is mighty dear."

Mrs. Mitchell asked Johnny where they would be able to find

a doctor in case the children got sick, and Johnny said that he figured the nearest doctor was likely to be in Kearney, about fifty miles from the homesteads.

"That's about the same distance as back here to Central City," Mrs. Mitchell observed. "That being the case, we would just have to come back and stay with the Gagles or some of the other neighbors till we were able to make the trip back."

Talk turned to the question of how much they could hope to get done before cold weather in the late fall. Johnny said that he hoped to begin breaking ground for some corn and a good garden, and he would plant some more trees. Mitchell deferred to his young partner to explain their plans.

"Luther and I have talked a lot about what we could get done this year. We figure, Mr. Bryan, that if the weather gives us any chance at all we should break about ten acres of bluestem sod, put it in corn, fence it, build a blacksmith shop, and put up our big combination sod house before the snow has a chance to pile up in December."

Johnny had not realized until the usually quiet Ketchum spoke up with such clarity and confidence how important he was in the Mitchells' plans. Aloud he observed that it sounded like a mighty busy summer ahead on Clear Creek.

"Just as Ami says," Mitchell added, "we figure to get a lot done this year. This is really the big year for us. If we can harvest a good corn crop in the fall, build our house, and do some blacksmith work we'll go into next winter not wanting for a thing or taking orders from anyone. From then on it will be just a case of putting in more crops and adding a little more livestock. In five years we should have our farms in full use, not owe a cent to anyone, and start working only eight or ten hours a day. Not that I mind hard work, but in a few days I'm going to be sixty-three years old. The rest of you are young folks." Even Jane, his wife, was only in her forties, and the rest were just youngsters. He hoped in another year or two he could attend mostly to the blacksmithing and leave the heavy farm work to the others.

Ami Ketchum laid out the work by months. He hoped even in

April to get a lot of bluestem broken for the corn ground. They would try to have half the corn planted by the middle of May and the entire crop by Memorial Day. In June they would fence the cornland and build a workshop. In July they would only have to keep the weeds out of the corn and garden, and then would get started building the big soddy.

Tamar Snow spoke up. "We will not work all the time, Mr. Bryan, even if you might think so, the way Ami and my father talk. We'll take some time to have fun too. There'll be times, just like there have been here, when the weather will be rainy, and we can go fishing or gathering wild plums and grapes."

"You'll be after Ami to take you down to Sweetwater when Mr. Hodges just happens to be playing his fiddle for a square dance, too," said Lydia.

"I have that in mind," returned Tamar, "but that won't be until next fall and winter. I'm thinking of the fun we will have before that. We will not work on the Sabbath, even if there is no church to attend on Clear Creek. We can invite the neighbors for a picnic. There will be the Herringtons, the Murphys, and maybe the Bakers, all close by."

"That is right, Tamar," said her mother, "Sabbath is the Lord's Day and a day of rest. With all of us working from sun to sun through the week, it's a good thing we have the Sabbath," she added. "It allows time to give the children a little special attention, too. Elizabeth and Henry work just as hard as any of us." Elizabeth was getting along well with her reading, Jane went on, but except on Sundays, no one had time to help her. Having the creek nearby was good for Henry, who wanted to learn to swim. He, too, would turn Sundays to his purposes.

As Johnny was leaving after breakfast the next morning, Luther Mitchell asked, "Mr. Bryan, is the offer to let us use your dugout house still good?"

Johnny assured him that it was, adding that he was anxious to see how the house had withstood the winter.

Mitchell said that he would like to work out the arrangements for the use of the dugout, especially for the benefit of Mrs. Mitchell and the children.

"Homesteading is a difficult business for everyone," Luther observed, "but for the women who have to get meals every day, do the sewing and the washing, keep garden, do the drying and canning for winter, and keep their menfolks straight all the while, it's about the hardest job there is in the whole country. Having a house to move into sure would be a big help, Mr. Bryan. What sort of an arrangement could we make with you until your family comes from Lincoln in the summer?"

Bryan explained that his brother had decided against coming that year, so the dugout house would be available for as long as the Mitchells needed it. They would not have to hurry with the building of their own sod house.

"As to the arrangements, Mr. Mitchell," Bryan said, "I'll be so glad to have someone living close by that you are welcome to use the dugout. I sure did get lonesome at times last summer. No, you folks will be welcome to stay as long as you need the place; and there will be no charge."

"That wouldn't be fair, Mr. Bryan, but Jane and I have talked it over, and we wondered if you would like to sit up to our table at mealtime and just become one of us. We would keep your horse well shod, and maybe we could help you with some of your heavy jobs around the homestead."

Bryan quickly agreed to the arrangement. Mitchell said he thought he and Ami could get their blacksmith work in the Central City neighborhood done by the end of the week. They might be on Clear Creek as early as the twelfth, he thought, but surely they would be there by the fifteenth of April as they had planned. He explained that his family knew that they could not bring all of their things to Clear Creek until they had built their sod house, so they had arranged to store at the George Gagle place all of the things they would not need until winter. They would also leave the gun collection at Gagle's place until the soddy was completed.

Mitchell asked Johnny Bryan if he had seen the guns. He explained that there were a couple of trunks filled with them besides the ones hanging on the wall in the racks. "Most of those guns are just junk. Some of them could be used, but most of them haven't been fired for a long time—some of them not since the War of 1812," he explained.

"They really are Ami's guns now," he went on. "Being a gunsmith most of my life, I've had a chance to pick up strange guns, especially during the war when a lot of the fellows brought their own firearms with them. Lord, at Pittsburg Landing there was one pile of guns high as a baggage wagon, and considerably longer, that men who started in that battle were never going to use again.

"I was never much of a hand at using a gun, mostly just repairing or rebuilding them for someone else. But Ami's different. He is the best shot with a short gun I've ever seen, and in the army I saw some good ones. Ami could be good with a rifle too, but he never shows much interest in them or in shotguns. Guess one reason could be that when you are as good with a short gun as Ami Ketchum, you don't have much reason to use a rifle or a shotgun.

"Before Christmas I gave all my guns to Ami. I'm getting along now, and I'm glad to have a young fellow like Ami to take an interest in the collection. Oh, I kept the short gun I carried through the war and an old sawed-off shotgun that isn't much good for anything but bringing down a rabbit or a bird, and even then they have to be close; but all the rest belong to Ami," Mitchell concluded.

Two days later Johnny Bryan rode up to his dugout house on Clear Creek. Everything was in place just as he had left it the September before. The key worked easily. Everything inside was completely dry. Through the chimney, apparently, the winter storms had set up air currents that had moved dust around inside the dugout, and Johnny could write his name in the dust that had settled on the black stove. The Herringtons, who had wintered in their dugout house half a mile to the north, told Johnny they had not seen any sign of life other than a few longhorns around his homestead since he left. They doubted if another man had set eyes on it.

Late one afternoon the middle of the second week in April,

the wheels of the Mitchells' covered wagon cut the first wagon tracks of the spring across Clear Creek and rolled up in front of the Bryan dugout. Johnny was still clearing the place where he planned to plant his corn and garden when the wagon came into sight. When it rolled up to the dugout, he was at the door to welcome the new homesteaders.

The children, Henry and Elizabeth, had remained with the Gagles in Central City for a few days. Several trips would be necessary, since with all five adults in the wagon, there was not much room left for supplies and equipment. They had brought only household goods on this first trip, cooking materials and bedding mostly—and the grasshopper plow used to cut the sod for building soddies. They had also brought their extra horse and two milk cows tied behind the wagon. Luther would leave again in the morning to go back for such necessities as the breaking plow and the blacksmith equipment. Meanwhile, Ami would use the extra horse to begin cutting sod for a blacksmith shop.

Johnny had been keeping a fire in the dugout stove, and in a remarkably short time Mrs. Mitchell and her daughters had their first homestead supper ready. Afterwards the homesteaders talked of their blessings and made some plans. Since the Mitchell and Ketchum homesteads were more than half a mile north of the Bryan house, the men decided it would be best to build the blacksmith shop at the Bryan place, where they would be living, so that they could better use short intervals for smithing. Too, they could keep a better eye on the equipment if it was close to their temporary home.

[13]

WHO'S WHO ON CLEAR CREEK

So BY MID-APRIL Johnny Bryan, the Mitchells, Tamar and Lydia Snow, and Ami Ketchum, settlers brought together on the bluestem by the circumstances of Johnny's horse having thrown a shoe a year earlier, were ready to turn the virgin soil of the Platte country, just as Americans for more than 250 years had been doing farther east. From the New England shore the awesome task of transforming a wilderness into secure homesites, churches, schools, and places of commerce had continued, decade on decade, with tents, dugouts, log houses, and soddies, always moving farther west.

Most of the settlers moving up the Platte were coming as a result of dislocations spawned by the great war. Men who had gone through the wrenching experience of the war found it hard to settle back into old situations, always different, many now nonexistent. All too frequently there really was no place for the returning soldier, and many chose to move on. Sluggards and cowards would not try, however, and the weak soon faded under the pitiless rigors of the frontier. Only the strong in spirit and body could expect any measure of success as pioneers. Most homesteaders, consequently, were capable, ambitious men and women, seeking greater independence and new opportunity —and homesteading was a family enterprise.

In terms of ability and achievement, the new settlers on Clear Creek had especially important assets. They were educated, skilled, and experienced at homesteading. Jane was a schoolteacher when she met Peter Snow. Born in Ohio in 1831, she married in 1853 and became the mother of four children, two sons and two daughters in that order, in a little more than five years. She had not intended to marry, so much had she enjoyed her teaching, until she met Peter. Snow, too, was educated

Jane Snow Mitchell, widow of Peter Snow and Luther Mitchell, as a young schoolteacher in Indiana.

and on his way to a promising professional career when the war began. Natives of Ohio, the young couple moved with the westward tide to Indiana to establish their home.

Jane and Peter Snow were typical of most of the young

families across the North. With four children under the age of six years and little in the way of financial reserves when the war broke out, they considered only one course. Peter put his affairs in order as soon and as best he could and joined Company C of the 84th Indiana Volunteers. Jane gathered up her

A photo copy, actual size, of a letter Peter Snow mailed to his wife Jane in the spring of 1862 from Franklin, Tennessee.

children and went back to Ohio to live with Peter's elderly parents.

Peter was in the war by the fall of 1861. His regiment was on the move so constantly in Kentucky that his Christmas presents did not catch up with him until February in a southern Ohio camp where the 84th Volunteers stopped en route to a terms of duty in western Virginia. Both capable writers, Jane and Peter maintained a steady correspondence that helped ease the strain of separation. Peter's letters, penned in a small, neat script that stretched his writing paper to the limit, were newsletters, sermons, and love letters combined. He thought his captain deserved to be turned out of the army; he considered Grant solid but slow. At the close of each he gave Jane directions where she might write to him next, and his final thoughts were always of "my devoted wife and our four beautiful little children."

COVINGTON, KENTUCKY—*November 24, 1861*—. . . came across Jacob Denice and gave him $7.00 to give to you. . . . The 30th of this month is our payday again and then I will send you more money.

CAMPSVILLE, VIRGINIA—*December 25, 1862*—. . . went to Lt. Taylor's tent for Christmas dinner and I tell you it was just like home to have so many nice things. Your last letter came nearly a week ago and I read it over and over three or four times a day and will until I get another."

FRANKLIN, TENNESSEE—*March 11, 1863*—. . . Tell them three years is all we enlisted for and if the rebellion is not put down by that time we are coming home and enlist again. . . . I would rather have five years and have it done up right than to have it slip now half done. . . . *April 3*—I think one more hard fight will settle it. Whether it will be here or where I cannot tell. It may be at Vickburg and it may be in Virginia. . . . Starvation is staring them in the face. . . . They are almost at the point of starvation. *April 11* —Our advance lines attacked by rebels about 1:00 o'clock yesterday . . . with the intention of taking Franklin and destroying the railroad and our provision stores. . . . We passed over the battle field where the dead rebels were still lying . . . their own relatives would not have recognized them. . . . When the rebels got in town some fifteen or twenty of them made for our hospital to destroy it, but our sick men, having their pistols, defended themselves and drove

Battle at Pittsburgh Landing.

Oct 16 1862

Camp in Ohio near Point Pleasant

Dear wife and Children

I take this opportunity to write you a few lines to let you know that I am in good health with the exception of a lame ancle, it has been for a few days that I could harley walk but it is about well now or so near so that I am able for duty again — now my dear wife I had begun to think the time quite long since I herd from you, I would have wrote to you but I did not knu where to write but yestarday evening deny Richardson reached the regiment and brought me tidings from you

Typical of the weekly letters from Peter Snow to his wife and children written during the more than two years he served in the Civil War.

the rebels back, killing several of them and wounding others—good for the sick boys. *May 21*—Jane, it does make me feel truly grateful to you to think you take such an interest in the welfare of our dear little children. . . . I wish Lydia would take an interest like the boys do . . . encourage her to learn her letters.

WARTRACE, TENNESSEE—*July 7, 1863*—Camped on the Nashville and Chattanooga Railroad. We are guarding the railroad so the rebels can't damage it. . . . The people are near starvation. Flour is selling at $40.00 a barrel and can't be had at that.

ESTILL SPRINGS, TENNESSEE—*August 17, 1863*—. . . this railroad [Nashville and Chattanooga] has got to be defended to keep the bands of guerrillas from destroying it. It is a very useful road to the government. . . . Well, my dear wife I will have to stop pretty soon. I want you to write to me as often as you possibly can and let me know all about the dear little children.

Peter fought through the Battle of the Clouds in November. Then in early December, as the 84th Volunteers moved into Georgia on the way to Atlanta, the war was suddenly over for Peter Snow, killed in a skirmish with the Confederate rear guard. He had already written and mailed his Christmas letter to Jane and the children, delivered after the War Department notification of his death and a letter from his commanding officer asking whether Jane wished Peter's personal effects shipped home.

When the numbing grief began to subside, Jane realized that it was up to her to provide what Peter had most valued for their children: an education and an appreciation for growing up in a united and peaceful country. She read to them from his letters frequently, keeping his memory—and his counsel—alive. In a few months she arranged for their care during the day so that she could go back to teaching school.

Luther Mitchell was a short, slight man with a round, kindly face. Born in 1815, he was already forty-five, well beyond military age, when the war began. But he had volunteered because he believed in the Union, and since the war effort moved forward on horses' hooves, blacksmiths were indispensable. He had lost his first wife years before the war and had no dependent children, so he had volunteered. He shod horses and mended guns four years for the Union, all the way south to Mississippi and east with Sherman to Atlanta and the sea. Back from the war, he met Jane Snow, widowed by the war, with small children to support and little family to lean upon for help. They were married in 1866.

Luther Mitchell was nearly fifty then, and Jane, just thirty-five. He became as devoted as any father to Jane Snow's little girls, Tamar and Lydia. Now, a dozen years later, the Mitchells were on Clear Creek with two children of their own in addition to Tamar and Lydia, who had grown to young womanhood.

By this time many things had happened. Jane's eldest son, Darius, was dead. Sam Snow, her second child, had stayed in Ohio with Peter's family. First Henry and then Elizabeth had been born to Jane and Luther, and they were now ten and eight years of age. With Tamar and Lydia, the family circle was complete.

In the last two years Jane Mitchell had perfected the complex skills of a homesteader's wife. She could manage a garden that would provide fresh vegetables for her family every day of the year. Her wild-plum jam and wild-grape juice were the talk of homesteader get-togethers. Her greatest skill, however, lay in organizing, planning, and executing the countless responsibilities of a homesteader wife and mother. She was the calendar, alarm clock, and sundial for all the members of her family, especially for her husband, who could otherwise become so engrossed in his blacksmithing that time almost ceased to exist.

Jane and her daughter Tamar seemed to enjoy a special relationship that had flowered at the time of Peter's death. Though only six at the time, Tamar had been a great comfort. She never knew the luxury of prolonged childhood, reared as she was in a time of constant crisis. Jane always said, "Tamar was a woman at six. I have no idea how I could have gotten along without her." When Sam and Darius went to live with Peter's family, Tamar seemed to understand how much her mother depended upon her, and she assumed a responsibility far beyond her years. As she grew up, she was in no hurry to invite the company of young men; she did not wish to leave her mother until the Mitchells' fortunes were more stable and secure. Now, marriage to Ami Ketchum, her stepfather's partner, would allow her to remain close to her mother.

Tamar looked younger than her twenty years. She was just over five feet tall, slight, and athletic. Her face was round like Peter's had been, and her eyes were the same deep blue. Her hair, almost auburn in the summer when she was in the sun, darkened to chestnut in the winter, when she also had more time—and inclination—to brush and coil it. Everyone thought that the taller and more reticent Lydia was the older, that Tamar was "sixteen or seventeen," though in fact Lydia was seventeen months younger than her sister.

Their schoolteacher mother had instilled in both girls the same respect for learning she had shared with their father. They read everything that came within reach and could write expressively in a firm, clear hand. Lydia was also good at sums, but Tamar preferred to spend her time with books, especially books about the war or distant places. Her mother continued to plan and organize, but it was Tamar who supplied the balance wheel for the Mitchell-Ketchum enterprise and saw that the plans were actually carried out. Engaged to Ami, adored by her stepfather, enjoying the full confidence of her mother, maintaining a bantering closeness with Lydia, she was Henry's closest confidant and the person into whose apron Elizabeth could cry.

As for the men in this homesteading venture, Luther Mitchell wanted nothing but peace, a home for his family, and a chance to work (Jane often called it puttering) in his blacksmith shop. Ami Ketchum wanted to marry Tamar Snow and give her a good home such as he himself had not known since his brothers went to the war with the Iowa volunteers. He had come to Nebraska from his home in Iowa. He had been reared in the same community as Robert Hodges, who was now homesteading in the Sweetwater community about twenty miles south of Clear Creek, the same Robert Hodges who would later become a circuit-riding minister, forming new churches in several plains states and preaching for forty years.

Ami was the youngest of four brothers. When the two older boys came back from the war, the family farm could not provide a living for all of them, so Ami worked at the blacksmith shop in town, learning the trade well. Finally it was agreed that the oldest brother would stay in Iowa to take care of their elderly parents and operate the farm, freeing the other three to come west to the Platte and homestead.

Lawrence and Samuel Ketchum had homesteaded south of Kearney, but Ami had happened onto the Central City blacksmith, Luther Mitchell, who had more work than he could handle, and they agreed to become partners. Ami stood six feet two inches tall, with powerful shoulders and arms, a long lean face, fair complexion, blonde hair, and blue eyes. Usually quiet-spoken, he rarely used profanity and did not drink. He seldom talked about himself or referred to his own past. Instead he had become an expert at asking questions—short, probing ones that could be funny or deadly serious, and he learned a great deal from the answers. He held strong convictions, and when he felt an occasion required him to take a stand, he could be decisive with a bluntness that was jarring.

The use of a six-shooter, or a short gun as Luther Mitchell called it, was Ami Ketchum's only sport. He rarely went hunting except for table meat. Then he would use a rifle for big game, but for small game he preferred a short gun. Of all revolvers he used at one time or another, he always preferred the heavy, .45-caliber pistol for what he called its "greater authority."

Ami practiced shooting practically every day when he was

not working on the homesteads. He would even practice in the rain occasionally because he contended that light conditions and the dampness in the air required compensations on the part of a marksman. He would aim from a prone position at both still and moving targets. Standing, or on horseback, he was equally skillful.

Ami had lived with the Mitchells more than a year before he took any special interest in Tamar. In fact, during much of that year he and Lydia seemed to have more in common than he and Tamar. Perhaps this fact accounted for Lydia's occasional acid-tinged remarks to Tamar about him. Tamar's ability to do many things well, her good humor, and, above all, her courage drew Ami to her. She was not afraid of the dark. She would pick up a field mouse or drive a rattlesnake to cover; yet she was no daredevil or tomboy. One evening when they were at a church party in Central City Ami suddenly realized that Tamar Snow was the most remarkable young woman he had ever known. On the way home he told Tamar of his discovery. A month later they were engaged.

By five o'clock in the morning the day after their arrival, Jane, Tamar, and Lydia had breakfast ready; the Clear Creek homesteading operation was ready to begin. Jane proposed that since they were all taking their meals together, they should also share their gardens this first year. Vegetables used fresh, like lettuce and peas, could be planted in Johnny's garden near the house, while storage vegetables, like potatoes and turnips, needed in large quantities, could be grown up at the Mitchell-Ketchum site. The idea won immediate approval. Since Johnny had laid out his garden and had spaded a part of it last fall, Jane could plant the first lettuce and radishes that very day, April 12, and with any luck at all, they would be eating their first crop within a month. She would take a chance, she declared, and plant some peas, as well. If the good weather continued, these might even be ready for the table by Memorial Day.

Luther and his wagon team were on the way back to the Gagles' for another load of supplies by the time it was fully light. He asked Jane if he could bring Henry and Elizabeth this time, but she said no, not unless the children were simply too lonesome for the family or were making life difficult for Mrs. Gagle. Three or four round trips would be necessary, and if the children came later, she and Tamar and Lydia would have a chance to get a lot done beforehand.

With Luther on his way, Jane brought out her list of things to be done, the one she had made and discussed on the way from Central City. All the work fell into three categories: tasks inside the dugout house, such as preparing meals and canning; jobs in the farmyard, such as milking and gardening and smithing; and heavy work on the farm that included breaking ground for corn, planting the crop, and building a fence.

Thunderstorms slowed Luther's progress, lengthening his trip by a full day. When he got within sight of the Bryan dugout, he could see that the Clear Creek skyline had already been altered. He found that Ami and Johnny had finished laying up the sod for the blacksmith shop, even putting on the roof. Besides, Ami had begun breaking the bluestem for Johnny's corn crop, eager to see how difficult the job would be. Since Johnny intended to plant at least three acres, and Ami himself was determined to get in ten, the task would be demanding, he knew. The bluestem grew thicker and tougher here than at Central City.

The early garden crops were all planted. Some warm, light showers had fallen, and Tamar and Lydia had laid wagers on which morning they would first see the "green snakes," that enchanting morning when the garden surface, which had been smooth and unbroken at sundown the evening before, would be split open by tiny green shoots. The radishes would appear any morning now.

Some system for dividing the tasks had begun to develop quite naturally while Luther was away. Jane would get breakfast, and under her efficiency program, the meal would be ready just before dawn so that every minute of daylight could be spent planting. In mid-April, breakfast was ready at 5:30, but the hour would become earlier as the days grew longer, until May, June, and July would mean fourteen to sixteen hours out of doors. Although Jane and Tamar helped, Lydia took charge of the other meals. Dinner was served promptly at noon each day, and supper at dark. Lydia, soft of voice and gentle, could work well outdoors, but she preferred the more domestic chores. Tamar, on the other hand, milked the cows which were kept on the Bryan property for convenience. Johnny, when he was not tending his corn, built additional furniture for the dugout. Bunk beds, useful while the Mitchells were with him, would be essential when Joseph and Mary and their children arrived the following year.

[14]

MASTER HENRY, WHERE WERE YOU?

FOR THE TIME BEING, Luther would do most of the blacksmith work, just as he had in Central City. Two homesteaders and one cowboy had already stopped at the smithy while he was away. But he did not like the idea of working at the forge all during the spring and summer, unable to help with the big jobs of plowing, planting, and fencing; so in June the men built a second shop at the Mitchell-Ketchum homestead. Here Luther could leave the farm tasks when he was needed at the forge, returning to help Ami as soon as a job was done.

Luther delayed his next trip to Central City so that Ami could hitch the heavy team-to the plow and speed the breaking up of the soil. If the good weather held, Ami might use the team for a week.

Jane planned to have Elizabeth and Henry come to Clear Creek on the next trip from Central City. The children added work for the Gagle family as long as they lived there, and now that things were getting organized, there was work for them to do here. Elizabeth was old enough to take care of the hens, feeding them and gathering the eggs. As for Henry, an equally important job awaited him. Longhorns, most bearing the Olive brand, were to be seen on the high ground west of Clear Creek every day, and some late afternoons they would be down in the bluestem next to the creek. If there was going to be any food from the garden and any harvest from Johnny Bryan's sod

corn, someone would have to keep those longhorns back. This
would be just the job for young Master Henry.

Before the children's arrival, though, Luther and Ami, with
Johnny's help, spent two days laying out the Mitchell-Ketchum
homestead. On both days Lydia and Tamar brought dinner to

Elizabeth Mitchell Marvin, daughter of Jane and Luther Mitchell, with her husband, William Marvin, and their first child.

the men at noon. Jane, who brought an afternoon snack, stayed to help with plans for the two-house soddy, yard area, blacksmith shop, corncrib, barn, chicken house, field layouts, and other features of the new homesteads.

They planned the double sod house with special care. The structure would be sixty feet long, east to west, and more than twenty feet wide, the west half on the Ketchum homestead, the east half on the Mitchells', and a partition would be placed in the middle, exactly on the line dividing the two homesteads. They planned to place an outside door on either end, the Mitchells' facing east and the Ketchums' west toward Clear Creek. They marked out three fields on the bluestem to the north. One of them would be put in sod corn this year, the others being plowed up for cropping, perhaps one each year for the next two years, since they probably would not be able to buy the fencing for more then one ten-acre field at a time.

About the twentieth of April Ami began breaking up the bluestem on the ten acres designated for this year's corn. The field was north and a little west of the house site, about an eighth of a mile away at the closest point from the place where the sod house would be standing by the time the corn was ready to harvest. Since Ami and Tamar did not plan to be married until Christmas, the corn could be brought into their side of the big sod house and dried down with the aid of the heating stove. Once it was completely dry, it could be moved to any kind of sheltered storage outside without impairing the quality, so long as it was kept dry.

Ami and Johnny worked from the middle of April until the last week in May battling the Clear Creek bluestem on their sod-corn ground. The men agreed that it was the hardest work they had ever done. There were days when Ketchum was in the field before sunup, working until darkness made it impossible to see where to set the plow. Tamar brought his food to the field, and he ate while the team was fed and watered at the nearby creek. Ami thought the Clear Creek water was good enough for him to drink, too, but Tamar would not hear of it. She brought him boiled water from the Bryan dugout along with the food.

Luther helped when he could, but Ami discouraged his handling the breaking plow. The work was too hard for a man of Mitchell's age and weight, Ami said. A man who could rebuild a gun and fashion tools was too valuable to risk injuring himself when there were stronger shoulders available for the task. Besides, Luther's forge was seldom cool, his hammer rarely still, and during a forty-day period he had been back to Central City twice.

It rained several times during the ground breaking and corn planting, but only once heavily enough to stop the work completely. Ami and Johnny were determined to have their own crops in by Memorial Day.

The corn was planted in three stages. By the time Luther was back from Central City the first of May with the seed corn—and with Henry and Elizabeth—some of the ground of both fields was ready to plant. A second planting was made on the tenth and eleventh of May. Johnny and Tamar, with some help from Henry, had the Bryan field planted by the fifteenth. Each morning, from the middle of May on, the ground broken on one day was seeded on the next, until the entire Mitchell-Ketchum field was sown. Late in the afternoon of the twenty-eighth, the Clear Creek homesteaders sat down to supper knowing that the first white man's corn crop ever to be planted on upper Clear Creek was in the ground. Johnny Bryan paced off his field, and it measured almost four acres. The Mitchell-Ketchum field was more than ten acres, but about half an acre was given over to potatoes and other winter garden crops.

Adding to their sense of achievement and satisfaction was the fact that the corn planted the first week of May was already up to a good stand. This proved that the seed was good, promising a fine crop over both fields and assuring security for the winter. The seed had come from Ami and Luther's crop at Central City the year before, which, even on the poorer soil they had farmed in Merrick County, had been the talk of the neighbors. That corn was the result of crossing the sod corn planted by the Gagles and other homesteaders in the Central City area with a white corn that Luther had seen produced exceptionally high yields back in Ohio.

After six weeks of uninterrupted labor, all the homesteaders welcomed Tamar's suggestion that they spend Memorial Day visiting their neighbors in the Clear Creek area. They had seen no longhorns for ten days now, and they concluded that the Olives must have begun the spring roundup. It seemed like a safe time for everyone to be gone for a few hours.

Stopping first at their own fields, they took a complete inventory. The early May planting was up to an excellent stand, and some of the mid-May planting was above ground. Almost all of Johnny's crop was up, a little taller than the corn in the larger field to the north. No question about it, the Bryan corn was coming a little faster. Luther had opined that buffalo must have sought the protection of the bluff during winter storms, judging from the fertility of the soil and the unusual number of buffalo skulls and bones. Johnny thought that perhaps the Clear Creek bluffs might also protect that tract somewhat against the cool nights.

After they had surveyed their own handiwork, Ami, who was doing the driving, turned down the valley for a call on the Herringtons and Murphys. Jane next asked Johnny, who knew the area best, to take them where he had seen the wild plums, gooseberries, and grapes the fall before. She would be making hundreds of quarts of preserves, and she wanted to see where the fruits grew and how they were coming along.

They returned to the Bryan house in the afternoon for an early supper. Since the weather was warm for May and the evening was clear, they moved the table to the yard and ate in the open, enjoying the balmy twilight. After supper Jane asked Tamar to get the letters Peter Snow had written during his three years in the army. It had been her practice to read from them each Memorial Day, and now the first holiday on Clear Creek closed on a quiet note of remembrance.

A few days later, gathering together every cent he and Ami had made from smithing, Luther made another trip to Central City, this time to buy enough wire to fence in their entire cornfield. More money would be coming in, to be sure, now that people were stopping at his blacksmith shop every day or two. There would be money to buy sugar and flour and other necessities, which cost little enough when compared with fencing. They had won the battle with the seasons, breaking ground and planting in time to get a crop. Now they were racing to get the fence up before the longhorns came back after the spring roundup—before the corn was high enough to attract the cattle. Luther and Ami decided the posts should be set three feet deep, fifteen feet apart, and Ami set to work digging.

Men stopping at the smithy often reported that cattlemen in parts of Valley, Sherman, and Buffalo counties were annoyed at the homesteaders "messing up" the range, but even they recognized the legality of the fencing, however much they might object. The Olive men, with headquarters on the South Loup, were the largest operators in the Platte Valley and were always mentioned among those who were determined to keep the range free.

Whenever Luther, Ami, or Johnny questioned their informants, the answer was always to the effect that "I didn't talk to the Olives themselves, naturally, but this is what I heard, not once but several times." Gradually, the Clear Creek homesteaders formed the impression that most of this kind of talk was circulating in the saloons of Kearney and Plum Creek, and that a man variously described as "one of the Olives" or "Bob Stevens, who came up the Chisholm with the Olives" or "Bob Stevens Olive, who is one of the principals in the Olive brothers' operation" was doing most of the talking.

All during June the reports kept coming. Their greater frequency indicated not so much that the situation was changing, but that the traffic to the Bryan and Mitchell-Ketchum homesteads was constantly increasing. Although most of the visitors were folks who needed some blacksmith work done and generally waited close to their horses until it was completed, it was Ami Ketchum's view that some of the cowboys were just looking for excuses to talk to Tamar and Lydia. For whatever reasons, the Bryan and Mitchell-Ketchum homesteads were becoming something of a community center, a place where a man could get his horse shod promptly while he met friendly people and exchanged news.

Several of the visitors seemed to come a little too frequently, however—men like Manly Caple and Jim McIndeffer. Caple lived on Clear Creek fifteen miles or more to the south, almost at the point where the creek crossed the Custer-Sherman county line. McIndeffer lived on Muddy Creek near the little settlement of Mason City, about ten miles south of Johnny Bryan's homestead and just a little west. Both Caple and McIndeffer were homesteaders, but both had cattle interests which always seemed to be more important than their farming, though the nature of those interests never seemed entirely clear. Both were pleasant men in their mid-thirties; both rode exceptionally good horses. And they always had substantial sums of money in their pockets.

Johnny Bryan had met Jim McIndeffer the summer before. They had talked then about possible conflict between the cattle-men and the homesteaders in eastern Custer County. McIndeffer had told Bryan then that he did not believe there would ever be the kind of trouble that had broken out farther up the Platte near Ogallala, where the Texas Trail came through, and up in the Wyoming Platte country. Both Caple and McIndeffer did agree, however, that it would be best for homesteaders to fence their crops and be prepared to invoke the Nebraska herd law that had been passed several years earlier. The law had never acquired much meaning, however, outside the "Lincoln justice" region in eastern Nebraska, where the counties were better organized and law enforcement was a full-time occupation rather than the evenings-and-Sundays hobby of a few home-steaders or cattlemen.

During May and June, Jim McIndeffer stopped at the Bryan

place three or four times—once or twice to have blacksmith work done, but occasionally just to see how everyone was getting along. McIndeffer, unlike the other news bearers, gave the impression that he had seen and talked directly to Olive men. There were three Olive brothers, McIndeffer said. Print was the eldest; and although he had little to say, he was definitely the man who ran things. Print had been in the war on the Confederate side and still proudly wore his holster with the letters "CSA." The second Olive brother, Ira, did not talk very plain and was not seen on the range very often. The youngest was Bob Stevens Olive, twenty-five years old at most. He was the one who did most of the talking. McIndeffer had heard that there was another Olive brother still in Texas, but he did not know his name.

"Things have changed a lot since you and I visited last summer," McIndeffer told Bryan on one of his stops. "The Olive cattle had not come into eastern Custer County much then— not until fall, in large numbers.

"This Olive outfit is big. I'm told they already own more cattle than any other single outfit on the Platte, but they talk about running another twenty to thirty thousand head up here next year. A fellow down in Plum Creek told me that last summer the Olives drove longhorns and horses through Plum Creek every day for nearly two weeks after they split off the Chisholm Trail with their Texas cattle and brought them together with their Colorado herd," McIndeffer added.

"With cattle herds like that," he went on, "the Olives need all the grass in Custer County. There just isn't going to be any room for us little cattlemen now. I think that's why the Olives are so upset about the big homesteading operations you folks are starting here on Clear Creek."

When Manly Caple stopped by, he always claimed to have some pressing blacksmith work, though sometimes Luther Mitchell thought the job could have waited. Caple seemed always on the move. He talked as though he knew people in Kearney, and he frequently referred to having talked to Bob Olive in a saloon there. Caple would report that Bob Olive often asked him how much corn was going in on Clear Creek and how the Mitchells and Ketchum were getting along with their planting.

When these reports came up for discussion around the supper table, Ami Ketchum showed his irritation. Reference to the Olives' keeping Custer County for cattlemen or the Olives' concern about the activities of the homesteaders along Clear Creek so angered him that he spoke sharply to all those who brought the reports. On occasion he would assert that if the Olives and their cowboys had any idea of taking things into their own hands, they would find they had cut into a hornets' nest. Tamar and the others wished that Ami had not talked that way, but they all realized that he had borne the heaviest tasks, both putting in the big sod-corn crop and building the strong fence around it.

The first longhorns appeared on the Custer hills to the west of Clear Creek the last of June, but by that time the fencing of the big sod cornfield was almost complete, so the homesteaders were not particularly alarmed. Nevertheless, young Henry Mitchell went on the alert, and each evening he reported on their approximate numbers.

June had been dry, favorable for the corn crop, since the roots would go deep into the soil, assuring that the crop would be better watered later in the summer. The Bryan corn continued to advance a little more rapidly, but as June passed, the Mitchell-Ketchum plants began to catch up.

Tamar proposed that July 4 should be observed like Memorial Day—that they all take a wagon trip as they had before. With the biggest jobs of the year behind him, Ami was quick to second her suggestion. Once again the first stops were at the cornfields, where the corn slogan, "knee high on the 4th of July," was easily fulfilled. Some of the tallest came to Elizabeth's shoulders. The party continued on its rounds, elated at the obvious rewards for their hard labors. Visits to the neighbors took longer than they had little more than a month earlier, since homesteaders had staked out two new locations south of

Johnny Bryan's place. The men had met, but this was the first opportunity for "woman talk."

Jane wanted to visit the gullies where the wild fruit was growing to see if she could tell when the first plums would be ready to pick. They were already showing color, and Jane judged that they might be ripe enough for making jam by the middle of August. The gooseberries were not as far along, but the wild grapes looked promising; a big crop was in prospect.

Once back at the Bryan homestead, Lydia served the supper, after which Ami put on the biggest shooting exhibition of the summer. Tamar split the tip of a willow sprout, inserting the silver dollar that Ami Ketchum kept for target practice. First she set the stake fifteen steps away, and Ami dropped the dollar in three successive shots. Splitting new shoots each time, Tamar moved the target to a distance of 25 yards, then to 35, and finally to 50 yards. At 50 yards Ami was still able to hit the dollar three times in seven. After this exhibition, Ami shot holes in objects that Henry and Elizabeth tossed into the air, and because it was the fourth of July, Henry was permitted to fire the big six-shooter himself, just once.

Then one morning in the middle of July, when Lydia went to the garden for the day's vegetables, she made a discovery that sent her running to summon Johnny. In minutes they were back at the cornfield, with Jane, Tamar, Elizabeth, and Henry at their heels. Luther and Ami had already gone to work up on their own property.

Tracks told the story: longhorns had moved into the field during the night and destroyed about one-fourth of the corn. The tallest stalks were the most badly damaged. The stricken little group was speechless. Not even the children could find words. Johnny Bryan finally broke the dazed silence.

"Master Henry, where were you?"

"Mr. Johnny, the corn was all right last evening, honest it was, Mr. Johnny," the boy blurted.

"I know the corn was all right at dark, because I was here to see how much it had grown in the last couple days. No, it wasn't your fault, Henry boy. I've been afraid of this all along, especially when you counted more than seventy longhorns on the hills yesterday. Henry, I think cattle can smell a growing crop the way we know when Lydia is cooking supper. My guess is we'll have more night visits from the longhorns," he concluded.

Henry Mitchell, son of Jane and Luther, with his wife, Mary. Both children of Jane and Luther Mitchell married children of William Marvin, Jane's third husband.

"I could sleep out here at night, Mr. Johnny," offered Henry.
"That's about the finest offer anyone could make, Henry; but
you mustn't think of doing that," answered Johnny. "For one
thing, in the darkness you might get hurt. For another, I doubt
whether we could keep them out in the darkness. I've tried
getting a few milk cows out of a cornfield back in Illinois,
and in the darkness a cow in corn will be so completely quiet
that she can be within arm's reach and you still can't find her.
If we had a couple of good dogs used to handling livestock, then
I'd take you up on your offer, Henry. But as it is, you just keep
the longhorns out in the daytime, and we'll see if we can save
the rest of the crop and the garden."

Luther and Ami learned of the destruction of the corn from
Tamar when she took their lunch up to them. At supper that
evening Johnny attempted to keep the conversation away from
the loss of his corn, but finally Ami could stand it no longer.
"I wish I could convince myself that those longhorns didn't have
any help finding your cornfield, Johnny. I've been worried about
them, and I've been checking every evening at sundown, when
you can see them so easily, just to figure how far away they were
from that corn. Last evening there were more longhorns around
than usual, but they were nearly half a mile away. They can't
smell that good. I figure those longhorns had help.

"Some of the folks who have been stopping here recently have
been hoping out loud that those longhorns wouldn't get into
Johnny Bryan's corn. I can't figure out whether fellows like this
McIndoffer are reporting the gossip or just hinting to us what's
going to happen. We've got things going pretty good if these
cowmen will just leave us alone," he ended fiercely.

Three nights later the longhorns were back in Johnny's corn.
Before the end of July, it was almost all destroyed. Luther now
shared Ami's suspicions, but Johnny believed that the tender
corn was just more attractive to the longhorns now that the
hot weather of July had begun to toughen the range grasses.
At least that was what Johnny steadfastly maintained each time
the subject came up.

Manly Caple knew a little too much too soon when he stopped

within a week after the first longhorn visit, Ami was convinced. Caple, McIndeffer, and some others who stopped by so regularly, were coming for more than hot iron work: they were learning what was going on at the homesteads and carrying rumors— perhaps rumors they were instructed to spread. As a result, Ami Ketchum became less communicative. When he spoke, his tone was often bitter. One afternoon he told Caple, "Nobody agrees with me here, Caple, but I think those longhorns had some help finding Johnny Bryan's cornfield. I can tell you one thing: these cowboys better not get any funny ideas about visiting my homestead to look over my corn crop. If I had caught anyone in or near Bryan's corn when those cattle were there even in the dark, he'd have still been there on the ground in the morning." He continued, "These cattlemen better wake up to the fact that homesteaders can use guns. At least this homesteader can, and while I don't usually figure to shoot first, I always plan to end the shooting," he added, and Caple had reason to wonder whether the warning included himself.

As July progressed, the Mitchell-Ketchum corn, behind a stout fence, grew so rapidly that everyone observed it was the best field of sod corn they had ever seen in the Platte Valley. Work on their double soddy had also begun, once the partners had completed the second blacksmith shop. Before the end of July the walls of the new home were going up, and its unusual dimensions were taking form. Everyone was keenly interested, but no one else could match Tamar's excitement. She now spent most of her days helping the men with the house. "After all," she said, "how many women get to help with planning and building their own house before they're even married?"

The first Sunday in August 1878 fell on the fourth. That afternoon the Herringtons drove up to the Mitchell-Ketchum homestead to see the corn that stood shoulder high, a budding ear on every stalk, occasionally two. Johnny was there too, and while the women looked on from a distance, the men went out to the field. How much the acreage would yield was the big question. A good first-year crop would be twenty-five bushels per acre. Bigger yields usually came the second and third year, when the old grass roots had decayed.

"Looks like we're getting set to harvest about two crops in one," said Luther. To a man, they agreed a crop of forty or fifty bushels to the acre was in the making, more than enough for johnnycakes, hominy, and half a dozen other wintertime favorites. There would be enough left over for the cows to assure plentiful milk and better calves, come spring.

Work on the big soddy progressed on Monday and Tuesday. Ami and Tamar held target practice each evening after supper. On Tuesday Johnny Bryan hitched the teams to the wagon and took Jane, Lydia, Tamar, and the children to gather wild plums and gooseberries and see how the wild grapes were coming. That same evening Tamar accompanied Ami on horseback to see what the men had accomplished during her absence.

The next day was the longest of the year.

The women were working with the plums while Henry and Elizabeth played down at the creek. Luther and Ami had gone up to work on the soddy shortly after sunup, and Tamar planned to take dinner up to them as usual and stay to help them in the afternoon. About midmorning Johnny stopped in for a cup of coffee.

Suddenly Luther Mitchell appeared at the dugout doorway. He appeared pale and feeble, like a man in the advanced stages of a long illness. Jane moved quickly to support him, helping him into a chair by the table. Putting his head down, he broke into convulsive sobs. Gradually the sobbing subsided, he regained control of himself, and he spoke, holding his head in his hands as he struggled to contain his grief.

When he and Ami had gone to work that morning they had not looked at the cornfield right away. Later he had gone around the soddy walls looking for something—he couldn't remember what—and he had glanced in the direction of the field. "Most of the corn was gone," he said as sobs once more shook his body. The cornfield was filled with Olive longhorns, he went on, in the voice of a man dazed and only half comprehending.

[15]
POINT OF NO RETURN

WHERE WAS AMI, Tamar demanded to know, and Luther said that he was still "up there." Tamar seemed to reach the door of the dugout as the words were spoken, and Johnny could see her still running when she was half a mile away.

"What did Ami do?" Jane asked.

"Didn't say a word for a long time, just kept looking at those longhorns eating his corn—what was left of it. He just stood there clenching his fists.

"At first we thought the fence had broken down; but when we got there we learned the truth. The fence had been cut all along the west side, toward Clear Creek. The wires were clipped between every other post by those goddamned Olives."

Jane suggested that Luther drink some coffee and then go with her to talk to Ami and Tamar. Johnny and Lydia stayed at the Bryan place. Johnny kept an eye on the children and tried to figure out what the homesteaders should do, now that the cattlemen had deliberately thrown down the gauntlet. No one came back for the noon meal, but Lydia fixed something for herself and Johnny and the children. Johnny explained to the children as best he could why their mother and Tamar were away.

As the hours of August 6 ticked away, Johnny Bryan wrestled with the great question: Was homesteading practical in Custer County, especially in eastern Custer County, now that the cattle kings had committed themselves to the use of force to keep the buffalo grass and bluestem? Apparently those long-horns that destroyed his own corn so methodically had, as Ami had insisted, been driven into his unfenced field.

Reports of harassment of homesteaders had increased. One of the most recent stories linked Print Olive himself with a brutal attack on a homesteader twenty-five miles south of Clear Creek, on the Custer and Buffalo County line. Olive, the accounts said, accused old Ben Christiansen of stealing the cattle in his corral from the Olives and demanded that he produce the bill of sale. When Christiansen went into his sod house for the papers, Olive followed him and attacked him savagely, breaking the man's jaw and leaving him unconscious in a pool of his own blood. Christiansen, a day's ride from the nearest doctor, was unable to get medical help. The jaw was not set, and he was never able to open his mouth more than a crack again. Christiansen, the reports said, had put his claim up for sale and was leaving the Platte country. For the first time it occured to Johnny that the reason the cattle kings had so far kept their distance was fear of Ami Ketchum and his "short gun." If Christiansen and the other targets of violence had been experts with six-shooters, maybe they would not have been so brutally molested, either. There was no question about the rights of homesteaders, Johnny knew; these rights were clearly written into law. But there was as yet no law enforcement here. The Olives and other cattle kings ruled Custer County with wire snippers and guns—and the men who would use them.

At supper, in spite of any effort at conversation, the silences grew longer after each attempt. When the meal was almost over, Jane asked Johnny what they were going to do to get them through the winter, now that their corn crops had been destroyed. For the first time a note of desperation crept into her voice.

Johnny had done a lot of thinking during the day. He acknowledged that he had moved much closer to Ami's view that they were being persecuted.

"It looks now like the cattle kings are determined to drive us homesteaders who won't work with them out of Custer County, whatever it takes. I'm sure they won't get away with it for long, but right now they're holding the high cards," he said. "I think about the only course open to us is to go back where we came from for the winter and be here next spring for a fresh start."

Silence followed. Tamar, who had been crying, stared down at the table. Luther Mitchell sat with elbows on the table, his head in his hands. Ami Ketchum, who had not spoken a word since the meal began, slowly raised his eyes to meet Johnny's. Speaking as though it was a great effort, he said, "Johnny, we came here to make our living and to have homes of our own. We've worked mighty hard, and we figure to stay right here. If that's the way the Olives want to play, all I've got to say is it's a game two can play. There's a lot of 'slow elk' in these Custer County canyons," he went on, "and I've heard there is a big demand for meat in Kearney. If those Olives won't let us be farmers, we'll be hunters. It's hard work. Those long wagon drives to get the meat there fresh will be difficult, especially until the weather cools off; but it can be done.

"We'll need two to four elk a week, depending on the size. Luther and I will hunt late in the afternoon so we can have the meat loaded by dark. That way the meat will have a chance to cool during the night." Ami, too, had been doing a lot of thinking since morning.

Luther Mitchell said nothing.

With a rested team, Ami figured, he could drive straight through to Kearney, a distance of about fifty miles. The night and morning would be cool, so the meat would only travel in the heat of one day.

If it arrived in good enough condition, Ami thought he might get back to Clear Creek with $15.00 to $20.00 clear, deducting expenses for one night at the livery stable for the team, a night's lodging for himself, and meals. Even if the meat had to be sold at a lower price—to Indians instead of the butcher shop—he still might bring back $5.00 or $10.00.

Ami announced that he would do his first hunting on Saturday and plan to be in Kearney with the meat when the stores opened Monday morning, returning home Tuesday night. The team could rest three days before starting the next long trip to Kearney.

"I won't bring back all the money, as a usual thing," Ami concluded, "because I will buy flour, sugar, yard goods, and other things we need here. Between the elk and the blacksmith work, we'll get through the winter."

Tamar, listening to Ami's words carefully, asked if he thought it would be difficult to find enough elk to fill a wagon with meat once a week. Ketchum said that after the weather turned cool so that animals could be killed and dressed over a period of twenty-four or even forty-eight hours, it would be no problem at all. Until then, he and Luther would both have to hunt the day the trip was planned and do the best they could.

Johnny thought the idea was sound, and he hoped it would work out well. As for himself, he thought the best thing for him to do would be to go back to Lincoln and teach music again during the winter months. He would plan to leave about the middle of September as he had last fall and return early the following April. He could live with his brother, and make enough money to pay for his keep, with a little left over. Ami Ketchum and the Mitchells, however, had no place to go, no house waiting for them, and no winter job, aside from smithing. Moreover, Ami and Tamar were planning to be married during the coming winter; if they were to retreat from Custer County their wedding might not be possible.

The word soon got around that the big cornfield on Clear Creek had been destroyed by night riders and longhorns. Homesteaders came from miles around to see for themselves, going away silent and serious. Ami predicted that Jim McIndeffer, Manly Caple, and the others who were in cahoots with the Olives would never mention the night raid and the destruction of the big corn crop.

Ami was right about everyone except Caple, who came to get the facts and to extend congratulations to Ketchum. "After all," he told Ketchum, "if it were not for your being so clever with the six-shooter, they would have walked right in on you like they did on Old Man Christiansen and the others."

Luther Mitchell and Ami Ketchum sent their first load of meat into Kearney the second week of August. By traveling the first night, Ami was away only Sunday, Monday, and Tuesday. The meat made the trip well, and Ami reported on his return that he was able to sell the elk to Gebhardt's Butcher Shop in Kearney. After expenses, he had cleared about $15.00. He brought back sugar for canning and a little gift for Tamar.

Work on the Mitchell-Ketchum soddy advanced rapidly those days that Ami Ketchum was on Clear Creek, but with him away three or four days a week, Luther said the house could not be finished before the middle of October. Ami made his second trip to Kearney shortly after the middle of August, detouring slightly to go through Sweetwater on the way home and visit Robert Hodges. Once more he had realized a profit.

On the last Saturday of the month, Ami and Luther announced at breakfast that they were going hunting and hoped to start another load of meat toward Kearney during the night. The weather had been hot for many days, and there was no sign of change. By midafternoon everyone looked forward to sunset and the comparative cool of the evening. Young Henry, who had begged to go on the hunts from the first, was allowed to go this time, on condition that he stay behind the men with the guns. Jane, Tamar, Lydia, and Elizabeth stayed inside the dugout with the door closed to keep out the heat. Lydia was preparing supper, and Jane and Tamar were preserving fruit.

Johnny Bryan had been cleaning up his garden and cornfield, cutting the weeds that had grown up since the longhorns ate the corn, and generally getting the area ready for fall plowing. About midafternoon, deciding to take a few minutes' rest, he climbed the bluff above the dugout in search of a little breeze. He sat down with his back to the sun so that he had an unobstructed view across Clear Creek to the canyons on the other side. He had been resting only a few minutes when he noted activity across Clear Creek. There, in full view and in good light, Johnny Bryan saw Luther Mitchell and Ami Ketchum drive several longhorns into one of the small canyons. Moments later young Henry brought up the team and wagon. No wonder, thought Johnny, that Luther let the boy go hunting with them; they needed him. He saw Ami take the rifle out of the wagon and point it in the direction of one of the longhorns. There was a puff of smoke—he was too far away to hear the shot—and the longhorn went down. Johnny watched while the men skinned and butchered the animal. He saw them shoot and dress a second, and yet a third. As darkness approached, Luther, Ami, and Henry drove up to the dugout with the load of meat.

"Why couldn't they have told me the truth?" Johnny wondered. What he had seen had made him a stranger in his own house. Johnny Bryan knew that the point of no return had been reached on Clear Creek.

He was heartsick on two counts. Killing Olive longhorns was a dangerous business that could touch off a wave of shooting and terror between the cattle kings and the homesteaders that could engulf all of Clear Creek and spread far beyond. But serious as was the killing of Olive longhorns, it was the imminent collapse of his relationship with Ami Ketchum and the Mitchells, especially Tamar, Lydia, and the children, that hurt Johnny most. He knew he could not ignore or postpone the showdown. There might be little enough time to escape the Olive holocaust.

Bryan went to supper that evening knowing that it was the last supper he would ever take with the Mitchells and Ami Ketchum. By meal's end, he was sure that Tamar and Jane knew well what had been happening. He tried to figure out whether Elizabeth and Lydia were aware of the "slow elk" fiction; and though he was convinced that Elizabeth had not been let in on the deception, he could not be sure about Lydia. At last the meal was over. He waited until the children had gone out to play before he spoke.

"Luther, aren't you fellows likely to get us all killed? I saw what you and Ami did this afternoon," he said. His words struck everyone dumb and motionless—everyone except Lydia, who looked questioningly, first at her mother and then at Luther; Johnny was convinced then that she had been kept as much in the dark as he.

It was Ami Ketchum who finally broke the silence. Looking unflinchingly at Johnny, speaking with the voice of a stranger, Ami asked, "Johnny, you've heard it said that dead men tell no tales?"

Bryan was stunned by the open threat on his life, and this from a man who had been his friend. Looking around the table, he knew he could count on no help there. Only Lydia seemed shocked by Ketchum's malice. Everyone else sat eyes downcast and motionless. Retreat was his only recourse.

"Yes, I have, Ami. That I have—and I'm here to tell you fellows that I never saw a thing this afternoon."

But Ketchum was still not satisfied. "Now, Johnny, are you sure about that? Are you real sure, Johnny?" pursued Ketchum in a voice that was, if anything, more threatening than his first verbal thrust.

Now Bryan was convinced that he was in fact pleading for his life. In an unsteady voice he declared, "Why yes, fellows, that's the way it is. I never saw a goddamn thing this afternoon." This is the only time in Bryan's life that anyone could recall his having sworn.

Ketchum eyed him suspiciously, seeming to toy with his quarry. In the end he appeared satisfied. "All right, Johnny," he said softly, "if that is the way it is. But I can tell you that it damned well better be that way."

Now it was Johnny Bryan whose suspicions were aroused. Ami Ketchum seemed satisfied; but suppose he should change his mind? He would have many opportunities to murder Bryan and dispose of his body; perhaps even the Mitchells would be none the wiser. Only one certainty emerged from this exchange: it was that Ami Ketchum was calling the turns, perhaps to such

an extent that even the Mitchells and Tamar were just following his instructions.

Leaving the dugout, Bryan lay down on his pallet in the yard.
He stared at the sky as the last light faded. The stars came out
against a black expanse, but still Johnny could not sleep. One
thing was certain: he must get away at once. Ami Ketchum
had announced he would not start for Kearney that night. Delay
could mean the loss of the entire load, since it could not withstand two days of such punishing heat. Why had he considered
it necessary to postpone his trip? Was he unconvinced that
Bryan was trustworthy? Might he be changing his mind on that
score?

About three o'clock in the morning, Johnny decided to make
a break for freedom. Ketchum was sleeping soundly on a pallet
several feet away. Now was his chance.

Johnny made a practice of putting a hobble on his saddle
horse in the evening so that the animal could graze and yet
not wander too far from the dugout. In the morning the horse
was usually within a few hundred yards of the place where
Johnny had left him.

Johnny had not yet realized how short the days had become.
Only a month ago he could have seen his mount half a mile
away at three in the morning; now, on this moonless night, he
could "see" his hand before his face only if he raised it to block
out the stars. He could have found the horse by calling to him,
but, hoping to leave undetected, he would not risk waking
Ketchum.

Johnny began his search methodically. Starting from the
point where he had left his horse the evening before, he was
sure he would not lose his bearings even in the dark. Using
the stars as a guide, he walked three hundred yards in one
direction, retraced his steps to the starting point and then
walked three hundred yards in the opposite direction. The
next time he walked to the left of his original course, the fourth,
in the opposite direction once again. Still he did not find his

horse. He widened his circle, repeating the process, but it was nearly six o'clock before he caught sight of the animal grazing nearly half a mile away.

By the time Bryan reached his horse and returned to the dugout, both Mitchell and Ketchum were in the yard looking for him. In response to their obvious curiosity, Bryan said that, thinking about things during the night, he had concluded he would get on down to Lincoln right away and start his classes.

"Now are you sure that's what you are going to do, Johnny?" Ketchum cut in. Bryan could see all the distrust of the previous evening still in Ami's eyes.

Luther turned to Ketchum. "Ami, I think Johnny is telling us the truth. We don't have any reason to think that he hasn't always told us the truth. We must help him get away today if that is what he wants to do."

Ketchum accepted the older man's verdict, and Mitchell turned to Johnny. "Johnny, we've had our breakfast already, but Jane is expecting you in for pancakes."

Luther Mitchell followed Johnny into the dugout while Ami Ketchum began preparations to hitch the team to the load of meat. Jane, Tamar, and Lydia all talked to Johnny freely, as though they were trying to rid the dugout of the ugly atmosphere of the evening before.

"When will you get to Lincoln, Johnny?" Tamar asked.

"I always try to do better, but just about anyway you cut it, Tamar, it takes three days. If there is a little weather or something, it becomes an easy four-day trip," Johnny replied.

Breakfast over, Johnny turned to Luther. "Now, Luther, you folks are welcome to use the dugout as long as you like. Use it all winter if it will be of any service to you. The dugout would be better with some heat in it anyway. But if you finish your sod house in the fall, as I am sure you will, then just lock the door and throw the key away. When I come back next spring I'll come prepared to change the lock and have a new key.

"I'll just leave everything of mine here. There isn't much that would be of any use to me this winter anyway—except that overcoat. Maybe I should take that along, even if it is a burden," Bryan mused. "No, it's too much trouble carrying that heavy coat all the way to Lincoln with all the other things I need. I have another lighter one there. I'll just leave the coat here."

Jane thanked Johnny for his friendship, for the use of his dugout, and especially for his interest in Henry and Elizabeth. "We will all miss you, Johnny, but none as much as Elizabeth. In a case like this, we all wish we had done some things differently. We can't be too hard on Ami. He worked his heart out on that corn crop—worked harder than any man I ever saw.

"He keeps his thoughts to himself so much that sometimes he gets ahead of you; before you know it, it's too late to reason with him. He will regret this terribly. You have always been one of his favorite people. He's told Tamar several times during the summer that 'Johnny Bryan is the finest man I've ever known.'"

Johnny Bryan embraced everyone, kissing Tamar on the cheek ("a kiss for the bride," he said). As he shook hands with Luther, he turned to Jane. "Take all the blankets up to the new soddy with you if you need them. After all, you're going to have two families to look after during the winter, so just take anything out of the dugout that will be of use to you. And the best of luck to all of you."

Most difficult was shaking Ami Ketchum's hand. The handshake was firm, but neither man could say a word. As Johnny walked toward his horse that Henry had brought up for him, Ami called, "Good luck, Johnny."

Even so, Johnny Bryan could not rid himself of the fear that Ami Ketchum might suddenly change his mind, pick up that rifle, and fire a slug into his back at a distance of half a mile. He kept his horse to a walk that first half mile just to make sure that nothing in his manner would prompt Ami to reconsider.

The "slow elk" meat continued to be delivered in Kearney regularly as the weeks of autumn passed. The income from the venture surpassed Ami Ketchum's first estimates. He was able to buy many things for the soddy—wall racks for his guns, additional windows for the kitchen work areas, numerous small items that having a regular income in hard cash each week made possible.

The big double soddy was completed in late October. On the twenty-ninth, Lydia had married Asa Gipe in Loup City, so when moving day came, the first week in November, only Jane and Tamar remained to supervise the household. That evening Luther Mitchell asked Jane if there was anything else to be moved. When she said "no," he turned the key in the lock, tried the door to see if it was securely locked, turned toward Clear Creek, and threw the key fifty yards or more into the bluestem.

[16]
THE OLIVE LINE

THE OLIVE OPERATION on the Platte represented a consolidation of ranching interests stretching from Texas all the way to Colorado, Kansas, and Nebraska. In the fall of 1877, the Olives had begun to market longhorns by the trainload through Omaha and into Chicago. For one whole week, during October of 1878, six trainloads of cattle were moved through their Plum Creek pens and onto Union Pacific cattle cars without ever freeing the dock facilities for another cattleman, so large had the Olives' operations grown.

Over in Kansas, the brothers' Dodge City operations were also prospering. Here, Jay's herds were multiplying to the benefit of his widow and family.

Print's capacity for hard work and his keen business judgment had led to a number of other business ventures as well—several of which were highly successful. Because he did not have to pay taxes, he was able to keep the records of his holdings secret, and he did—sometimes even from his own family. He owned at least one hotel in Colorado, meat retailing and livestock feed businesses in Kansas, and partial interests in a number of widely scattered taverns.

Prentice Olive planned to establish the headquarters of his empire on the Platte. Realist that he was, he was neither surprised nor disturbed to discover that there were a few hardened cattle rustlers like the affable David Cherry "Doc" Middleton and—he suspected—Manly Caple in the area. Men like Middleton and Caple posed no long-range threat; their kind could be handled in the normal course of things, as experience had shown in Texas. The others—the homesteaders who insisted on coming across the "Olive Line"—would have to be discouraged or absorbed. Without sizable capital, they would either move on or drift back east. Those who remained could, he was confident, be induced to supervise his local operations on terms similar to those arrived at with Jim McIndeffer. No voice was raised against Print's logic. His father, with his quiet, perceptive counsel, a steadying influence in Texas, had remained behind. Jay's moderate voice was forever still. Now Print's only close advisers were Bob and Ira. Bob had always been headstrong and impulsive, and Ira preferred leaving things in Print's hands. Thus, more and more Print came to rely solely on his own judgment.

Olive cowboys had reported in May that three homesteaders, all living together in one unusually large dugout jammed into a hillside, were plowing for crops on two homesteads. The plowing operations appeared to be joint ventures, and the one farthest northwest seemed destined to encompass many acres.

From the first report, Print and his associates on the South Loup had recognized the upper Clear Creek sodbusting as a serious problem. First of all, it was taking place miles within the "Olive Line," the supposed separation between farming and cattle country; and in addition, a cooperative or joint operation could involve substantial numbers of homesteaders. Print Olive had directed Fred Fisher to see that their cowboys rode through Clear Creek Valley every week and reported as quickly as possible exactly what was taking place.

By June the Olive command had a fairly clear picture of developments. They knew that three homesteading ventures were in progress, that two others were beginning, and that several more seemed contemplated. In addition to the work on the Bryan, Mitchell, and Ketchum homesteads, the Charles Baker homestead farther north and the Elbert Herrington enterprise just down Clear Creek from the Bryan dugout were taking shape. With good weather to encourage these sodbusters, Print speculated, this could mean the beginning of a new community that, even if it were not permanent, could destroy several miles of valuable bluestem up and down Clear Creek.

Good weather had continued; by the first week in June the plowing was done. The big field had been expanded to about ten acres, the largest farming operation reported by Olive cowboys riding the Custer County range. Sod breaking near the Bryan dugout was limited to the usual two to three acres, and crops were being planted near both the Baker and the Herrington homesteads.

By mid-June, when work on the buildings had begun, the extent of the Clear Creek homesteaders' intentions was clear. Print heard first that two workshops were up, the smaller near the Bryan dugout. The other, large enough to back in the end of a farm wagon for repairs, was located on the Mitchell and Ketchum homesteads near the site of a proposed sod dwelling. This soddy would probably be the largest in eastern Custer County, rivaling the Olive headquarters on the South Loup. As summer advanced, work had also begun on a large barn near the Mitchell-Ketchum sod house.

Work on the buildings had given way abruptly, about the first of July, to another homesteader activity even more alarming from the Olive point of view. Luther Mitchell had returned from a trek to Central City with enough wire to fence the entire ten acres. By the middle of the month, three strands of heavy-gauge wire, stapled to posts only fifteen feet apart, protected a corn crop which was growing so rapidly it covered the ground by the time the fence was up. Another rain or two, and the Clear Creek homesteaders would have their crop made.

Late in July, Print, Ira, and Bob Olive, accompanied by Fred Fisher, Jim Kelly, and a few other trusted cowmen, had gone to Clear Creek to have a look for themselves. They had not ridden onto the Mitchell and Ketchum homesteads, but from the high ground close by, they had gotten a clear picture of

213

what they wanted to know. They had seen no cattle, Olive branded or otherwise, about the homesteads. All that the cowboys had been reporting was found to be true. With progress like this, the homesteader foothold on Clear Creek could bring a flood of settlers, render the "Olive Line" meaningless, and perhaps make it impossible ever again to fix a boundary between homesteading and cattle operations in the Central Platte country.

Bob immediately began to press Print to let him take some of the cowboys and clean out those homesteaders' crops. Although Print was worried, he was not yet ready for that kind of action. All during the last ten days of July, they discussed the best way to meet the Clear Creek threat. Bob argued for six-shooter action, since these sodbusters appeared not to heed the cowboys' hints. The time had come, Bob argued, to make an example of the Mitchell and Ketchum farming operations so that settlers would know that when they entered Custer County they might just as well "prepare to meet their God." (Years later, when the Burlington Railroad built its line into Custer County and across the Clear Creek Valley, the passenger conductor called out to his passengers as they approached the eastern boundary of Custer County, "Prepare to meet your God.") Among Print Olive's top aides there was some support for Bob's proposal, but just as many urged more cautious approaches.

The final decision lay with Print. Finally, in the last days of July, he yielded to his fear that they would lose all the bluestem and buffalo grass of the Central Platte if he allowed the homesteaders to move their fences into Custer County. He agreed to defend the "Olive Line." He knew he was embarking on a collision course. For the first time he was shifting from defense of what could rightfully be considered his to attack upon what clearly was not his in the eyes of the law, however ineffectual that law might be.

Bob took personal charge of the attack. Destroying the big corn crop on the Mitchell and Ketchum homesteads would not be a simple thing to accomplish in the few hours of total darkness afforded by an early August night. A man or a horse moving about could still be seen against the western sky after nine o'clock, and light tinged the east once more within a few hours. Only in that interval could the raid be perpetrated. Their scheme profited, of course, from the fact that the homesteaders were sleeping and taking their evening and morning meals at the Bryan homestead. Even so, the cowboys knew that two or three carloads of steers would hardly inflict significant damage to such a large field of corn. They would need hundreds of hungry steers in order to do the job quickly.

Under Bob's eager direction, the plan was executed. Then they doubled the watch on the homesteaders to learn how the settlers would react. Would some means of retaliation be launched by a confederation of settlers? Conceivably, homesteaders in eastern Custer County and adjoining portions of Valley, Sherman, and Buffalo counties could cause the cattlemen and their cowboys a lot of trouble. Any move of this sort would come quickly, the Olives believed, or not at all. More probably the Clear Creek homesteaders would just retreat, causing no more trouble, at least until the next spring.

Bob sought to learn through the Kearney taverns' rumor mills whether news of the raid had spread. No one seemed to have heard a word. This worried Print because it indicated that Ami Ketchum and Luther Mitchell were confiding in no one.

On Sunday the eighteenth of August, some of Olive's cowboys noticed smoke rising, plume-like, to the northwest on the Thomas-Hooker county line. This could only mean an early-season range fire. Thunderstorms, welcome for their summer moisture, had for weeks passed over a wide strip in the southern sandhills, and now the grass stood tall. The fire, first sighted a little before noon, began in the Dismal River bottoms near where North-Cody and Olive operations joined. No one ever admitted seeing it start, but the blaze probably spread from the campfire of some Indians or cowhands celebrating the weekend. The big prairie fires, terrible at any season, did not usually occur until after the heavy freezes in November had crisped the dry grass.

Ranchers and cowboys watched the smoke towering on the

horizon that hot, still Sunday afternoon. So long as the smoke mushroomed lazily into the sky, there was a chance that the fire would be contained and burn itself out in the area where it started. But toward evening a cool front, without clouds or rain, moved through the sandhills and brought with it a brisk northwest wind.

During the night the flames rode the wind down the Dismal to the east, hurdled the sandhill ridges, and ignited the heavier bluestem in the valley of the South Loup River. Even had there been a firebreak, there would have been no way to man it. Every available man and horse was needed to drive the cattle out of the path of the inferno. Despite all their efforts, longhorns bellowed and perished in the flames.

All day Monday the holocaust continued—a raging, twisting, all-consuming, constantly advancing tide of fire. Flames raced down the Middle Loup into Custer County, through and past the soddies of Callaway, until by evening they were within sight of Olive headquarters eight miles farther down the river.

As the wind subsided, the fire also reached the bluestem, which was too green and wet to burn without the tremendous draft which the wind had been providing. As the fire wavered, hundreds of cowboys, joined by ranchers, began dragging green cowhides behind their ponies with separate ropes tied to each front leg of the skins. They raked the earth all through the night and most of Tuesday before the fire was finally extinguished.

The men had arrested the conflagration, saving a few thousand acres of grass and the lives of most of the cattle, but not before five thousand square miles lay blackened. From Grant, Hooker, and McPherson counties, across the western and southern sandhills, eastward through parts of the Platte country counties of Logan, Lincoln, Blaine, Custer, and Buffalo the desolation stretched. All the cattle kings—Cody and North, the Olive brothers, and a score of smaller ranchmen—had lost an important part of their feed supply for the fall, winter, and early spring to come; and worse, they had lost it three months earlier than the prairie-fire hazard generally had to be reckoned with. Economically, this meant that thousands of longhorns, perhaps half a hundred Union Pacific cattle-train-loads—would not be marketed on schedule. Instead the Olives and other cattlemen would be forced to move thousands of cattle east to bluestem still too green to burn. Everyone forgot the Clear Creek homesteaders during this flurry of activity.

Thus obscured, the measures taken by Mitchell and Ketchum in retaliation for the August night raid on the corn crop went undetected. Until the summer heat was over, the partners worked on a tight schedule in order to deliver fresh, salable meat to their Kearney clients, and had it not been for Manly Caple, little might ever have been known about the trade in "slow elk."

Shrewd and cunning, Caple had recognized the Olive raid for what it was: an effort to drive out not just Mitchell and Ketchum, but all homesteaders in eastern Custer County, and to keep the bluestem for their longhorns.

Manly Caple, reputed to be a rustler in his own right, saw at once that here was a fight he could promote. Whatever strife ensued could afford a screen for his own operations. Moreover, he seems to have enjoyed incitement for its own sake. In any case, he set about systematically promoting a feud between Bob Olive and Ami Ketchum and encouraging partisan attitudes among normally disinterested groups. For example, Caple represented to Sheriff Anderson and to his Kearney drinking companions that Ami Ketchum was a giant of a man, never without his six-shooter, that he could use his left hand or right with deadly effect, that he feared no cowboy, and that he openly exhibited a desire to cross guns with Bob Olive.

Bob was susceptible to such talk. He had long been a violent man, and he felt a particular annoyance that a homesteader should excel at marksmanship, a skill he regarded as more appropriate in a cattleman.

All during the late summer and early fall, Print listened to his brother's threats against Ami Ketchum, Manly Caple, and others, always admonishing him to keep out of further trouble on Clear Creek, at least for the present. Print was not too much concerned about the loss of a few longhorns, and he was still sure that the homesteaders would soon leave and not be back to plant more crops next spring. This conviction was strengthened when he learned that Johnny Bryan had left for Lincoln.

Print, however, sought to protect himself further. He decided to make a strong bid for support from the ranchers in Wyoming whose "cattlemen's association" seemed to be coping successfully with both rustling and the intrusions of homesteaders. But first he must get the fall marketing work underway.

Late in October, Print, Ira, and Bob each accompanied a trainload of their cattle to the Chicago market via the Union Pacific and the Chicago and Northwestern railroads. Bob, however, did not return immediately to Plum Creek, heading south instead to visit his parents. He was still on the Texas Rangers list of "most wanted men," but by now he was confident that if he would stand trial on charges of murdering cattle rustlers in Williamson County, he could clear his name, as his accomplice Sam Carr had done a few months earlier.

His parents welcomed him, of course; but his father, who had lost none of his acumen, advised Bob not to stay and face the charges—not at this time, anyway. So Bob returned to the Platte, his name still on the "Fugitive List of the Texas Rangers."

Returning from Chicago, Print and Ida took the morning Union Pacific passenger train up the Platte. The ride gave the brothers a chance to talk more leisurely than they had done for months. Print always enjoyed these trips, contending that the major difference between a small cattle business and a large one was that a large longhorn enterprise made it necessary to travel, and travel provided time to think about the future of the business.

Ira voiced his concern over the increasingly crowded condition of their range and their losses to rustlers. Though Print acknowledged the seriousness of both problems, his primary worry was the steady influx of homesteaders pushing across their line.

UNION PACIFIC RAILROAD

TIME SCHEDULE No. 4

TO TAKE EFFECT

SUNDAY, DEC. 2nd, 1866, 6 P. M.

*For the Government and information of Employees Only. The
Company reserves the right to vary therefrom at pleasure.*

Trains leave Omaha & North Platte Daily, Sunday excepted.

Bound West.		Distance from Omaha.	NAMES OF STATIONS.	Distance from North Platte.	Bound East.	
TRAIN No. 3.	TRAIN No. 1.				TRAIN No. 2.	TRAIN No. 4.
6.00 P. M.	12.00 M.		OMAHA, 12.5	290	6.30 A. M.	11.40 A. M.
7.10 "	12.50 P. M.	12½	PAPILLION, 16.3	277	5.40 "	10.55 "
8.40 "	1.55 "	28⅞	ELKHORN, 17.8	260	4.25 "	9.45 "
10.10 "	3.10 "	46⅝	FREMONT, 14.7	243	3.10 "	8.35 "
11.30 "	4.10 "	61¼	NORTH BEND, 14.3	228	2.05 "	7.35 "
1.05 A. M.	5.05 "	75½	SHELL CREEK, 15.9	214	**1.05** "	6.40 "
2.40 "	6.10 "	91¼	COLUMBUS, 17.7	198	12.00 P. M.	5.35 "
4.20 "	7.30 "	109	SILVER CREEK, 22.5	180½	10.40 "	**4.20** "
5 55 "	**9.05** "	101¼	LONE TREE, 22.	158	**9.05** "	2.50 "
7.40 "	10.35 "	153½	GRAND ISLAND.	136	7.45 "	1.20 "
8.10 "	10.40 "	153½	GRAND ISLAND, 18.	136	7.30 "	1.15 "
9.40 "	**12.00** "	171½	WOOD RIVER, 18.5	118½	6.25 "	**12.00** P. M.
11.20 "	1.10 A. M.	190	KEARNEY, 21.	100	5.20 "	10.50 "
1.00 P. M.	2.35 "	211	ELM CREEK, 19.	79	4.00 "	9.30 "
2.50 "	3.50 "	230	PLUM CREEK, 20.	60	**2.50** "	8.15 "
4.10 "	5.10 "	250	WILLOW ISLAND, 18.	40	1.35 "	6.55 "
5.40 "	6.25 "	268	BRADY ISLAND. 22	22	12.20 "	**5.40** "
7.30 "	8.00 "	290	NORTH PLATTE.		11.00 A. M.	4.00 "

REGULAR MEETING PLACES ARE INDICATED BY FULL FACED FIGURES.

SEE RULES ON BACK.

A. A. BEAN,
Master of Transportation.

SAM'L B. REED,
General Superintendent.

A Union Pacific schedule in 1867, the year Nebraska became
the 37th state of the Union, covered 290 miles (from Omaha to
North Platte) in 20 hours. *(Union Pacific Railroad Museum)*

219

Since the Olive interests were more extensive than those of any other cattlemen in Custer County, the solution of these problems fell on the brothers' shoulders more than any others. The greatest natural asset of this country north of the Platte, the bluestem grass, was an enemy of the sodbusters but the best friend of the cattlemen. This fact alone, the Olive brothers agreed, made the area cattle country. It was up to the cattlemen to protect the bluestem—and the homesteader too, who they felt would plow it up and starve his family to death in the struggle. Since their destruction of the Clear Creek homesteaders' crops had failed to dislodge them, something would have to be done about Ami Ketchum, the man most responsible for stiffening the sodbusters' backbone.

By the time their train reached Kearney, Print had decided on a new approach. His father had always urged working as closely as possible with representatives of law enforcement, so when Print got off the train at Kearney, he went to see Buffalo County's sheriff, David "Cap" Anderson, a big, friendly man who had been a Union army captain. Olive and the sheriff had met before, but now Olive was careful to keep the conversation focused on cattle rustling, avoiding any mention of homesteading in Custer County. He explained that he was enlisting Sheriff Anderson's aid because most of the stolen Olive longhorns coming out of Custer County were sold in Kearney. Anderson assured Olive of his support. From this beginning, Olive pursued his advantage. He portrayed not Manly Caple or David Cherry "Doc" Middleton as the greatest menace, but Ami Ketchum, persuading Anderson that so long as Ketchum's six-shooter remained at large, no cattleman, cowboy, or sheriff could safely perform his function in Custer County.

Anderson agreed to issue a warrant for Ami Ketchum's arrest, charging theft of cattle. As finally issued, listing no specific instance, time, or place, the document charged Ketchum with cattle stealing in Custer County on a complaint signed by a man from Dawson County, before the sheriff of Buffalo County. Cap Anderson was not too fastidious in these matters. He did balk, however, at arresting Ami Ketchum himself, since he would not physically confuse the boundaries of his jurisdiction. This scruple was offset by his willingness to appoint as his special deputy for the task anyone whom Print Olive might suggest. The cattle king proposed that his younger brother, Robert Olive, be named.

That settled, Cap Anderson gave Olive a handful of signed forms that the cattleman could use to deputize each of the cowboys who would ride with Bob Olive in the posse. In this way the move against the Clear Creek homesteader could be taken in the name of "law and order."

Cap Anderson knew that Print Olive could, if the need arose, put more guns at any given point along the middle Platte—and in less time—than anyone in Nebraska except the U.S. Army commandant at Fort Omaha. Yet Anderson, had he possessed the inclination and the courage, could have tempered the Olive demands. He had the strongest jail in the region; he had the facilities of Fort Kearny, though it was no longer heavily manned. Cap Anderson had the largest body of town citizens, independent of cattle and cattle kings, to be found between Omaha and Denver. He had an established newspaper, known for its crusades for law and order, ready to support him. Telegraph lines reached directly into Lincoln and the office of Governor Silas Garber, with whom Anderson was acquainted, and the Union Pacific afforded rapid transport between Fort Omaha and Kearney.

But Cap Anderson was a limited man, seldom leaving Kearney and almost never looking beyond the obvious for facts. The cattle business made sense to him, perhaps because he could understand its tools: horses and guns. And so his sympathies were with the Olives and their brand of justice.

By the time Bob reached home it was the week before Thanksgiving. Print was in Wyoming, hopeful of extending the confederation of cattlemen to the Central Platte after the removal of the Clear Creek homesteaders. Besides discouraging homesteaders, such a move, he felt, would serve to rally the support of the other ranchers, whose combined holdings exceeded the

Olives'. So not until the weekend did the three Olive brothers get together. The brothers decided to move quickly. The discussion was so matter-of-fact that it might almost have concerned the control and extermination of calf-destroying coyotes. No need, they concluded, to wait until after Thanksgiving to pick up Ami Ketchum. Preliminaries could be completed on Monday, the twenty-fifth of November. The men could leave early Tuesday, arrest Ketchum on Wednesday, and be back home by Thursday. As for the number of gunmen to be used, Bob thought too much was being made of the affair. He was sure that with Barney Armstrong and perhaps another cowboy or two, he could handle the job himself. If Ketchum submitted to arrest, there would not be much to do; if he made any motion to resist, Bob would empty his six-shooter, in which case there would be little for "Sheriff Anderson's deputies" to do beyond reporting the quick end to the affair. Ira, on the other hand, thought the job might develop into a major undertaking and that it called for a posse.

Print's talk with Cap Anderson had convinced him that Ami Ketchum must be overwhelmed from the beginning—hit with such a show of force that even a madman would see that resistance of any sort was hopeless. Print was unusually brusque about the matter. He said that the Olives did not have as much right on their side as he would have liked and he was determined there would be no bloodshed. The way to prevent violence, Print reasoned, was to swoop in on Ketchum quickly, surrounding him in such strength that unless Ketchum lost his head and resisted, no gunplay should be necessary.

Bob yielded, agreeing to lead a posse to arrest Ami Ketchum; but with so small an area as the Mitchell-Ketchum farmyard to cover, five horsemen, he felt, would be the most that could be used effectively. But Print was still not satisfied. These homesteaders might have worked out cooperative plans for resistance, he cautioned.

So final plans called for not one, but two Olive posses. The main one would consist of five men, four Texans and the Nebraskan Jim McIndeffer, led by Deputy Bob Olive. Bob would select three more men, preferably Barney Armstrong, Fred Fisher, and Pete Beeton if they were available. Print and Ira would have felt easier if Bob had included Jim Kelly in his plans.

The second posse would be held in reserve against the possibility of some unforeseen circumstance, stationed out of sight but no more than one minute away from the yard. Five men, all of them Texans, including Jim Kelly, would comprise the backup posse, directed by Print Olive himself.

Hours were required for the Olive brothers to complete plans for the expedition. Both Clear Creek posses would leave early Tuesday, arriving by early evening at the little settlement of Mason City across thirty-five miles of range. Jim McIndeffer, the Olive contact in the area, lived nearby, and from his place it was only a short distance to the Mitchell and Ketchum homesteads. Seizing Ketchum before noon on Wednesday, the combined posses would accompany him down the Elm Creek trail—now Nebraska Highway 183—to the point in Buffalo County where the trail crossed the South Loup River. Keeping out of sight would forestall any countermove by the homesteaders at the same time that the prisoner would be transported from Custer County into Buffalo County, whose sheriff had issued the warrant.

At the South Loup, Ketchum's arms could be bound behind him so that only three of the cowboys would have to accompany him into Kearney and turn him over the Sheriff Anderson. The Olives could turn west and be in Plum Creek to have Thanksgiving with their families.

As Bob and Print led the company out of their South Loup headquarters in the early morning darkness of Tuesday, the twenty-sixth of November, 1878, one of the Texans observed that this was a reenactment of the War Between the States, with the Confederate cavalry planning a surprise attack on prepared Union positions. Print Olive found no humor in the jest. During the ride, he engaged in little conversation; indeed, he was lost in his own thoughts, hardly aware of the others riding with him. Print was not disdainful of Nebraska law. It was only that enforcement was as yet too tenuous in that part of the state. Used in conjunction with the power of the cattlemen, perhaps law could fashion the area's future; alone, it seemed quite powerless. Print shared with most cattlemen the conviction that grasslands were meant for grazing, and that for the good of everyone, a boundary must be established on the Platte beyond which farming would not expand and the cattle business could flourish. They were convinced that in time everyone would accept and defend such an arrangement.

There might be several incidents such as the one which they were now undertaking, he thought, but properly handled, these would affect only a few homesteaders and be relatively painless. Then the great cattle industry, the only enterprise capable of bringing real prosperity and money into the plains, could thrive unhindered. In his mind's eye as he rode across the Custer County range on his favorite horse, "White Flanks," Print could see, based on the Platte, the greatest cattle empire on the American plains—from Kearney and Plum Creek to the sources of the river's tributaries rising in the snowy mountains of Wyoming and Colorado—supplying beef for tables all across the nation.

Shortly after sundown the Olive posses reached Mason City and sought out Jim McIndeffer to explain their mission. After supper, Deputy Sheriff Bob Olive discussed the strategy for the next morning. He wanted Armstrong, Fisher, Beeton, and McIndeffer to ride with him when he went to Clear Creek to arrest Ketchum. He gave each of them a certificate deputizing them for the occasion.

McIndeffer described in detail the layout of the Mitchell-Ketchum homestead. Clear Creek ran almost south through the homesteads of Mitchell and Ketchum. The large soddy was located several hundred yards east of Clear Creek, he said, but a ravine deep enough to hide a man on horseback extended almost due north and south only about two hundred yards west of the Mitchell-Ketchum soddy. The soddy, roughly thirty by sixty feet, ran east and west with the door on the east, and hence out of view from the dry ravine west of the sod house. A little north and thirty to forty yards east of the big sod house stood the smithy, open on the south side.

Print talked very little during the evening. When he did, it was usually to emphasize that they had brought along enough men to enforce their will quickly and bloodlessly. Ami Ketchum was to be arrested—and nothing more. It was Bob who laid out the plan of attack. The posse would use either the half circle or full circle pattern to cover Ketchum, depending on where they encountered him. If they found him in the blacksmith shop or in the soddy itself, the deputies would quickly form a half-circle around the homesteader. If they caught him in the open, they would encircle him.

In either case, everyone would come in with guns drawn in hopes that Ketchum would see that resistance of any kind was useless. Deputy Sheriff Bob Olive would explain their mission to Ketchum. If Ketchum reached for his gun or showed any other sign of resistance, the deputies were ordered to shoot to kill. If Ketchum were taken outside the soddy, he would not be permitted to go inside—where there were guns.

Print talked about the second posse. Its members would remain in the dry ravine west of the Mitchell-Ketchum soddy, far enough apart so that they could follow any action that might develop, whether on the north or south side of the soddy.

In the discussion the men questioned whether they should reveal their full force before they knew definitely that Ketchum was at the homestead. It was decided that Pete Beeton, the least likely to be recognized as an Olive man by the Mitchells or Ketchum, would go to the homestead in advance and inquire about getting his horse shod. This way he would learn Ketchum's whereabouts.

Print set up the schedule for Wednesday. Everyone would be ready to ride at daylight. They would be in the dry ravine on the Mitchell-Ketchum homestead about ten o'clock, and they should be away again in little more than half an hour. They would ride back to McIndeffer's place before stopping to eat. If trouble with other homesteaders was going to develop, it should have occurred by that time.

Ketchum would be offered the same food as everyone else and would not be tied up, so long as he behaved, until they stopped for the night. With luck, that stop would be made some-where near the South Loup, where the party was scheduled to separate, the smaller contingent taking Ketchum on to the jail in Kearney.

Wednesday was a mild day for the end of November, and clear—too good to last long, the cowboys said. The two posses were riding at daylight. They stayed west of Clear Creek until they were well north of the Herrington dugout which, like Mitchell and Ketchum's, had a view only to the east. A little before ten o'clock, while the main group waited on the range west of Clear Creek and counted Olive longhorns to pass the time, Pete Beeton rode ahead to the Mitchell-Ketchum home-stead a mile to the northeast. McIndeffer explained to him ex-actly where to cross the creek and enter the dry north-south gully so as not to be seen from either the Mitchell soddy or the Her-rington dugout. Print called after him, directing him to keep his eyes open for everything they needed to know.

Beeton reported back in twenty minutes. Yes, Ami Ketchum was there. He had found him in the blacksmith shop doing some repair work on his own wagon. Ketchum had said he was too busy to shoe Beeton's pony that day but he would be glad to do it if Beeton would come back after Thanksgiving or, better yet, the following Monday or Tuesday.

Print and Fred Fisher questioned Beeton closely. Was Ket-chum wearing his gun? Did he have other guns nearby? Were there obstacles in the yard? Was Mitchell around? Had he seen Mrs. Mitchell or the kids? Was there a window on the east side of the soddy? How steep was the bank of the dry ravine?

Yes, said Beeton, Ketchum was wearing his six-shooter, but there were no other guns in sight. The wagon, which Beeton thought to be empty, was in the yard about midway between the repair shop and the soddy door. Old Man Mitchell was there. He seemed to be mostly waiting around to help Ketchum with the wagon repairs. Beeton had not seen Mrs. Mitchell, but Tamar Snow had run from the repair shop to the soddy as he rode up. The slope of the ravine was gentle and could be scaled on horseback with ease. Beeton did not think he saw a window—there was none, in fact—in the east end of the soddy, facing the repair shop. Bob called for the half-circle formation; Print's reserves were marshaled, and the ride on the homestead began.

Beeton's report to his posse was remarkably accurate for a man who had just ridden in and out again. However, the attacking force had no way of knowing the precautions Ami Ketchum and Tamar Snow had taken against just such a visitation.

Tamar had left the blacksmith's shop and run to the soddy by prearrangement: at any time unknown visitors approached, the two of them would not be found together, and one of them would always be close to the guns and ammunition in the east section of the soddy. In this way each could come to the aid of the other if the need arose.

Ami Ketchum quickly sensed the real nature of Beeton's mission. The moment Beeton disappeared into the ravine—it was about ten fifteen—Ketchum called to Luther Mitchell and went into the soddy. He reported to Tamar and her mother that their caller was an informer for the Olives and that they should count on having more visitors, perhaps soon.

Ketchum laid an extra six-shooter and some cartridges on the table near the soddy door. Jane Mitchell moved the children into the area farthest from the soddy door as she tried to calm their fears. Luther Mitchell found and inspected his old sawed-off shotgun, the one firing in a wide pattern so that the meat of rabbits and other small game would not be too badly torn up for table use. It was an old gun. He had not aimed a firearm at another human being since the spring of 1865, at the close of the war; but if there was going to be real trouble, at least he would be ready.

Mitchell and Ketchum had done their weekly butchering the afternoon before, and the halves of beef were on the wagon that Beeton thought was empty, under a protective cover of bluestem hay. Now that the weather was cool there was more time to transport the meat, and Ketchum had decided to repair the wagon brakes before setting out for Kearney.

The wagon was typical of the ones used by homesteaders on the plains. It had two brakes, each about the size of a brick that, when applied from the driver's position at the front of the wagon, would clamp on each rear wheel in much the same manner that the steel brake shoes operate on a modern railway car. Ketchum had completed repairing the brake on the left rear wheel before Beeton's visit and was fashioning the necessary parts for the other when the Olive scout rode up.

The wagon position in the yard was not, as Beeton described it, on a straight line between the soddy and the repair shop. Rather it was considerably south and much closer to the soddy than to the blacksmith shop.

Except for Jane's assurances to the children, there was no more conversation on the part of the homesteaders. None was needed. Ami Ketchum returned to the repair shop, where he gathered up parts and tools he needed to finish the work on the wagon—the repairs on the right rear wheel brake, the wheel nearest the soddy door and clearly visible from it. Luther went with him, helping to carry the things to the wagon. Both men got down under the wagon, but Ketchum asked Mitchell to go into the house and stay with the women and the children.

Luther Mitchell had just passed through the door, leaving it purposely a little ajar, when suddenly the yard was full of horsemen. Ketchum, under the wagon in the yard, reached for his gun but held his fire. This was not the time for him to start the gun fight; his opponents must spend their ammunition first if he were to finish the fight, and that he meant to do.

Deputy Sheriff Bob Olive had signaled with his drawn six-shooter for the charge across the two hundred yards separating the dry ravine from the Mitchell sod house. Barney Armstrong at his side, he galloped around the north side of the soddy. The mounts of Fisher, Beeton, and McIndeffer leaped from the gully together, racing around the south side of the sod house and heading for the blacksmith shop.

In their haste, the posse had moved past the soddy and the wagon and were almost to the blacksmith shop before they were aware Ketchum was no longer there. They wheeled as Fred Fisher, riding behind McIndeffer and Beeton, made the discovery that Ketchum was under the wagon. Quickly the posse formed a circle around the wagon.

The men realized instantly that if Ketchum chose to resist, the wagon would shield him from their fire and provide a barricade from which he could pick them off. However, they were sure he would not have ammunition enough to fire indiscriminately.

The posse moved in close to the wagon in order to provide no easy targets in the event there was shooting. Olive moved near the right rear wheel, the one on which Ketchum had been working. Armstrong was so close to the wagon's endgate that he could have kicked it. Beeton was near the left back wheel, Fisher, near the left front wheel and McIndeffer, in front of the wagon.

Bob Olive called out to Ketchum, "You're under arrest. I am deputized, and so is the entire posse. I have a warrant for you. Throw out your guns."

"The only thing I'll throw to you or any of your Texas friends is hot lead from a six-shooter," came the response.

Infuriated, Bob lost his temper and any pretense of being a law enforcement officer. He was Bob Olive, Texas killer.

"You goddamn, homesteadin', cattle stealin' son-of-a-bitch, we'll kill you right where you are. We'll pump lead through this wagon until all your blood is on the ground," shouted Bob as he opened fire.

"He can't have more than a couple of guns," he called to his gunmen. "Run him out of ammunition, and then we'll go in under the wagon after the son-of-a-bitch, if there's any life left in him."

More from fear than inclination, the other members of the posse moved even closer and began firing into the wagon box in hopes of driving slugs through the floor and into their quarry. Only McIndeffer, farthest away and protected by the front end of the wagon, had any strategy of his own. He cautiously moved toward the west side of the wagon, hoping to fire at Ketchum's gun hand as the homesteader attempted to get a shot at Bob. He dared not move too far from the front panel, or he himself would become a prime target.

Ketchum was slow to return the posse fire, indicating his determination to wait for good shots. Meanwhile, no member of the band had noticed that the soddy door was ajar. Only Beeton and Fisher could have a view of it, closed or open. Armstrong and Olive had their backs to the soddy, and McIndeffer was out of range at the far end of the wagon. All of them were perplexed at the apparent futility of their shots. The sides of beef were taking up the slugs, but they saw only the bluestem hay on top, and could not understand their failure to penetrate the wagon floor. Now, Luther Mitchell, his sawed-off shotgun gripped in both hands, had moved unnoticed into the doorway, set back in the two-foot-thick soddy wall.

Print Olive and Jim Kelly, from their positions west of the soddy, could not see the entire action; but they could see the wagon and McIndeffer and Fisher firing into it. They concluded Ketchum was under the wagon, but could Mitchell be there too? If not, where was he? Print ordered the reserves out of the ravine to attack the defenders in case the tide of battle should turn against the cattlemen.

A slug from the gun of one of the cattlemen suddenly struck the iron on a wagon wheel, glanced off at an angle, and drove through Ketchum's forearm with such force that it shattered the bone. Ketchum's gun dropped to the ground. Even Bob Olive, who was closest to Ketchum, did not see the gun fall. Other members of the Olive posse were not aware of the injury, and all of them continued firing into the wagon.

But Ketchum's injury and the gun dropping had been seen from within the shadow of the soddy doorway. The homesteader's arm had hardly gone limp before Tamar Snow, watching from behind Mitchell, darted around her stepfather and into the open yard. Heedless of the gunfire around her, she raced across the yard and threw herself under the wagon beside

Ketchum, putting a fresh gun in his good hand. Then she snatched his gun from the ground, wiped the blood from it, reached in her dress pocket for cartridges, and began reloading the six-shooter.

Everyone except Bob Olive in the cattlemen's posse saw Tamar join the battle. And her act of courage seemed to trigger a re-

Tamar and William Wall, after they had moved to San Antonio, Texas. Tamar had already contracted tuberculosis, which would cause her death.

sponse in the immobilized Mitchell. Luther Mitchell did not know one posseman from another. He did not realize that the horseman nearest him, firing his six-shooter through the wagon wheel in an effort to kill Ami, was one of the cattle kings. It did not matter who he was, Mitchell recalled thinking to himself, because this was the only raider within range of his old sawed-off shotgun. The older man, his faculties now fully functioning, steadied his hands, took aim, and pulled the trigger.

The pattern of his number-four shot formed a circle about a foot in diameter across the back of Bob Olive's coat, squarely between the shoulders. Mitchell remembered being well pleased with his handiwork.

Shoved forward by the force of the blast, Bob Olive crumpled, his six-shooter slipping from his hand.

Print Olive heard but could not see the blast from Mitchell's shotgun. The corner of the sod house prevented him, Jim Kelly, and the other cowboys in the reserve posse at the dry ravine from knowing that Bob Olive himself had taken the slugs from Mitchell's shotgun. Print knew there was something wrong, very wrong, when he saw Fred Fisher spur his horse in front of the wagon and disappear from sight behind the house. Print was spared the sight of Fisher and Armstrong, disregarding their own safety, rushing to Bob Olive's side to hold him in his saddle for a retreat.

Just as Print ordered his reserves to move in, three Olive horses came around the corner of the soddy, advancing in measured steps as though they were lashed rigidly together. Barney Armstrong and Fred Fisher, on either side of the slumped form of Bob Olive, were retreating toward the protection of the dry ravine. An instant later Pete Beeton and Jim McIndeffer moved in behind them to provide a rear guard.

Again Print Olive ordered his fresh posse toward the sod house to re-establish Olive control and finish the job of arresting Ami Ketchum. Again it was a development at the corner of the soddy that gave them pause.

With the slowly retreating posse no more than forty or fifty yards from the wagon, Ami Ketchum, supported by Tamar Snow, moved into view. Ketchum moved cautiously, his injured arm doubled tightly against his right side. He leaned heavily on Tamar, who walked at his left side, her arm around his waist and his arm around her shoulders. Ketchum's left hand held a six-shooter. Seeing the retreating posse, Ketchum laboriously went to his knees for greater steadiness. As Tamar stepped behind his shoulders to provide added support, Ketchum opened fire on the posse, by now far enough away to be a better target

for a rifle than for a revolver. His first or second shot hit Armstrong's lower left leg, ripping through the boot and inflicting a
crippling and painful wound. As he emptied his six-shooter,
another slug tore away the scarf from Fisher's throat.

Photographed
Aug 4th 1885

Luther Mitchell and Ami Ketchum erected a unique, duplex
soddy intended to serve both families, exactly half its length on
each of the two homesteads. (*Nebraska State Historical Society*)

Tamar counted the shots; with the crack of number six, she
slipped a fresh gun into Ami Ketchum's hand so smoothly there
was hardly an interruption in his firing. While holding her rigid
stance as a prop for Ketchum, she took fresh cartridges from her
pocket and reloaded the smoking six-shooter.

By now the oncoming posse had stopped, and the retreating
horsemen were nearing the ravine. Ketchum emptied his gun,
shredding the rim of Beeton's "ten gallon" Texas sombrero.

Ami and Tamar saw the fresh Olive posse moving in to attack, but they were not frightened into retreat or inaction. If the fresh posse wanted to carry on the fight, it would have to come closer, the young homesteaders knew, and they could deal with it then.

Print Olive and his reserves realized all this too. But for the first time in all their gunfights up and down the plains, the cattle king from Texas and his cowboys faced a woman who if they moved into range would unflinchingly help kill them like so many loafer wolves.

Tamar Snow had become the "unforeseen circumstance" that had worried Print Olive all along. To be sure, she was engaged to Ami Ketchum and was defending him and the rest of the family, but many another woman in such circumstances would have covered her face or looked helplessly on.

"It was lucky for us that Ketchum was injured," Jim McIndeffer explained to Johnny Bryan later. "Otherwise he and that Snow girl would have killed every one of us. That Snow girl was a tiger."

Once back in the protection of the ravine, Print took command. He ordered everyone to follow him as he set off on a dead run to the Herrington homestead half a mile away down Clear Creek. He ordered the homesteader to harness his beautiful matched sorrels to his wagon, fill it with bluestem, and drive on a dead run with Bob Olive toward Kearney. Herrington protested that this would kill his team. Olive shouted that the Olives had hundreds of horses, and he could have his pick in addition to the gold he would be paid.

As each member of the Olive contingent reached the Herrington farmyard, Print dispatched him on some separate errand. Some dashed down the trail to arrange with settlers along the way to Kearney for fresh teams. Clearly the wagon trip from Clear Creek was to be made in far less time than any wagon had ever traveled this distance before. One horseman rode to Plum Creek to notify Bob's wife and Ira of developments. Print ordered others, including Barney Armstrong and Jim Kelly, flying back to Olive headquarters on the Middle Loup to organize a new posse to continue the war with the Clear Creek homesteaders. Armstrong, of course, needed the ministrations of Jim Kelly, who could be an effective corpsman when anyone was hurt on the trail. Armstrong's wound would not be dangerous once Kelly stopped the bleeding.

But the run toward Kearney was shortened. After they had traveled less than two miles, it became evident to Print that his brother was dying. He ordered the wagon stopped, the hay removed and put on the ground near a tree half a mile from the new Murphy homestead, the first one southwest of Johnny Bryan's dugout. Here Bob lay—on his deathbed. Bob asked Print to explain things to his father—to explain that he, Bob, had done what he had only because he had wanted to be like Print. This assertion only added to Print's anguish.

The sun over the Olive cattle empire had passed high noon; the shadows were beginning to lengthen.

[17]

SEARCH EVERY SODDY

WHEN BOB DIED ON CLEAR CREEK, Print sat wordlessly beside his brother's body. After about half an hour he got up and, with the others, lifted the body into the wagon. He directed Herrington to start at once toward Kearney. He was going to accompany the body, he said, but Herrington should go ahead; he would catch up after he had talked to his men and made some plans.

At Kearney, Print would have the body prepared for shipment to Texas, he told his men, and he would wait there for Ira and Bob's wife to arrive to accompany the body south. Print himself would then return from Kearney, reaching McIndeffer's place by Saturday. Meanwhile, Jim McIndeffer was instructed to ride to Plum Creek and break the news to Ira.

Another cowboy was dispatched to the headquarters on the South Loup to report Bob's death and Print's plans. The cattle king directed that a new posse hunt down Mitchell and Ketchum; but this time the outcome was to be different. The posse was to engage in no new fight with the homesteaders. They were merely to find their quarry and watch to see that they did not get away. Clearly Print Olive intended to deal personally with the men who killed his brother, just as Bob had avenged Jay.

These plans made, Print turned toward Kearney to catch up with the wagon. Another wagon waited about five miles to the south, with others at regular intervals. Changing teams frequently, Print and the wagon arrived before midnight. By the time Ira arrived on the train from Plum Creek the next day, the embalmer's work was done.

Ira reported that Bob's wife would come to Kearney on the morning train one day later. Ira asked if Print had sent word of Bob's death to their parents. Print said he had not, thinking that Ira would send the telegram from Plum Creek. The two tried to compose the difficult message.

Ira thought that Print should go home with the body since it was he who had been so close to Bob all of their lives. Everyone, especially their parents, would expect Print to attend the services. Print came straight to the point. He could not go to Texas, but he could hardly explain the reasons to his parents.

"I've got work to do for Bob here," Print said. He would never rest until he had personally settled the score with these cattle-stealing Clear Creek homesteaders who had killed his brother. Ira suggested that hunting down the homesteaders could wait until after the funeral, but Print said that every passing hour made the task more difficult.

As always, Print's will prevailed, and Ira agreed to accompany Bob's widow on the mournful journey. The telegram was sent to Julia and Jim, breaking the news of their son's death and advising them that Ira and Bob's wife were on their way. The message suggested the service and burial in Lawrence Cemetery might take place one week later, on December 6.

The injured Armstrong, Jim Kelly, Fred Fisher, and the others had arrived at the South Loup late in the night following the fight on Clear Creek. About two hours later, the special messenger brought news of Bob's death and the fresh instructions from Print. Once they had Mitchell and Ketchum under surveillance, they were to meet Print at McIndeffer's place Saturday noon.

Barney Armstrong's wound was too painful for him to consider riding with the fresh posse. Fred Fisher was sure that this would become a manhunt calling for all hands available, and that the hunters should not expect to find their game at the big soddy. Dennis Gartrell, Bion Brown, and Sam Carr were back on the South Loup from herd inspection trips. The weather was fair when they joined the posse that left soon after daylight the next morning.

At midday, as the cowboys approached Clear Creek and the Mitchell-Ketchum soddy, they noticed, from a distance, that the wagon was gone. There was no sign of life, but the posse took every precaution against being surprised before forcing open the soddy door. The teakettle and stove were cold. There was no trace of warmth—not even in the ash box under the grate. The Olive men concluded that the homesteaders had probably left shortly after the shooting two days ago.

Members of the posse fanned out in three directions—north, east and south. They would range as far as they could and be back at McIndeffer's place sometime Saturday morning with all the information they could gather, ready to meet Print when he arrived from Kearney. They visited all of the Clear Creek homesteads, even the Bryan dugout. The Herringtons, the only settlers who could see the Mitchell-Ketchum soddy from their place, said they had not seen the wagon or any activity since the morning of the shooting.

Olive men riding as far north as Arcadia found no one who had seen the Mitchells. The men rode around every building in the little town to make certain the wagon was not hidden away in some protected spot.

Meanwhile, two men rode east to Loup City, arriving about nightfall. No one could be found at Judge Aaron Wall's home; and although they asked several persons in town if they had seen a wagonload of settlers going east sometime after Wednesday noon, no one could remember seeing an unknown wagon within the past week.

The detail that rode as far south as Muddy Creek, talking to homesteaders who either could not or would not give any information about Mitchell and Ketchum, was mainly interested in questioning Manly Caple. His being absent from home raised the suspicion that Caple and Ketchum were working together in some way. The search did not extend to Robert Hodges' place at Sweetwater, so it was from neighbors who were contacted that

Hodges learned of the gun battle on Clear Creek and the death of Bob Olive.

Saturday morning Print's men reported back to him. Fred Fisher told him they had covered the area from Arcadia in Valley County to Loup City in Sherman County to the Sweetwater community in northern Buffalo County and searched every soddy in eastern Custer County without finding any trace of Mitchell or Ketchum or their wagon. Print's reaction disturbed his men. Some of them had worked for the Olive brothers five years, some, ten, and a few, like Jim Kelly, considerably longer. This was the first time the veteran cowboys got the feeling the cattleman might be buckling under the strain. For one thing, he had been drinking heavily. He talked, but it was increasingly difficult for him to listen, and he had always been a good listener. His attention seemed to wander; his eyes got misty. Jim Kelly, Fred Fisher, and others concluded they must get him home to Plum Creek as soon as possible so he could rest. He resisted such suggestions with an uncharacteristically bad temper. Heretofore his men had been accustomed to saying anything they wanted to him without fear of reprimand. The men who had been with Print and had known him intimately years earlier recognized that after Jay's death he had reacted in much the same way. Here, again, was the concentration on avenging a brother's death—a lack of interest in anything else. But Jay's death had not been entirely unexpected; there had been more time for Print to prepare himself for the possibility that one brother or another—himself, perhaps—would fall in the Texas confrontation. Now, in the case of Bob's death, Print felt that he himself was largely to blame. He had decreed that the Clear Creek battle would be joined, and he had placed Bob in jeopardy.

Print concluded that information was scanty because the men whom the possemen did not see were hiding or aiding the homesteaders. Aaron Wall and Manly Caple must be found and made to talk; then the cattlemen would know where to look for the homesteaders. Still, no clue must be overlooked. Search every soddy again, Print told his men.

"Just to speed up this job," said Print, "we're going to offer a reward of $1,000 to anyone who brings these rustlers to ranch headquarters. That offer goes for everyone, you fellows included. You all get your regular pay, and you get the $1,000 in addition if you bring Mitchell and Ketchum in."

Print figured the posting of such a large reward would turn every cowboy and homesteader into a one-man posse looking for the Clear Creek homesteaders. Instead, the offer heightened the resentment among the homesteaders, and the reaction among his own men was mixed. For the first time, some of the Olive cowboys felt uneasy about their orders.

Print split his men into two groups—Fred Fisher leading one contingent south to hunt for Manly Caple, Print riding to Loup City to question Judge Wall.

As the last of the Olive men retreated down Clear Creek from the gun battle, Tamar and Ami retreated toward the sod house. Before they got to the door, Jane and Luther met them, Jane carrying a blanket, a sheet, and some of the bandages which she always kept on hand for emergencies. With a doctor fifty miles and two days away, homesteaders had to be ready to provide their own medical service; and with a family to care for, Jane often said she should have been trained to be a doctor rather than a teacher.

Spreading the blanket on the ground, Tamar and Luther helped Ami onto it. Better to be on the cold ground in good light, Jane said, than indoors in the dark, at least until she learned how serious the wound was. Fortunately, the arm was still somewhat numb from the shock of the bullet, making examination easier.

Jane found that only the smaller bone in Ketchum's lower arm had been broken by the Olive slug. She sent Tamar to get some whiskey in water and asked Luther to make some splints. The two frightened children, Henry and Elizabeth, looked on from a distance.

Jane asked Ami whether she should clean the wound and put on the splints now or wait a while until the whiskey had taken more effect. Ketchum directed her to begin. Now that he was lying down, the bleeding had almost stopped, making it much easier for Jane to dress the wound.

Now came the difficult and painful moment. Jane directed Luther to take Ami's wrist and be ready to pull, so that the pieces of bone could fall back into a position as nearly normal as possible. On the same signal, Tamar would apply two splints. Then Jane would wrap the wound and apply the outer bandage.

At the signal, Jane's first-aid team went into action. Even Ami said it was not long, but he did ask Tamar for another draught of the whiskey. Luther and Tamar helped Ami move to a chair inside the soddy. Jane directed him to hold his bandaged arm above his waist to stop the bleeding and minimize the pain.

By now it was noon. Tamar put the food on the table, and Jane insisted that everyone, including Ami, eat something. They could decide while they ate, she said, what move they would make next.

"The only thing we know for sure is we can't stay here," said Luther. "As soon as the Olives organize, they will be back and kill us all." Turning to Ami, Mitchell asked, "Who was that cowboy I hit?"

"That was Bob Olive. He was running the show. You hurt him. He could be a goner," Ami replied.

Everyone agreed that they must hide somewhere immediately. The Olives would, of course, expect them to go east. Consequently it would be best to drive north ten miles to Charlie Dowse's homestead, see if they could arrange to stay there overnight, and then go on north to find a doctor for Ami's arm and to get farther out of Olive territory. Jane thought it most urgent that Ami and Luther get away, and Tamar should go to take care of Ami. She and the children would stay on at Clear Creek for the present. But Luther and Ami wouldn't hear of that. The Olives would not believe anything Jane or the children said but might torture them in an effort to learn where the rest of the family had gone.

Luther Mitchell and Henry hitched the team to the wagon. First the two of them took the load of bullet-pocked meat, the buffer that had saved Ami Ketchum's life, a short way up Clear Creek and dumped it. Then Luther put the canvas cover on the wagon to keep the wind out while Jane put a fresh dressing on Ami's wound. Next they arranged some blankets so that Ami could rest in the wagon, taking others to bundle themselves against the early winter cold. Tamar packed some food, and less than two hours after the gun battle, the Clear Creek homesteaders were moving north.

As Luther took up the lines, Jane told him he was not dressed warmly enough to do the driving. "Go in and get that heavy overcoat of Johnny Bryan's so you will be warm," Jane directed. Luther said he did not think it was going to get that cold this early in the season, but Jane was adamant, so he did don the gray overcoat he had borrowed for the planned Christmas trip to Central City.

As the Mitchells' covered wagon was leaving Clear Creek, one of the Herrington boys came riding up to tell them that the Olive man who was hit in the gun battle was dead. He had lived until the wagon got to Murphy's beyond the Bryan dugout, the messenger said. In answer to the Herrington boy's question as to where Luther was going, the homesteader said, "Got to get Ami to the doctor. He's not hurt bad, but he got nicked in the arm." He was careful not to indicate where they would go for a doctor, and young Herrington did not ask.

In mid-afternoon, the Mitchell wagon pulled up in front of the Dowse soddy. Both Charlie Dowse and his wife were there. Luther and Jane went in to talk to the Dowses, explaining what had happened on Clear Creek and asking them for a night's lodging. Charlie Dowse said they would be glad to help, but the Olives would track the wagon to the Dowse place in a few hours and "kill all of us." He suggested that the fugitives cross the Middle Loup at the fording place nearby and then get their wagon tracks lost on the trail down to Arcadia. From there he urged them to go to Loup City to see Judge Aaron Wall who had helped homesteaders more than any other lawyer in the area.

Mrs. Dowse set some food on the table. Ami, Tamar, and the children came in for a quick lunch before resuming the journey. As evening came on, the ground began to freeze, so the team made better time. By seven o'clock the Mitchell had passed through Arcadia and into Valley County. Just before midnight the Mitchell wagon was nearing Loup City, and Luther was back in familiar surroundings. So many times had he passed through Loup City on his trips to Central City for supplies, there was no need for him to ask directions to Judge Wall's home. Everyone knew that Judge Wall lived in the imposing white house set back among trees just off the main street at the west side of town. Ami's arm was more painful as the night in the wagon wore on, but Jane was pleased that the swelling was moderate. This was a good sign, she kept reminding Ami.

Judge Wall was already in bed when they arrived, but he and Mrs. Wall invited the homesteaders into the warmth of their comfortable home. When the weary group had told their story, Judge Wall said he had been fearing something like this ever since he had heard about the night raid on their cornfield.

"You folks were working too hard and making too much progress not to draw Olive gunfire. They are determined to keep homesteading out of Custer County, and those Confederates out of Texas will never have any respect for decency and the law until someone teaches them a right good lesson. You may have started their education today, but you probably haven't finished the matter," Wall added.

"I'm a marked man with the Olives," the judge continued. "I've been fighting them ever since they drove those longhorns onto the range in Custer County. My guess is that since you killed Bob Olive, the 'Texas Cavalry' will counterattack quickly. They will figure that the first place you would come would be to my place, so we must get you out of here."

While Mrs. Wall fixed something to eat, her husband continued to counsel the homesteaders. He suggested that they drive on east of Loup City immediately and stop at the home of his brother John, who taught in the school recently established on Oak Creek and lived with Rev. John R. Baker, who could also

Judge Aaron Wall of Loup City saw the injustice of the cattle kings and sought to protect homesteaders.

be counted on to help. Wall wrote a note to his brother acquainting him with the travelers' plight.

"But where are you going from there?" the judge asked, pointing out how difficult it would be to hide from the Olives for very long anywhere along the Central Platte. The Olives' control in Custer County was well nigh complete, he went on, extending into areas of the counties bordering Custer County: Sherman, where Wall lived, and Valley to the east of Custer, and Buffalo County to the south.

"But that's not all," Judge Wall continued. "On a raid-and-retreat basis, the Olives could strike a major blow another twenty-five miles beyond this large area that they rule outright. This means that they could capture someone they wanted here in Loup City; they might even be able to operate as far east as St. Paul, and that's a good twenty-five miles east of here, in Howard County.

"I understand that the Olive brothers got involved in a gun battle something like this before they left Texas and that one of them was killed in that shooting match," he went on. "I am told that they murdered everyone they thought was involved in the battle as a means of avenging their brother's death. This man Bob Olive that you shot today was the man who did most of the murdering. So you can expect to be hunted like rattlesnakes till they get you," he concluded.

The homesteaders sat glumly around the table, Elizabeth dozing on Jane's lap, Henry stretched out on the floor near the stove asleep. Suddenly Judge Wall's round face lit up, "I've got it!" he exclaimed. "You fellows have the law on your side. Those Olives attacked you twice. They will deny that they attacked you in August, but no jury or judge will believe them. Now, this time they rode in on you and began the shooting. You can let the law protect you."

The more Aaron Wall thought of his plan the more excited he got. "You can accomplish two ends at once. You can get protection from the Olives, and you can force them to come into court and answer for their crimes. This is what we've been hoping for, an opportunity to bring these big cattlemen into court. You can be the means of stopping the fence cutting, the destroying of crops, the gunwhipping of old men like Ben Christiansen, and the killing of homesteaders as they like."

Nebraska law provided for protective arrest, their host explained. A man who believed that his life was in danger could go to the county jail or even the state prison and become an inmate with the full protection of the police or sheriff—even the United States Army if the state authorities should deem it necessary

Jane Mitchell and Tamar sat forward to catch every word. Luther Mitchell was watching his host eagerly. Ami forgot about his painful arm as he listened.

"Here is what I suggest you do," Wall summarized. "Go on to Oak Creek tonight and get some rest. You will be safe there for at least a day. If the Olives come this far—and my guess is that they will—I can keep them confused and occupied for at least a few hours and send a messenger on to warn you. But they probably won't get here until sometime tomorrow, since you left a body for them to deal with. And they aren't apt to ride farther east looking for you without paying me a visit first. If they come here, I will get word to Sheriff Crew.

"The children will be ready to travel by the middle of the morning tomorrow," Judge Wall continued. "Then you can drive on in to St. Paul and see Sheriff F. W. Crew. He lives on a homestead outside St. Paul. Stop at the county jail and see if he is there. If he's not, you will have to go to his farm. He is a friend of mine. Tell him I sent you to him for protective arrest. Now Crew may feel that even Howard County is too close to the Olives, and if he does, he will work something else out. He might send you on to Sheriff Bill Letcher at Central City. You probably know Letcher. He's a fine fellow, too—veteran of the war and won't allow any monkey business in his county.

"You'll need a lawyer, and I can't help you because I've had too many battles with the Olives already to be considered fair. Ask Crew or Letcher to get you a lawyer; they'll do it."

Jane protested that they did not have any money to pay a lawyer, but Wall said that would make no difference. Any good lawyer would help them: first, because freedom in Nebraska was at stake, and also because when they got back on their feet, Ketchum and the Mitchells were the kind who would pay for the services.

About midnight the homesteaders, fed, warmed, and heart-

246

ened, left Loup City and drove east to Oak Creek. With some difficulty, they aroused John Wall and Reverend and Mrs. Baker. Mrs. Baker got them bedded down by about four A.M. By noon of Thanksgiving Day, the Mitchell's covered wagon was headed toward St. Paul, a four-hour ride away.

Luther, with occasional help from Tamar, did the driving. Ami Ketchum sat on a blanket in the center of the wagon, midway between the wheels, in order to reduce the road shock, since the wagon had no springs. Jane rode at the back of the wagon and played games with Elizabeth and Henry. Later she talked about Thanksgiving the way she used to each year with children in her classes at school, describing conditions that first Thanksgiving on Cape Cod.

On arriving in St. Paul, a plains town of about a hundred buildings, they first sought out Dr. Barnes. Jane went in with Ami to consult the doctor, a capable man who displayed a gruff exterior to prevent everyone's intruding too quickly on a generous nature. Examining Ketchum's wound, Barnes expressed amazement that the injury should have been so well handled by persons untrained in medicine. The bones were already properly in place, he announced. He disinfected the wound, put on more professional splints, bandaged the arm properly, and provided a strong sling that he ordered Ami to use faithfully for the next six weeks.

The doctor talked frankly when he had completed his work. He told Ketchum that although he had on occasion amputated arms following wounds no more serious than this, Jane's first-aid treatment had been so expertly applied that no permanent impairment would result, provided two conditions were met: the arm must be kept in the sling and free of stress, and infection must be controlled. They should know in three days whether it would be possible to control the infection. However, Ketchum should expect some permanent enlargement at the point where the break occurred, he added, since the bullet had left little bone chips and slivers that could not be absorbed. Those on the open side of the wound had been removed, but there were undoubtedly as many embedded and inaccessible. Dr. Barnes directed Ketchum to see him again in three days.

The homesteaders did not find Sheriff Crew at the Howard County jail on Thanksgiving Day. It was evening before they pulled up in front of his farm house. After reading the note Judge Wall had sent, the Crews insisted the Custer County homesteaders come in and eat Thanksgiving supper with them. After supper, when Sheriff Crew had learned the whole story, he suggested that the visitors take over the county jail for the night, since it was unoccupied at the time. The Mitchells could fix breakfast in the morning, Crew proposed, and he would be in to talk with them as soon as he had finished his morning chores on the farm.

"Do I understand that one of the Olives was killed in the gun battle the day before yesterday?" Sheriff Crew asked the next morning.

Jane summarized the events that preceded their flight.

"This may be the situation we've been waiting for," Crew said. "The Olives rode in on you and started the gun battle. One of the cattle kings was killed, and you fought them off and escaped. That's something new. Yes, this may be just what we have been waiting for," he mused.

The sheriff said he thought Judge Wall's suggestion of seeking protective arrest was sound. The Olives would surely try to avenge their brother's death. "Those rebels are strong on that sort of thing, but they almost have to do this if they are not to concede they are whipped and pull their herds out of these parts. If you are under protective arrest and in a jail of your choosing," Crew explained, "the Olives will have to press their claims against you in court in the same jurisdiction." This could be the first step, Crew thought, toward ending the lawlessness that had existed along most of the Platte Valley for nearly a decade.

"You need the help of a good lawyer, and we have one here— Thomas Darnell; he'll help you. There is one danger in your seeking protective arrest here in St. Paul, though" Crew went on. "It's the same danger than Aaron Wall told you about in Loup

City: the Olives could take anyone out of our jail here in ten minutes. You can see that just from staying overnight. You need to go on to Central City to get your womenfolks located where they can be comfortable for a few days until we can get this thing worked out. You can be in Central City by tonight."

Turning to Mitchell, Crew said "Tomorrow I suggest you go to see Sheriff Letcher. You probably know him already. Talk this matter out with him. He has a better jail than we do, and he might have a good lawyer to help you, too."

Jane assured Sheriff Crew they knew Sheriff Letcher. "Luther and Ami have done blacksmith work for him," she explained. "and Mr. Letcher grew up in Ohio, not far from the home of my first husband, Peter Snow. The sheriff is a fine man. But we're fairly well acquainted in the Central City neighborhood, and I don't recall any lawyer there who would be likely to help us."

Sheriff Crew responded that getting their problems worked out in Central City would be better in several ways, regardless. Central City, he pointed out, was a little farther from Custer County and a little closer to the capital, Lincoln, a factor which might eventually assume importance. If for any reason they could not work matters out with Letcher, then they should certainly come back to St. Paul and meet Darnell.

Sheriff William Letcher had lost his left arm about six inches below the shoulder; and although everyone assumed that the proud veteran had been a war casualty, he had, in fact, lost the arm in a hunting accident near his home while on leave. His actual war injury was concealed by a built-up heel on his right boot which compensated for a shortened leg. A Confederate rifle slug through his hip had almost cost his life before army doctors were able to stanch the flow of blood from a ruptured artery in his thigh. Now serving his sixth year as Merrick County sheriff, he knew his job well. The ten days that followed the homesteaders' visit Sheriff Letcher would remember all the rest of his life, and he never tired of telling the Mitchell-Ketchum story and the part he played in it.

After hearing the account of events on Clear Creek, Letcher

agreed that this could be an opportunity to limit the cattle kings. They must learn to respect the rights of homesteaders. The sheriff did not think the Merrick County jail would afford Mitchell and Ketchum adequate protection, however, if an Olive posse elected to come in force to get them.

"I like to tell my friends that my daughter was born in jail, and that about explains the situation. Our county jail is really just a good-sized house. We live upstairs, and the office and confinement areas are on the first floor. I don't think any of the county jails in this area are much better. The only good jail anywhere along the Platte River is at Kearney.

"You folks know as well as I that we do not have a lawyer here capable of helping much in this kind of a situation. Those Olives will have the best lawyer money can hire if they need one, and before this situation is over, they may need several. What I know of this man Darnell at St. Paul, I agree with Sheriff Crew. Darnell could help you," Letcher concluded.

Quickly the plans were made. Mitchell and Ketchum would go back to St. Paul, traveling on Sunday, December 1, so as to be there first thing Monday morning. They would meet with Sheriff Crew and Darnell.

"If Darnell thinks you should have protective arrest and go to the jail in Kearney, come back here. I'll arrange the arrest papers, and as soon as I do that, Merrick County can pay for your transportation and food expenses to Kearney. I probably will go with you just to see there isn't any funny business until you are safely in the Kearney jail," Letcher promised.

Ami Ketchum went to see Dr. Barnes Monday morning and proceeded to the meeting Crew had arranged with Darnell. The lawyer, a man in his early forties, consented at once to help. He knew something of the problems homesteaders were having in Sherman and Valley counties with the big cattle operators, and he regarded the cattlemen as more dangerous than the Indians had been.

Mitchell, in turn, told Darnell the full story of the destruction of the corn crop and the "slow elk" operation which subsequently paid for food and kerosene. Figuring three steers for a load and a total of twelve trips to Kearney, they had butchered thirty-six steers in all.

Darnell halted his visitors' report of the gun battle to ask, "Ami, did they fire the first shot?"

"They fired at least a dozen times before I had a chance to return their fire," Ketchum replied. The cattle kings were going to have to become reconciled, Darnell said, to buying their range land, fencing it, and paying taxes, just like homesteaders.

"This isn't a fight between Mitchell and Ketchum and the Olives," Darnell declared. "This is a fight between law on the Lower Platte and lawlessness on the Central and Upper Platte that started when the Union Pacific began attracting Texas cattle and Texans up the Longhorn Trail."

Their lawyer agreed that the place for the homesteaders was in the jail at Kearney. Only the state prison at Lincoln, and the prison maintained by the army at Fort Omaha were stronger, and they were too far away.

Darnell went on to say that in Kearney they would be in the hands of the most courageous judge on the Central Platte. "When Judge Gaslin takes the bench and lays that six-shooter on his lap, respect for law and order gains considerably," he said. "I think I know the man who can see that your case comes up in his court: E. C. Calkins in Kearney."

Darnell also urged Mitchell and Ketchum to accept Sheriff Letcher's offer and get themselves locked up in Kearney as soon as possible. He wrote a letter for the homesteaders to take to Calkins, explaining the situation and proposing that Calkins secure a lawyer from Plum Creek, if one could be found to represent their interests. Before leaving Darnell's office, Luther Mitchell asked the lawyer about the fee for his services. Darnell said for Mitchell and Ketchum not to worry about that now. When they were back on Clear Creek and when they had brought in a crop, they could discuss payment for services.

Tuesday morning the two men reported to Sheriff Letcher, who busied himself immediately in their behalf. "I will send

Sheriff Anderson a telegram immediately and tell him to expect us tomorrow. The train leaves for Kearney at ten-thirty in the morning, and if you'll meet me at the jail at nine-thirty, I'll have the arrest papers ready, and we'll be ready in plenty of time," he said.

The ride on the Union Pacific was Ami Ketchum's first on a

Kearney Jail, from which Sheriff Anderson took Mitchell and Ketchum and turned them over to Olive men. *(Nebraska State Historical Society)*

passenger train. He was impressed by the luxury of its furnishings and the speed at which it traveled. The car was not crowded, and Letcher sat facing Mitchell and Ketchum so that they could talk. Though the men discussed Calkins and Gaslin, for the most part conversation during the three-hour trip dealt with Letcher's and Mitchell's experiences in the war.

Sheriff David Anderson was at the train with a rig to meet Sheriff Letcher and his prisoners. From Anderson's manner and the number of persons at the station when the train came in, it appeared that Anderson thought he would be assisting Sheriff Letcher in transferring two desperadoes from the train to the jail. He seemed surprised and puzzled to see the two men without handcuffs, wearing clean clothes, and showing every evidence of being well fed and generally confident.

Letcher told Anderson that he would stay overnight so that he could meet with lawyer Calkins, who would represent the homesteaders. Anderson gave Letcher the guest room at the jail and assigned a large cell suitable for two or three inmates to Luther Mitchell and Ami Ketchum. Letcher explained to Anderson that Mitchell and Ketchum were only technically prisoners in Merrick County, the homesteaders having come to him seeking an arrest so that they might have protection and a court hearing about the difficulties they had encountered with the Olive brothers. He then explained the reasons for selecting the Kearney jail for their safekeeping.

Calkins came to the Kearney jail on Thursday, the fifth, where Letcher introduced him to Mitchell and Ketchum. This done, the sheriff promised to keep Mrs. Mitchell informed of developments if the men would get word to him back in Central City, and he took his leave.

Calkins believed he could get the services of a good lawyer in Plum Creek to represent the homesteaders. He telegraphed C. W. McNamar. By the next morning, McNamar had wired his acceptance, asking for further information. Much of Friday was devoted to consultations between Calkins and the homesteaders as they mapped their strategy.

On Saturday, December 7, Robert Hodges appeared unexpectedly at the Kearney jail. He related how he had learned of the battle on Clear Creek from neighbors after Olive's men had stopped at Sweetwater a week earlier. Thinking he would hear more, Hodges said, he waited from Friday until Tuesday before going to see if he could be of any help to Jane, the girls, and Henry. Arriving early in the afternoon, he found the soddy undisturbed except for the lock on the door. Ketchum inquired about his gun collection on the wall. Hodges reported there were two empty places in the racks, but Ami said those were the holders for the two guns he and Tamar used in the fight—the same guns he took when he left.

Failing to find anyone at home on Clear Creek and deciding the homesteaders might have gone to Aaron Wall for help, Hodges followed his hunch and their trail. The cautious judge, taking a considerable time to be convinced that Hodges was not an Olive spy, finally said reluctantly that Mitchell and Ketchum were reported to be in the Kearney jail.

"That's all I know, Mr. Hodges, and I don't know that these reports have any substance, but if you are that interested you might stop at the jail in Kearney and make inquiry," Wall told Hodges. The words "if you are that interested" convinced Hodges that the judge was trying to convey information in a manner that would in no way implicate himself.

At the conclusion of his story, Bob Hodges asked if there was anything he could do to help. Luther asked him to send a telegram to Jane in care of Sheriff Letcher at Central City so that the women might know their men were being well treated and expected to get a court hearing during the coming week. Hodges left, saying that he would be back the middle of the week.

PART FIVE

JUSTICE ON THE PLAINS

[18]

A CATTLEMAN'S REVENGE

FROM THE MOMENT of the disastrous Olive defeat on Clear Creek, the Olive men speculated as to how Print planned to avenge his brother's death. The Olive cowhands, especially the veterans, knew that conditions in the Platte Valley were totally unlike those in the San Gabriel country in southern Texas where the Olives had had to defend themselves and protect their property at the risk of an occasional gunfight. But until coming to the Platte, the business of the Olive cowboys had been cattle, not murder.

Now things had changed. Print Olive had changed, and his Texas veterans were increasingly apprehensive. When Bob was permitted to destroy the corn crop, the cowboys showed little enthusiasm for the job. Some of them had visited Clear Creek to get blacksmith work done for their ponies, and they had found no evidence that these settlers had any interest in cattle aside from keeping them out of the crops. Moreover, they knew that as a rule Platte Valley homesteaders were not gunmen. They stayed at home and worked hard. None of them had ever heard Ami Ketchum brag about his marksmanship.

The Olive men sensed an increasing personal danger. This business of holding the Olive boundaries and reserving the vast stretches of Custer County as open range for cattlemen against homesteaders involved great risks, not only to the cattle kings but to the men who did their bidding and accepted their wages.

The men knew that in court their Texas backgrounds would argue strongly against them. They had no desire to get themselves shut up in northern prisons or to fight off a hangman's rope for carrying out orders to preserve the bluestem and buffalo grass of Custer County as free range. The Olive cowboys watched anxiously during this long first week in December as Print sat glumly in his headquarters, whiskey close at hand. He made no effort to see his neighbor, County Judge E. J. Boblits, whose ranch was only a few miles down the South Loup. This would have been the first step, had he any intention of proceeding legally.

Friday, the day Bob's body was being buried in Texas, Print stayed near the ranch headquarters, speaking hardly a word to anyone. His men hoped that as soon as the funeral hour had passed, he would leave from Plum Creek, as he often did late on Friday. Instead, Print stayed on at the ranch until Saturday morning. When he did call for his horse and start south down the trail to Plum Creek, Henry Gesner, one of the ranch hands who lived in Plum Creek, rode along, leaving him only when they had entered the town. Print rode directly to Green's Saloon to buy a drink and hear the news. He had been out of town nearly two weeks.

Bill Green immediately motioned Print to the end of the bar for private conversation. Green said a report had been circulated at the Kearney Saloon the previous day that the cattle rustlers, Luther Mitchell and Ami Ketchum, had been brought into the Kearney jail. His informant did not know exactly how the homesteaders got there, but apparently some sheriff down the Platte had brought them to Sheriff Anderson for safekeeping.

The cattleman did not have long to wait for more information. Later in the afternoon when it was known that he was back in Plum Creek, his neighbor, the lawyer C. W. McNamar, came to the Olive home, explaining that he had been retained to represent Luther Mitchell and Ami Ketchum. McNamar said that the Olive brothers would be invited to appear at the hearing in Kearney and state their case against Mitchell and Ketchum.

The ride from the South Loup to Plum Creek had cleared the whiskey haze from Print's brain. He could see beyond the calm words of McNamar. A full telling of the events on Clear Creek this year past would end not only with Mitchell and Ketchum going free, but also with homesteaders organizing against cattlemen all along the Platte. That court hearing in Kearney must not take place, he resolved, if free range were to survive in the Platte Valley. Going to the Union Pacific station, Print sent a telegram to his friend—the friend of all cattlemen along the Platte—Sheriff Barney Gillan at Ogallala in Keith County, asking him to take the next train to Plum Creek.

Early Sunday morning, December 8, Gillan, a big man with heavy black hair and chin whiskers, strode along the platform to meet his fellow Texan, Print Olive. Print recounted for Gillan the events since Bob's death ten days earlier, and the two men agreed that the court hearing in Kearney must not be held. The cattle baron planned to end the controversy quickly. Print meant to avenge his brother's death by lynching the Clear Creek rustlers.

Print thought there was a way the homesteaders could be gotten out of the Kearney jail. On a complaint signed by the Olive brothers, Sheriff Gillan could issue a warrant calling for the transfer of Mitchell and Ketchum from the jail in Kearney to Custer County for trial in the county where the shooting of Robert Olive had taken place. They knew Sheriff Anderson would help them.

By now the law enforcement officers of several counties were involved, but Print thought it best not to implicate the sheriff of Plum Creek's Dawson County or the sheriff of Custer County where the action had occurred. It might be useful to have Phil DuFran, a cattleman in Custer County and a deputy sheriff, accompany Keith County's Gillan to Kearney to lend legality to the proceedings.

Gillan hesitated. This was an ambitious plan—really the staging of a jail break, substituting forged legal papers for guns and horses. Print, noting Gillan's resitation, promptly offered him the full $1,000 reward for his participation, the sheriff to share the money with Sheriff Anderson, Deputy Sheriff DuFran, or anyone else at his own discretion. At the mention of money, Barney Gillan forgot his misgivings.

Sheriff Gillan drew up his papers and secured Print's signature as the complainant, while Print sent for Phil DuFran. On Monday the two lawmen would obtain the release of Mitchell and Ketchum from Anderson on the pretext that they were to be arraigned in Custer County for the murder of Bob Olive. In fact, Gillan and DuFran would bring the captives to Plum Creek either Monday night or Tuesday. Print would meet the train, and Mitchell and Ketchum would be driven north to Olive headquarters as quickly as possible.

One detail remained to be settled. Where would Print pay the $1,000, and in what kind of currency? Print replied that he would have the money for Gillan when Mitchell and Ketchum were delivered to the Olive ranch. Payment would be in double eagles—twenty dollar gold pieces—the only money Print ever really trusted. That same afternoon Print rode to the ranch on the South Loup. He had final plans to make.

Finding that the next train for Kearney would arrive in about two hours, Gillan went into Bill Green's Saloon. After he downed two or three drinks, he began to talk. Gillan, never a retiring type, became increasingly talkative, and before the train reached Plum Creek, Bill Green had learned everything of importance about the trip to Kearney. Gillan would be back late Monday or Tuesday and give Plum Creek its first opportunity to see two cattle thieves in the flesh. Green also learned that Gillan was turning them over to the Olives. As soon as Gillan had been joined by DuFran and both men left for Kearney, Green turned over the bar to his wife and went up the street to the Baldwin Hotel to relay the exciting news to Jack Baldwin. Both men admitted they had always wanted to see a lynching, and this certainly looked like their best opportunity.

Early Monday, the ninth of December, Gillan and DuFran

260

presented Sheriff Anderson with an authorization, issued on the signed complaint of "I. P. Olive of Custer County," calling for the transfer of Luther Mitchell and Ami Ketchum to Custer County to stand trial for the murder of Robert Olive which had occurred in Custer County on November 27. Sheriff Anderson's initial unresponsiveness misled Sheriff Gillan into assuming he was unwilling to share responsibility for the maneuver. Anderson quickly made himself clear. Certainly, he said,

Sheriff David Anderson of Kearney, a former captain in the Union army, misused his office scandalously. *(Nebraska State Historical Society)*

the Olives would reward the sheriffs for their aid, and he went on to drive a hard bargain with Gillan: he would turn over Mitchell and Ketchum for half the reward they collected,

William E. Letcher of Central City, sheriff of Merrick County, was a Union veteran and a cousin of President Garfield. *(Mrs. Elgin O. White, Central City, Nebraska)*

and he wanted the sum in gold coins which were to be dropped into one of the holster-and-cartridge belts that always hung just inside his office in the jail. Print Olive, Anderson observed, always paid off promptly. Gillan would undoubtedly have the money on Tuesday, and Anderson would look for the gold in

Barney Gillan, sheriff at Ogallala, was the Olive front man in getting Mitchell and Ketchum released from Kearney jail. (*Langford Collection, Golden, Colorado*)

his holster on Wednesday. Thus the transaction could be consummated before the affair attracted further notice.

Gillan complained that Anderson's take was too high, but Anderson rejoined, "Hell, Gillan, I'm taking all the risks. You and DuFran just have a couple days' time invested, and you fellows came to me; I didn't ask you to come. I'd just as soon you hadn't come, but I'll take the risk for half the reward money. The Olives and the other cattle kings have a mighty big stake in keeping those homesteaders from telling their story in front of Judge William Gaslin. If they ever do, there won't be any open range left in Custer County or anywhere else up the Platte where a homesteader decides to file," he continued. "Besides, this little gun battle over on Clear Creek has taken on a lot more steam than you fellows know. How do you think a couple of homesteaders, without money, suddenly have three lawyers working for them, including one right in Plum Creek?"

Feeling against cattlemen in Buffalo County and eastward was running higher with each passing week, Anderson reported. The farmers in the east end of the valley would like to see the cattlemen and their longhorns pushed all the way to Ogallala, and there was some talk that the Platte should belong to homesteaders all the way to Wyoming Territory. Sectionalism was a factor too, Anderson thought. The cattlemen from Texas faced homesteaders who were mostly Union Army veterans. "Homesteaders would like nothing better than to run you Confederates off the Platte and out of Nebraska," Anderson observed as he made one more stipulation: Gillan and DuFran would have to come to the jail about an hour before the departure of whichever train they planned to board, and they would have the full responsibility for the prisoners once they all walked out of the jail door. Gillan and DuFran decided that they would move the prisoners on the morning train Tuesday so that they could continue up to the Loup in daylight.

Sheriffs Gillan and DuFran did not fully understand Anderson's plight. Mitchell and Ketchum had been committed to the Buffalo County sheriff's care by Sheriff Letcher from Merrick

County, but there was no charge against them. Perhaps before the day was out, the two would be scheduled for a hearing in Judge Gaslin's court, in which case Anderson could expect to be served with a notice apprising him of the hearing. Once served, the sheriff would be responsible for seeing that the prisoners appeared on the appointed date.

Anderson decided that the best way for him to avoid being served was to be unavailable. As soon as he concluded his deal with Gillan and DuFran, therefore, he left the jail and did not return until late evening.

Darnell, arriving from St. Paul on Monday, asked Calkins whether he had told Judge Gaslin all of the important details in the Mitchell-Ketchum case. Specifically, had he reported that Mitchell and Ketchum had butchered thirty-five to fifty head of Olive longhorns after the Olives cut down the fence and turned their steers in to destroy the homesteaders' corn crop?

Calkins had discussed the case fully with Judge Gaslin. He told Darnell that Gaslin had been inclined to the view that the matter of property damage could be handled by a market-value settlement, the Olives paying for the corn crop lost and the homesteaders paying for the steers butchered. As to the gun battle, the court would first ascertain the validity of the deputization of the Olive posse on November 27. Sheriff David Anderson would have to prove that he had authorized the posse upon solid evidence that Mitchell and Ketchum had indeed been stealing cattle or selling stolen cattle. Without such evidence, the posse was trespassing, and the Clear Creek homesteaders were engaged in a legitimate defense of their homes, property, and persons.

Darnell was pleased with Calkins' report. Judge Gaslin, he noted, already had a reputation the length of the Platte for severe penalties—even death sentences—meted out to cattle and horse thieves. No one could accuse the judge of pro-homesteader or anti-cattlemen bias, but he had taken a dim view of cases in which cowboy night raids on homesteaders' crops were involved. The judge had come from a rural family in Maine and knew firsthand the incredible toil of settlers when they broke virgin land for crops.

Both Calkins and Darnell busied themselves with other matters for the balance of the day. Calkins would call on Judge Gaslin during the afternoon and arrange for the hearing papers; the only major matter yet to be settled was the date on which the hearing would be held. Since Gaslin would insist on giving the Olives sufficient advance notice, it was not likely, Calkins thought, that the hearing could be held before the following week.

Print arrived at the South Loup headquarters soon after dark on Sunday, reporting that Mitchell and Ketchum were in jail in Kearney and that they were to be moved to Custer County "this week." On Monday morning he was up before daylight. Saddling "White Flanks" himself, he was gone before breakfast was ready, returning in the late morning. On returning, his first request was for a drink. Jim Kelly tried to be tactful as he urged him to eat first, but Print sensed his disapproval.

As was the practice at the Olive ranch headquarters during the winter months, the noon meal was served from eleven-thirty to one, with the men drifting in between chores whenever they could. Some of the men began to come in as Print was eating. Print talked separately to Texans Dennis Gartrell, Pete Beeton, and Pedro Dominicus as they came in, directing them to stay close to the ranch Tuesday afternoon and evening. Although the other men surmised that Mitchell and Ketchum's arrival was involved, only to Gartrell did Print actually say this was so. He told Gartrell that he was riding back to Plum Creek in the afternoon and would send a messenger northward when the homesteaders' train arrived to alert the men at the ranch.

Before the noon meal was over, Judge Boblits drove up to the Olive headquarters and asked for Print. Print came out and somewhat stiffly invited the judge in to have something to eat, motioning to Si Hagadorn to put Boblits' horse in the corral for feeding.

Although a cattleman himself, Boblits looked upon cattle

merely as the best means of building a new country. Print, on the other hand, looked upon the new country as a means to building a larger cattle empire. Boblits saw roads and schools as a necessity on the bluestem and buffalo grass. Olive viewed the same roads and schools as signifying doom for the free range and the cattle empires.

Young Judge Boblits had driven his rig to the South Loup convinced that he could convert Print Olive to his point of view, not in one sitting, perhaps, but before the winter was out. By one-thirty Boblits was alone at the table with his host. He began by saying that he had wanted to call ever since he had heard about Bob's death. The tragedy would have lasting meaning, Boblits said, if those left in Custer County and elsewhere on the Platte realized the time had come to face up to the cattlemen-homesteader problems and work out plans to live peacefully and build together. Homesteaders had to know their crops were safe, and cattle had to be protected against rustling.

The first step would be for both to recognize the same laws and uphold them, Judge Boblits said. Justice before the law, he contended, would be the only foundation for lasting peace between the two groups. Print said he believed that too, but he thought cattlemen and homesteaders would always live apart because cattle raising and farming required different land and weather. Homesteaders would do nothing but starve to death in Custer County, and while they starved they would steal cattle from the cattlemen. Unsuccessful homesteaders turned rustlers had cost Bob his life, Print insisted. Bob and his own men had been trying to work within the law. They were deputies of Sheriff David Anderson in Buffalo County when they went to Clear Creek to arrest this cattle-stealing homesteader by the name of Ketchum.

Boblits agreed that Olive's view of cattlemen and settlers living apart made sense. But perhaps, he added, Custer County was too big to be generalized about. Maybe there were some areas in eastern Custer County where crops could be produced successfully. Print received this thought coldly, suspecting that

Boblits knew that Olive men had destroyed the crops on Clear Creek. The conversation, outwardly cordial to this point, began to chill. Print became grim and silent, but Boblits pressed him to give his word that he would help bring the homesteaders back into Custer County for a fair trial. Print tried to avoid a direct answer, hemming and hawing and raising objections. Boblits insisted on an answer. Print said he would cooperate.

The first step, Boblits said, would be to have the Olive family come into court, report the death of Robert Olive, and charge Mitchell and Ketchum with his murder. For his part, Judge Boblits would try to arrange a formal hearing by the middle of the week.

Exactly what took place in that room during the next few minutes never became clear. Suddenly a shot rang out, followed by the sound of a six-shooter falling to the table or the floor. the messroom door was flung open and Print, pale and wild-looking, rushed into the yard and disappeared into his living quarters.

Moments later, Boblits, his face white and his expression grim, appeared in the doorway, followed by Jim Kelly who was talking to the judge, telling him that Print had not been himself since Bob was killed. Print would be all right, Jim assured the visitor, after he had had time to think. But right now he was mighty upset. Just to make sure that no one got hurt, Jim suggested that Boblits wait in the saddle room by the corral while someone readied his horse. Jim added that since it would be a few minutes before he could bring the rig around, the judge might as well get some rest before starting back to his own ranch. Boblits wanted to leave, but seeing that Kelly had a six-shooter in his hand, he had no choice. Jim was determined to hide him until Print had set out for Plum Creek. Boblits, irritated with the delay, stepped out of the saddle room momentarily to ask why his rig was not ready, and confronted Jim Kelly. Still carrying his gun in his hand, Kelly told the judge to go back inside and wait to be summoned. A few minutes later Print called for his saddle horse. Heading south across the Loup, he was soon lost in the early shadows of the winter evening.

Now that he no longer feared any violence against Judge Boblits, Jim brought the rig, tucked the judge in with a robe as protection from the evening cold, and rode with him until Boblits could see the lights of his own ranch house.

The three men never again discussed the events of that December afternoon. Judge Boblits and Print Olive never again talked about the future of Custer County. Jim Kelly never rode

Eng. by E.G Williams & Bro. N.Y.

Eugene J. Boblits, first county judge of Custer County, argued for a fair trial for the homesteaders.

with Print again. Kelly and Boblits remained friends for the rest of their lives.

The train to Plum Creek was expected at ten-thirty Tuesday morning. As agreed, Gillan and DuFran went to the jail at nine-thirty, emerging a few minutes later with Luther Mitchell and Ami Ketchum, bewildered and handcuffed together. Sheriff Anderson did not even see them to the jail door. Gillan in front and DuFran behind, the four-man party walked to the Union Pacific station. Here Gillan purchased the tickets and offered Mitchell and Ketchum a drink. They refused.

A few minutes before the train pulled out, Calkins, having learned of the removal of his clients, rushed into the station. He demanded to know on what authority Gillan was taking such action. Gillan responded that he was taking the men to the county seat of Custer County to stand trial for the killing of Bob Olive, and that the proper documents were in Sheriff Anderson's possession.

Calkins assured Mitchell and Ketchum that he would arrange for McNamar or some other responsible person to make the trip with them from Plum Creek to Custer County. Turning to Gillan, Calkins charged him with full responsibility, shouting as Gillan and DuFran pushed their prisoners up the steps of the train, "You'll be met at Plum Creek by the lawyer representing these homesteaders. You better treat them and him well. If anything happens to these homesteaders, the grand jury will charge, and Judge Gaslin will treat you like anyone else breaking the law."

Calkins went into the station and sent a telegram to McNamar asking him to meet the train in Plum Creek and follow the party to Custer County. Calkins waited at the telegraph office for the confirmation he had requested, and it came within minutes. Thereupon he notified Gillan of these arrangements by wire, to be delivered when the train stopped at Elm Creek.

Once inside the railway car, as DuFran was to testify later under oath, the lawmen stepped away from Mitchell and Ketchum and conferred in private regarding how to deal with the homesteader's lawyer when they arrived in Plum Creek. They decided that they would not use the wagon and team that Print had promised to have at the station for them. Instead, they would secure the fastest rig available from E. O. Carpenter's livery stable and try to lose anyone who tried to trail them.

McNamar was at the train door when Sheriff Barney Gillan stepped out, followed by the handcuffed homesteaders and Phil DuFran. McNamar introduced himself and asked Gillan's plans for the prisoners. The sheriff said that he was taking the homesteaders to Custer County where he was to turn them over to Custer County authorities.

"Do you mean, Sheriff, that you are turning these men over to an elected official in Custer County?" McNamar asked. As Gillan hesitated, McNamar threatened to summon Nebraska's Attorney General-elect, C. J. Dilworth, who had already been informed of the transfer in progress. Gillan, anxious to avoid any involvement with Dilworth, blandly announced they would all get something to eat and then be on their way to Custer County.

"Sheriff, again I am asking you to state into whose custody you are delivering Mr. Mitchell and Mr. Ketchum. I have to have a satisfactory answer," McNamar insisted.

"Mr. McNamar, the reason that I insisted on Custer County Deputy Sheriff DuFran to help me in the transfer of these prisoners to Custer County is that—well, it is better for him to answer your question," Gillan hedged. "He lives in Custer County."

DuFran, attempting to allay McNamar's suspicions, declared, "We're taking these prisoners to Custer County by the shortest and fastest route, and you have my word that we will turn them over to Judge E. J. Boblits before the day is out." McNamar announced that he would ride along to make sure the homesteaders were well treated.

Meanwhile, Barney Gillan joined Print Olive, who was also waiting when the train pulled into Plum Creek. After a bite to eat at the Johnson House across the street, they planned to leave at once for the Loup River. Print was entirely agreeable to Gillan's hiring a faster rig. It could be returned by someone from headquarters.

Almost as the train pulled in, Fred Fisher appeared, exchanging a few words with Print. A few minutes later, shortly after two o'clock, he was riding north to Custer County with the message Print had promised to send to Dennis Gartrell as soon as the homesteaders arrived in Plum Creek.

While Gillan and DuFran were eating at the Johnson House, the Carpenter livery stable's light wagon with seats for four was brought up and tied in front of the hotel. It was drawn by a pair of matched bays reputed to be the fastest team in Plum Creek. Soon after, McNamar rode up in his sturdy rig. Entering the dining room, he asked Mitchell and Ketchum what he could do to make them more comfortable. Luther Mitchell was wearing a dark gray overcoat, a little heavy for the midday temperature which was well above freezing. Ami Ketchum's hunting jacket was pulled around his left shoulder and over the arm that hung in its sling. The temperature would fall as the sun went down, McNamar pointed out, inquiring whether the homesteaders needed another horse blanket. Ketchum did not think they would need it.

When they had finished with the meal, Sheriff Gillan directed Mitchell and Ketchum to get into the rear seat of the wagon. He then chained them to the side, mounted the driver's seat accompanied by DuFran, and set off. A brief stop at the Dawson County courthouse was never explained; they drove out of Plum Creek toward the north, with McNamar's rig following immediately behind. It was nearly three o'clock.

Though the trail was an indistinct line, the traveling was good. The fall had been dry and there was no snow on the ground. The bays were rested and at their best. Thus within an hour they had reached the Donald McLain ranch house, located at the edge of the flat bottomland where the South Loup trail led over the first hills to the north, just over eight miles from Plum Creek. Gillan drove into McLains' to water his team at the last well they would see before dark. McNamar's team pulled up to the watering trough a minute later, and the lawyer jumped out of his rig to exchange a few words with Mitchell and Ketchum. Again he inquired if they were cold, offering them one of his lanterns to put under the horse blanket to warm their feet. The homesteaders thanked him for coming with them, saying they were not cold but were withstanding the trip well so far. As the two rigs left McLains', early winter darkness was beginning to settle over the Platte country.

Immediately upon moving into the hills, abetted by early darkness, Gillan began to concentrate on leaving McNamar behind. For the next hour McNamar continued to see the forward wagon at intervals as he moved across the top of a hill and looked down into the valley beyond. About an hour and a half after leaving McLains' ranch, however, the fleeing rig dipped into a canyon and by the time it emerged, it was swallowed by the darkness. McNamar judged that he was about twenty miles north of Plum Creek.

Print had seemed in no hurry to leave Plum Creek on that afternoon of December 10. After the departure of Gillan and his prisoners, Print stopped at his barn and talked with his workmen for a time before setting out alone on a fast roan. He passed McLains' about four-thirty, half an hour behind Gillan and McNamar.

About a half mile farther on, Olive was joined by two horsemen who rode in from the side of the trail as though they had been waiting for him. One was Bill Green, and the other was Jack Baldwin. Although Olive had attempted to discourage their coming, they were determined to see what happened. Dressed as they might have been for a hunting expedition, they regarded the trip as something of a lark. Each had a gallon of whiskey slung from the saddle.

Just as darkness was closing in, McNamar's horses slowed down, tossing their heads to the rear as they sensed the approach of other horses. Olive and his companions, overtaking McNamar's rig in the semidarkness, hardly saw him before they were past him, whereupon Olive left the others and rode back almost to McNamar's buggy. Without saying a word, apparently satisfied that it was McNamar rather than Gillan and the homesteaders, he rejoined his companions and disappeared. It was now between six and seven o'clock.

In a little while, McNamar came to the point where the trail crossed the tiny Wood River. By prearrangement, neither Gillan nor Olive had followed the trail from this point. Instead, the team and the saddle horses had turned northwest and followed the dry Wood River bed to Devil's Gap, a shortcut to the South Loup headquarters.

McNamar could not know this, of course. He followed the trail to the ranch of Louis Wamsgans, where he stopped for the night. Wamsgans knew that Judge Boblits, following his clash with Olive on Monday, had ordered a preliminary hearing in Custer County Court for Wednesday, the eleventh, and had returned to the Olive ranch on Tuesday to serve notice personally on the Olives that court would convene at ten o'clock. He did not, of course, find Print there, but he left word with Jim Kelly and some of the other men.

Fred Fisher reached the ranch soon after seven o'clock with word that Gartrell, Pete Beeton, Pedro Dominicus, and Bion Brown were to meet Print at Devil's Gap at eight o'clock. The message surprised Brown, but when he demanded of Fisher to know what Print wanted him to do, Gartrell answered only that the boss needed some special help during the evening.

Meanwhile, Olive, Green, and Baldwin had outflanked Gillan and the homesteaders, reaching Devil's Gap by a shorter route which could be used only by men on horseback. Gartrell and the others had arrived only minutes before at the little adobe supply house. They listened as Print briefed them quickly. Then they moved to their appointed positions.

When Phil DuFran drove the wagon carrying the homesteaders through Devil's Gap, horsemen quickly surrounded the wagon, one of them ordering him to relinquish the reins and surrender the wagon and its occupants. DuFran and Gillan were then ordered to remove the chains that had bound each prisoner throughout the long ride and told to walk on up the trail to the adobe house, a distance of a quarter of a mile or more, and await instructions.

By the time Print had reached the canyon, Gartrell had pulled the wagon under a tree with a big limb—the tree designated earlier by Print. Print directed Brown to steady the team and ordered the homesteaders to stand up, nudging them with his six-shooter. He ordered Gartrell and Dominicus to put ropes around the necks of the homesteaders and throw the rope ends over the limb a couple of times. Just as it appeared he was ready to give the order to drive the wagon out from under his victims, Print suddenly grasped his rifle, rode around to Mitchell's back and fired at the blacksmith point-blank. The blast knocked Mitchell out of the wagon as far as his handcuff would permit. Ami Ketchum continued to stand straight and defiant.

For Baldwin and Green, who despite their ample supply, had not been drinking excessively, the expedition had suddenly lost all aspects of fun. Somewhat belatedly they realized that willing witnesses to a lynching might later be regarded as accomplices. For once, wise-cracking Bill Green was mute.

Print motioned to Gartrell to drive the wagon out from under the tree. An instant later the homesteaders were swinging in the winter wind. Mitchell's body was quiet from the first. Print's bullet had spared him death by hanging. The executioner sat on his horse, his gaze fixed on the homesteaders until all motion was gone from Ketchum's body. Smoke curled from Mitchell's clothing where the gun blast had entered his body. A member of the lynching party attempted to extinguish the smolder, but he found it difficult, from the saddle, to clutch a swinging body and beat out a fire in a heavy gray overcoat.

[19]

BODIES WITHOUT EVIDENCE

PRINT GOT OFF his horse outside the adobe supply house, calling to Sheriff Barney Gillan and drawing him aside. The two men talked in a tone too low to be heard clearly by Phil DuFran as he took over the wagon and the bays from Print's comrade, whom he did not know. Print told Gillan that Judge Boblits would be holding court at the log courthouse on the Young ranch just beyond the Olive headquarters the next morning. The cattleman told Gillan that it might be better all around if the sheriff appeared in Boblits' court and reported that Mitchell and Ketchum were taken from him by a posse and that he knew nothing of the prisoners from that time on.

Then Print handed the Keith County sheriff the reward money and invited him and DuFran to the Olive place for something to eat and a night's lodging. Gillan declined, explaining that they were close to DuFran's ranch, and they would go there to spend the night. Print himself was back at his ranch headquarters by nine-thirty and ordered supper.

Lawyer McNamar left the Wamsgans' ranch at sunup on December 11 and drove directly to the Olive ranch headquarters, a distance of about twelve miles. It was a little before nine o'clock when he arrived. He talked to some of the Olive men, and finally Print came out to talk with him. McNamar asked the cattle king where Mitchell and Ketchum were. Print fumbled for an answer. At first he said the prisoners had been taken away, he did not know where. Then he suggested they might have been taken back to Kearney. Finally he told McNamar to go and see Boblits—that the county judge had the return on the warrant and "knew all about it." McNamar next inquired where Gillan and DuFran were. Print said he supposed they had gone back to Plum Creek. Then Print attempted to find out from

Captain C. W. McNamar, Plum Creek lawyer, gathered evidence that eventually helped convict Print Olive. (*Nebraska State Historical Society*)

McNamar where he had spent the night. Fearing that the Wamsgans family might suffer reprisals from Print, McNamar evaded the question.

Louis Wamsgans finished his ranch chores that morning and rode upriver to the courthouse, arriving at about the same time as McNamar. When the two entered the courtroom, Gillan was testifiying that at about eight o'clock the previous evening he and DuFran, while bringing Mitchell and Ketchum to Judge Boblits', had encountered a posse of ten or more men, none of whom he knew. Gillan said that the posse seized the wagon and the prisoners, leaving Gillan and DuFran on the trail. After about half an hour a lone man with his horse trailing along behind brought the wagon and team down the trail and turned it back to them without a word. Gillan said he judged that the horseman was one of the posse but he did not know this for certain. Boblits asked Gillan if he recognized Print Olive in the posse, or if Olive was the man who brought the empty wagon back. Barney Gillan denied under oath that he had seen Olive during the episode.

McNamar testified to all that he observed from the time that the prisoners were brought to Plum Creek Tuesday afternoon until his final glimpse of them at nightfall. He also placed Olive at the scene, recounting how the three horsemen pursuing the wagon had overtaken him. He identified one of them as Print. He then said he had spent the night at Wamsgans' ranch. Wamsgans confirmed the statement, adding that it was about eight o'clock when McNamar arrived.

McNamar then reported that just before coming to the courthouse he had talked to Print Olive, getting no satisfaction as to where the prisoners were. He added that Olive had told him Judge Boblits would have the papers and would "know all about it." Gillan had, indeed, turned over the transfer-release papers from Buffalo County signed by Sheriff Anderson, Boblits replied, but the judge knew nothing of the whereabouts of the Clear Creek homesteaders.

Gillan said he had a long trip back to Plum Creek and left the courthouse late in the morning. By then, word of the proceedings had spread and a number of the small ranchers in the vicinity were in the courtroom. McNamar announced that it apeared to him that Olive had taken the prisoners, gone into one of those South Loup canyons, and murdered them. He would search for them, he told Boblits, and then he would be on his way to Plum Creek. The magistrate responded by proposing to adjourn court so that all who wanted to help McNamar might go with him. It was decided that since George Sandford's ranch was closer than any other to the place where Sheriff Gillan claimed the prisoners were taken, they would try to enlist Sandford's aid in the search. His knowledge of the area would prove useful.

Al Wise and Anton Abel joined McNamar, Boblits, and Louis Wamsgans. Reaching the Sandford ranch a little before one o'clock, the searchers accepted the Sandfords' invitation to warm themselves and to have something to eat before going on. Although the sun was shining brightly, the midday temperatures were in the thirties, a marked contrast to the balmy weather that had prevailed every day since the first of December. The judge assured Sandford that they were all mindful of the element of danger in searching the canyons, since the Olives might consider such a search an act of hostility. For this reason, and because he lived so close to the Olives, everyone would understand if Sandford chose not to risk reprisals by joining the group.

When the men left the Sandford ranch, George was with them. They went first to the spot on the trail north of Devil's Gap where Judge Boblits thought it most likely that Gillan and DuFran had turned over the homesteaders to the posse the evening before. Sandford said there were three or four canyons back of Devil's Gap, and he suggested that to save time the party split up and search all of them at the same time. It was Sandford himself who came upon the bodies of Mitchell and Ketchum within twenty minutes after the search began. He summoned the others immediately. They all gathered quickly in the canyon around the bodies.

The searchers had expected to find that the homesteaders had been lynched, but they had not expected the grisly spectacle they discovered.

"It was as gruesome a sight as I ever witnessed," said Judge Boblits, and he had seen plenty of horror in his time, especially at the Battle of Antietam. McNamar gave the most detailed account of the gruesome scene the searching party found in the Canyon on the afternoon of December 11:

> The body of Mitchell was partly on the ground, partly resting on the ground, and partly on one knee. The body was partially held up by the handcuffs, chaining his left arm to the right arm of Ketchum. The body of Ketchum was still hanging from the tree. Over the head of Mitchell was a rope hanging but burned off to within about a foot [of the limb]. Mitchell's clothing was all burned off, except the cap and the shoes on the feet. The body was burned black and in some places cracked open. I don't know whether they [the cracks] were the result of the fire or wounds. The body was burned very black only in portions. One place on the stomach some of the entrails came through the opening in the body . . . bloody mucous was coming from the mouth of each of them.

The horrible scene etched various details into the memories of the men. Abel reported the ropes used to lynch the homesteaders were hitched to the same limb, about three feet apart. Sandford noted that Ketchum's boots were about two feet off the ground and that his head was about one foot from the limb. Wise observed there was little evidence of fire on Ketchum's clothing and that there were few slashes in Ketchum's body. Another observed that the slashes had not bled, indicating the knifing had been done after the men were dead. Wamsgans observed that the rope used to hang Ketchum was tied with an ordinary choke knot so that the Clear Creek homesteader lost his life by long, painful strangulation rather than by a quick, more merciful death imposed by a regular hangman's knot. Another retained in his memory the picture of "Ketchum's head dropped forward with the knot on the back of his neck." One rancher reported that the grass under Mitchell was burned away in an egg-shaped patch only three or four feet across, and that there were ashes and blackened embers under the body.

Before leaving the canyon, Judge Boblits announced that an inquest would be necessary, and that since Custer County had not yet held an inquest and had no coroner the inquiry would be held in his own court the following Monday, December 16.

Shortly before dark, McNamar started for Plum Creek. He spent the night at the ranch of Boblits' sister Angelica and her husband, Henry Stuckey. Back in Plum Creek Thursday afternoon, December 12, he drove directly to the telegraph office and sent the first official report of the murders to E. C. Calkins in Kearney, asking him to perform the unpleasant task of breaking the news to the families. Then McNamar went to see Gen. C. J. Dilworth, public prosecutor for the Fifth Judicial District Court and attorney-general-elect of the State of Nebraska.

On the previous afternoon, December 11, Sheriff Anderson wrote Governor Garber's office on other matters but in the final paragraph reported that Mitchell and Ketchum had been lynched. No one else in Plum Creek or Kearney knew of the murders until the next afternoon. Apparently Sheriff Gillan paid Anderson off promptly.

Print Olive had taken advantage of the dry, mild weather both Wednesday and Thursday to ride through his herds farther down the valley. On Thursday he did not return until long after dark. He went immediately to the mess table and began his supper. While he was eating, he called for two of the ranch hands, Hagadorn and Young. Si Hagadorn was nineteen years old and lived in Plum Creek. He had been working for the Olives for a year and a half, almost since their big herds came through Plum Creek on the way to Loup range in July of 1877. Young, twenty years old, also of Plum Creek, had been working for the cattle kings about a year. These ranch hands rarely did any riding or herding, but spent most of their time working around the Loup headquarters.

"I want you fellows to go to bed right away so you can get a little sleep and be on the job across the river by three o'clock tomorrow morning. Those Clear Creek rustlers were strung up earlier this week. Their bodies are hanging in that canyon back of the gap that has the big trees. Take your shovels and axes with you and cut down the bodies and bury them," Print ordered.

"Better figure on having that job done by daylight. You can't tell who might be looking around up there, and you wouldn't want anyone to find you. They might think you fellows killed 'em," Print added.

Si Hagadorn often told friends afterward, "If we hadn't learned anything else working on the South Loup, we learned that when Print Olive gave an order it was final."

Print called after the startled young men, reminding them to take along two or three sharp axes. He knew that the weather had been turning colder, that temperatures below freezing had generally prevailed ever since the lynching. The continued absence of snow had permitted the ground to freeze.

Hagadorn and Young went to bed for only a few hours and were up at one o'clock in the morning. Real winter had moved in during their brief sleep. A snowstorm was in progress, and the ground was already covered with two or three inches of dry snow.

By the time the ranch hands had had their breakfast, had saddled their horses, had gathered the equipment for their eerie job, and had made their way through the storm to the canyon, it was nearly three o'clock. The snowstorm was subsiding and the wind rising. The snow cover made the light of their lanterns more effective. They could see the bodies swinging in the wind a hundred yards away.

As they moved closer, Young and Hagadorn saw that the bodies were handcuffed together and that one had been burned, and was now held up only by the handcuffs. Frozen hard in their death stance, the corpses swayed in the wind as though strapped to a single board.

The youths decided to dig the grave before lowering the bodies, both of which, they saw, would have to go into one grave. The canyon floor was hard and unyielding because of decades of flooding and the frost which reached a depth of three or four inches. After about a quarter of an hour the ranchmen selected a site in a protected area next to the wall of the canyon, about fifty yards down the canyon from where the bodies were hanging. They had to chop the hard ground with their axes before shovels could be useful at all.

After an hour or more, their feet were getting so numb that they had difficulty continuing their work. The idea occurred to Young to build a fire just upwind from the bodies. Perhaps while the diggers warmed their feet, the heat from the fire would thaw the bodies a little and make them easier to bury.

The men were careful to build the fire a few feet from the bodies where the smoke and heated air would circulate around them. After warming their feet, Hagadorn and Young returned to digging the grave, but not before they had found additional wood and piled it on the fire.

It was nearly five o'clock. The snow had stopped and the wind had continued to rise. The men realized that the job was taking much longer than they had planned, as they continued to work furiously, using the axe and the shovel by turns in a grave that was beginning to take shape. Suddenly both men caught the odor of burning flesh. They turned and ran to the fire. The flames had carried farther in the rising wind than the ranch hands had thought possible, and Ketchum's body was on fire. Mitchell's body, badly burned already, was alight again. Although the clothing on the lower part of Ketchum's body was burning, the flames were not near the rope from which the body hung from the tree. The men tried frantically to get in close enough to the fire to cut Ketchum's body down so it could be moved away from the fire. Young ran to his horse, thinking that he could, from the saddle, swing an axe accurately enough to cut the hangman's rope over Ketchum's head. But his horse refused to move close enough to the fire to make this possible. Hagadorn, long and lean of build, finally had to climb the tree, creep out on the limb, and use his knife on the rope suspending Ketchum's body. In all, nearly half an hour elapsed before Ketchum's body fell to the ground, the bodies were dragged away, and the flames were entirely extinguished on both bodies.

It was getting light by the time Young and Hagadorn were free to finish digging the grave. Time was too short to dig a grave as deep as it should be, though the men worked at the frozen snow-covered ground without rest for an hour more.

They used one of the saddle horses to move the bodies from under the hangman's tree to the grave. The heavy, stiff forms, still bound together by Sheriff Anderson's handcuffs, were not easy to handle. The men tried several ways to remove the handcuffs, even hacking at the links with their axes. Finally in desperation, they seized Mitchell's arm, cut it through, and slipped the handcuff off. Then they cut off the leg that, by its unwieldly position, interfered with quick burial in the single grave.

Since Mitchell's body was the smaller, and the shallow grave tapered inward toward the bottom, Young and Hagadorn placed Mitchell's remains in first and Ketchum's body on top, jumping on it to force it down into the grave as far as possible. Even so, when the dirt was spread, one of Ami Ketchum's toes stuck out of the mound.

In full daylight, the ghoulish task completed, the young cowhands hastily left the canyon, as fearful of being found there by Print Olive as by outsiders. On their way back to headquarters, they agreed that unless Print Olive should question them about their job, they would say nothing to their boss about the fire and the burning bodies. Print never asked.

Calkins saddled his horse and rode to the homesteads of Lawrence and Samuel Ketchum, south of Kearney, to tell the Ketchums about the lynchings. The families received the news in silence. Samuel's first words expressed concern for their mother, who was in poor health at their home in Iowa. Ami was her youngest, and his loss would not be easy to bear. The Ketchum brothers inquired about their brother's body and allowed that they should go to Custer County and bring it back for decent burial in the Kearney cemetery.

Calkins thought such shocking news should be conveyed to Mrs. Mitchell and her children by a friend rather than by telegram. He asked Sheriff William Letcher to go to see Mrs. Mitchell and Tamar Snow. Letcher got the message from Calkins late on Friday but decided to wait until Saturday morning to drive out to the George Gagle homestead where Jane Mitchell and her children were staying. Letcher would later describe his mission this December day as the "most painful of any I encountered in my eight years as sheriff of Merrick County."

Tamar saw the sheriff's rig coming up the road and recognized it while the buggy was still some distance away. There had been no word from Kearney all week, and she had been sure that they would hear something any day now.

After Sheriff Letcher entered the house, gave his greetings, and shook hands with George Gagle, he hesitated. Before he could find his first words, Jane Mitchell sensed bad news and asked, "Sheriff, is there more trouble?"

As gently as he knew how, Letcher stated his mission. "I must tell you that Luther and Ami are dead," he said.

Instantly, Jane Snow Mitchell turned to Tamar, who, as a child, had comforted her the day the news of Peter's death had come, and gathered her tightly in her arms. Today, Jane's grief was two-fold. Widowed a second time, she nonetheless wept for her daughter whose cherished dreams had died in a distant canyon. Once more a war had claimed her loved ones—not a big war, to be sure, but one as inexorable as the last, and like the last, its outcome would mold the lives of generations yet unborn. Still holding Tamar tightly, she asked, "Sheriff Letcher, is there more that we should know?"

The sheriff replied that he received only the barest news of the tragedy from Calkins in Kearney, and he related what he knew of the ruse by which Luther and Ami had been spirited to Custer County and murdered. He also asserted that he and Calkins were convinced that the Olives were implicated, a view with which Jane bitterly concurred.

Letcher promised that he would try to learn more about the tragedy and come back early in the week. There would be an inquest in Custer County, and then the bodies would be released for burial, he added. Mrs. Mitchell could be thinking in the meantime about where she would like Luther to be buried.

"I hope Luther and Ami can be buried together," said Tamar. "They were such good friends."

Custer County's first inquest closed with the verdict that "Luther Mitchell and Ami Ketchum came to their deaths by hanging in Custer County on December 10, 1878, by a party or parties unknown." This was all that the coroner's jury could assert. The way to grand jury action was now open.

"Gravestones cry out against you. Hell longs for you. The cries of these dying men will resound in your ears forever and ever and through endless eternity. . . . You will hang in burning chains over fires even as you hung these TWO INNOCENT MORTALS. . . ."

These were the conclusions of the important *Central Nebraska Press*, the Eaton family newspaper in Kearney. The *Press* account of the slaying was the first to be published, and it appeared nine days after the murder of Luther Mitchell and Ami Ketchum. The *Press* carried both a news story and an editorial comment. Union Pacific train crews within a few hours had carried copies of the December 19 issue of the *Press* to towns up and down the Platte. A copy of the newspaper was in Green's Saloon in Plum Creek late on the night of publication.

Print Olive read the Kearney newspaper account the next evening when he stopped in at the Baldwin Hotel to inquire if there would be the usual Saturday night card game. The cattle king was contemptuous of the newspaper articles. "How many six-guns does the Kearney press control on the South Loup?" he sneered.

On the basis of what Print knew, his sense of security and immunity from the law in Nebraska was justified. The homesteaders agreed with him as they discussed the tragedy on the

Caleb J. Dilworth, a lawyer from Lewistown, Illinois, who as Nebraska's Attorney General was most responsible for bringing the Olive group to justice. (*Nebraska State Historical Society*)

South Loup from soddy to soddy eastward down the Platte, and so did the cattle kings to the west. True, the power of cattlemen had been diminishing before the determination of homesteaders up the Platte. Cowboys were no longer shooting out the streetlights in the state capital as they had only five or six years before. But cattlemen, convinced that farming had no future west of Kearney, were determined to retain control under Nebraska law if possible; if not, under their own. They looked upon the murder of Mitchell and Ketchum as a necessity. The Olives, in the view of the other cattle barons, were merely manning the forward defenses of the grass empire that stretched to the mountains.

In the November elections General Sherman's former brigadier general, Caleb J. Dilworth, a lawyer-cattleman of Plum Creek, had been elected attorney general of Nebraska, though he would not take office until January 9. Dilworth raised cattle on his homestead southwest of Plum Creek, but he resided in town where, in addition to his own law practice, he had served as prosecuting attorney of Nebraska's Fifth Judicial District over which William A. Gaslin, Jr., presided. Disputes between cattlemen and homesteaders accounted for much of the litigation during the three years they had worked together.

Both had come from the East. Gaslin was from Maine, where he had gone to school and had first presided as a judge. Dilworth, a native of Ohio, received his education and practiced law in Illinois before and after his distinguished four-year career as a Union officer in the Civil War.

By the time McNamar returned to Plum Creek, Dilworth already had heard rumors of the murders from Olive sources. He was shocked by the brutality of the Olives, who maintained a respectable façade. The two men talked for several hours, reaching several conclusions. Plum Creek citizens, even those who had witnessed the murders, could not be counted on to help; the personal danger was too great. Little help could be expected from Judge Boblits or anyone else in Custer County, either. Boblits and his small-ranch neighbors, while not in sympathy with the Olives, thought that Mitchell and Ketchum were common cattle thieves; and though Boblits had wanted a trial, he seemed blind to the true motives underlying the lynching: the determination to prevent Mitchell and Ketchum from revealing the extent of provocation that preceded the gun battle in which Bob Olive was killed. Moreover, Boblits thought Custer County authorities could cope with the Olives; McNamar and Dilworth believed the entire plains area had a stake in the tragedy, and furthermore they were sure that the full power of the State of Nebraska would have to be used if the cattle kings were to be brought to justice. Under the state constitution adopted only three years before, the Governor could exercise many discretionary powers, including the provision of funds to implement justice.

Securing help from the Governor was complicated by the fact that in about three weeks Governor Silas Garber would be turning the office over to Governor-elect Albinus Nance. But the two Plum Creek men decided that there could be no delay. Response to the killing of Mitchell and Ketchum must be prompt and decisive to be effective. Dilworth would therefore request an immediate appointment with Governor Garber and be prepared to go to Lincoln as quickly as he received a reply.

McNamar, meanwhile, would work with Calkins, the Kearney lawyer, to find a way of moving the bodies of Mitchell and Ketchum from the canyon where they died to Kearney for burial. This move, Dilworth reasoned, would arouse people up and down the Platte to the plight of the homesteaders and the depredations of the cattlemen. McNamar and Calkins would also appeal to the Kearney newspaper to print a full account of the murders in its next issue.

Dilworth and Governor Garber met early in the week. The Governor listened intently and then came quickly to his decision. "The time has come," said the Governor, "to begin enforcing the laws of this state all the way up the Platte to the Wyoming Territory. Our state has only one set of laws, and they apply to every citizen—settlers, cattlemen, and townsmen."

The Governor proposed that Dilworth stop in Kearney to see Judge Gaslin on his way back to Plum Creek. The judge and the prosecutor should decide how best to proceed, and if emergency funds were needed, Dilworth should apply to the Governor's office.

On Friday, the twentieth, Dilworth took the morning train to Kearney and went directly to Calkins' office. Here he reported to Gaslin, McNamar, and Calkins the results of his visit to the statehouse. In conclusion, he said he was ready to move if Judge Gaslin would agree to hear the case in his court and issue warrants for the arrest of the outlaws responsible for the murdering of Mitchell and Ketchum.

The forty-one-year-old Gaslin expressed concern about his being able clearly to claim jurisdiction and about Dilworth's ability to arrest the killers. McNamar reported that despite mounting resentment against the Olives in Plum Creek, probably no one in Plum Creek—or all of Dawson County—would undertake to arrest Print Olive so long as the cattle king was armed. There was a rumor that the Olives had said they would cut the tongue out of any man who tried to arrest them.

Dilworth agreed that arresting the Olives was not a Plum Creek job. The Governor had offered to send state officers, but Dilworth feared that the presence of strangers might alert the Olives and send them into hiding. Kearney men would not attract undue attention; they would make the ideal posse. As for the trial itself, Judge Gaslin wanted to have a confidential talk with some of the Plum Creek men who had witnessed the killing of Mitchell and Ketchum before reaching a final decision as to his role. If the trial were to be held in his court, he wanted Print Olive and his principal accomplices arrested and jailed not later than January 10. The idea of Print Olive being delivered to the Kearney jail in handcuffs in less than three weeks startled even General Dilworth. Gaslin added, "I know that is only twenty days, but if we are going to bring an end to this war between homesteaders and cattlemen along the Platte River in this decade, we have to move quickly."

As they were leaving to take the train to Plum Creek, Calkins handed Dilworth and McNamar a copy of the Kearney newspaper with its first story about the killing of Mitchell and Ketchum.

In response to McNamar's appeal, Calkins had prevailed upon Ami Ketchum's two brothers, Lawrence and Samuel, who lived near Kearney, to go to Custer County and bring back the bodies. He told them to go first to Judge Boblits' ranch on the South Loup and let him direct them to the canyon where the bodies had been found. Judge Boblits would know, Calkins was sure, whether the Olives were likely to resist having the bodies moved.

In order to be prepared for any eventuality, the Ketchum brothers rode through the Clear Creek valley on their way and enlisted the aid of several homesteaders who had been Ami's friends. The Ketchum brothers rode north under a clear sky in cold winter weather. They stopped at Bob Hodges' homestead, but Ami's close friend was not at home. Lewis Bechtold, a leader in the lower Clear Creek Valley who had been a captain in the Union army during the war, provided the team and wagon and, with some of the neighbors, accompanied the Ketchums on their mission.

A posse of seven homesteaders left Clear Creek on the morning of the eighteenth, heading west across Olive territory in southern Custer County. Because of the sub-zero temperature, the men walked, taking turns driving the team and trailing the Ketchum horses behind the wagon. The men carried revolvers, most of them relics of the war. The wagon box was filled with hay weighted down by several rifles, just in case difficulties should arise in which six-shooters alone would not be effective. As if to make sure no one misconstrued the group's allegiance, Captain Bechtold wore his Union army officer's hat.

The trek took two days. On the second night, the party reached the Boblits' home. The judge mapped out a route to the death canyon where the bodies were, a route least likely to bring them in contact with any of the Olive men. At daylight on the twentieth, the homesteaders set out across the frozen South Loup. They had no difficulty finding the bodies: tracks in the snow led directly to the site.

The rope still bound Ami Ketchum's neck. Both bodies were burned—Mitchell's so badly that the homesteaders overlooked the gunshot wound in his back. Sheriff Dave Anderson's handcuff was still on Ami Ketchum's arm, and the sickened home-steaders made no effort to remove it.

The frozen bodies were laid in the wagon, covered with the bluestem hay from Clear Creek, the rifles stacked tentlike over the bodies to hold the hay cover in place. By early afternoon the homesteaders and their wagon-hearse were moving south-west on the sixty-mile journey across the open country to Kearney. Although the intense cold abated, below-freezing temperatures prevailed all during the three-day trip. On the afternoon of the twenty-third of December, the homesteaders de-livered the bodies to Coroner F. J. Switz of Buffalo County. Preserved by the winter cold, the burned and frozen bodies of Mitchell and Ketchum were laid out on boards back of the Switz undertaking rooms and remained there in public view until after Christmas.

By the time Judge Gaslin got to Plum Creek on Monday, the twenty-third, Dilworth and McNamar could report that the Ketchum brothers and the Clear Creek homesteaders had reached the canyon, taken up the bodies, and were well on their way to Kearney. The Olives had shadowed the party both com-ing and leaving but decided that their own best interests would be served by allowing the homesteaders to carry out their peace-ful mission.

McNamar had arranged for Judge Gaslin to talk privately with one of the witnesses to the slaying. The secret revelations were conclusive. Gaslin was ready to undertake the conduct of an Olive trial. He would issue the warrants for the men in the gang against whom Attorney General Dilworth thought there was enough evidence to present to a grand jury. He proposed that the Attorney General and McNamar come to Kearney on Friday to attend the inquest over the deaths of Mitchell and Ketchum, at which time Dilworth should be prepared to obtain the warrants and arrange for the arrests.

The next afternoon was Christmas Eve, and Judge Gaslin and Calkins went to the yard back of the Switz undertaking rooms to view the bodies of Mitchell and Ketchum. When they arrived, Lawrence and Samuel Ketchum were still there. The judge asked if the brothers were able to state unequivocally which of the charred bodies before them was that of their brother Ami. The Ketchums said that there was no question

Elmo E. Calkins, a lawyer and former captain in the Union army, settled on the Platte in 1873, and represented Mitchell and Ketchum. *(Nebraska State Historical Society)*

293

whatever, and they assured their questioner that they would identify both corpses formally at Friday's inquest.

Calkins suggested that it would be useful to have a picture taken of the bodies as an exhibit in any court action which might follow. Photographer H. M. Hatch came to Switz's place and took the photograph of the bodies, and within hours he had begun to exhibit the picture and take orders for copies. Within a week the photograph was being viewed in Plum Creek, Lincoln, Omaha, Central City and most other towns along the Union Pacific. The plains had known many shootings and some hangings, but burning bodies was without precedent.

The photograph produced a wave of revulsion not only in Nebraska but across the nation. In Lincoln, Johnny Bryan picked up the *Lincoln Journal* and with sadness read,

> We have before us a view of the remains of Mitchell and Ketchum, burned in Custer County. . . . The photograph is sickening to look at and shows the two men lying upon planks. One of the bodies [Mitchell] presents a shocking sight, both arms having been cut off and the body, from the arms to the lower part of the stomach, badly burned and the entrails protruding. . . .

After the inquest, Calkins sent word to Sheriff David Anderson asking him to bring the key to unlock the handcuffs from Ami's arm. Anderson sent a deputy with the key and the remains were placed in plain unpainted wooden coffins and released to the families. Lawrence and Samuel loaded Ami's coffin onto their farm wagon and drove to the Kearney cemetery. They lowered the coffin into the grave they had dug, packing the earth securely. They wrote their mother in Iowa that they had given Ami a good burial.

Travel was hard for women on the frontier. Whereas men could ride long distances on horseback, stopping off overnight if necessary, the womenfolk were usually too busy at home to travel much. Tamar knew Ami had a decent burial, and she knew where his grave was located; but she never fulfilled her wish to see the spot where he rested.

Luther Mitchell was buried with greater formality. On December 29, Jane Mitchell, accompanied by Tamar, Henry, and Elizabeth, met the morning train from Kearney. Also waiting on the platform were the homesteader-neighbors for whom the quiet little man had often blacksmithed into the night, replacing thrown shoes or repairing plows in order to conserve the daylight hours for getting in the crops.

The wooden box was lifted from the baggage car and placed on a wagon draped for the occasion. Sheriff Letcher and the president of the Central City Grand Army of the Republic post stepped forward and covered the coffin with an American flag. The veterans leading, the procession moved to the cemetery where a grave for Luther Mitchell had been dug on Lot 89. As the last act of the short service, the president of Buford Post 23 stepped to the head of the grave and pressed into the earth a simple iron marker of the type reserved for the graves of Union Army veterans.

Threats of violence against anyone helping to prosecute the murderers had made it extremely difficult for Dilworth to secure the evidence he needed against the whole lynch mob, but he now placed before Gaslin the names of cattlemen Print Olive and Bion Brown, and Plum Creek citizens William Green and John Baldwin. On the advice of Calkins, based on notes taken during his talks with Mitchell and Ketchum in the Kearney jail, the names of Fred Fisher and Barney Armstrong were added. Another meeting was set for the following Tuesday, the last day of December. Dilworth said he wanted to give Governor Garber a report of their progress and petition for additional funds, since the prosecution was bound to be costly.

By the time Judge Gaslin, General Dilworth, and the lawyers Calkins and McNamar, met in Kearney on Tuesday, the Governor's office had received Dilworth's report of the previous Friday and a copy of the picture of the burned bodies and had responded. The Governor had assured Judge Gaslin that he could draw as necessary upon the $10,000 State of Nebraska funds appropriated for the Fifth Judicial District, with assurance that when those resources were used up, the state would provide supplemental funds for the remainder of 1879. In addition, the Governor's office would immediately make available another $10,000 from executive funds appropriated by the Nebraska legislature for the purpose of maintaining order. Thus, Gaslin and Dilworth had $20,000 and the assurance of more, if necessary, with which to press their case, and the Governor's promise to send state marshals if they were needed. Speedy justice was their aim, lest the Olive outlaws commit some new crime or the Union Army veterans among the homesteaders decide to seek reprisals against the Texans.

Judge Gaslin produced from his ever-present small brown suitcase, the one in which he was known to carry a loaded six-shooter, warrants for the arrest of I. P. Olive, John Baldwin, Frederick Fisher, William H. Green, Barney Armstrong, and Bion Brown. As he placed the warrants on the table before Dilworth, Calkins, and McNamar, the judge pointed out that the next move—bringing about the arrest of these residents of Plum Creek and delivering them to the Kearney jail—was up to the prosecuting attorney. Dilworth announced that it was his intention to have all six of the men in jail at Kearney within one week. The best time to separate them from their guns and arrest them would come early Sunday, Dilworth said, the one time during the entire week when the suspects were most likely to be in town, apart from one another, so they could be surprised and arrested, one by one. He wanted every one of the six to be wearing handcuffs by nine o'clock Sunday morning.

If the capture was to be bloodless, Dilworth warned, complete surprise was essential. If word leaked out, the accused men might choose to battle in the streets of Plum Creek. If, on the other hand, they escaped north into the vastness of the open range, a small army would be required to bring them in.

McNamar and Dilworth agreed that it would be a mistake

to try to arrest the members of the gang in their respective homes where they might be encouraged to shoot it out with the deputies. Baldwin and Green were least likely to cause trouble, since they were not actually Olive henchmen. But the deputies must be prepared to wait until each of the Olive killers was alone and could be surrounded.

Dilworth outlined his plan, assigning roles with the same precision that he had exhibited as commander of the Army of the Cumberland's XIV Corps. McNamar was to have each of the men watched from Friday evening through Saturday. The Olive men usually came in from their ranch headquarters on the South Loup by early afternoon on Saturday, but in the winter they sometimes arrived home on Friday evening. Thus the hour of decision would come at three o'clock on Saturday afternoon. If Print Olive had not put in his appearance by that hour on Saturday, the arrests would be called off for one week. However, if he was in town, but some of the others were absent, the plan would be executed, and the others would be picked up later. McNamar would send a telegram to Calkins not later than midafternoon on Saturday—earlier if all of their quarry had arrived—with the single word "yes" or "no."

The team of deputies to make the arrests was being assembled by Calkins. He had talked to the Ketchum brothers, whose fearlessness to date certainly qualified them, and they had consented to take part. A minimum of twelve deputies would be needed to arrest the six men, most of whom could be expected to be armed. Dilworth would have preferred more, but the impossibility of secreting more than twelve deputies in Plum Creek limited the number. Besides the Ketchums, the deputies would be Kearney townsmen from the old Kearney Guards, organized six years before to protect settlers from gun-happy Texas cowboys who had come up the trail with herds of longhorns. A citizens' auxiliary for the reduced U.S. Army contingent stationed at old Fort Kearny, the Guards had been organized by Calkins, then a new lawyer just arrived from New York State. Made up of forty townsmen, mostly Union

297

Army veterans with battle experience, .the Guards had been issued fifty-three of the latest breech-loading Springfield rifles and one thousand rounds of ammunition. That first year, 1873, they had used 315 rounds of their ammunition in running fights with Texas cattlemen and their cowboys who overran the area, and had two of their number killed. The former members, then, were fitted by courage, training, and experience to perform the task for which they were deputized.

Calkins would have the Kearney men ready to board the evening train to Plum Creek. He would confirm the date when McNamar wired, and he would acquaint them with the exact time of departure at least two hours in advance. Except for the Ketchum brothers, who would ride in from their homesteads, the deputies would remain in their homes until time to go to the

Photograph by H. M. Hatch of the burned bodies of Mitchell and Ketchum caused newspaper headlines from coast to coast. (*Nebraska State Historical Society*)

station, to avoid anyone's discovering their plans. When the Ketchums arrived, they would go directly to the home of one of the deputies located on the outskirts of town where their coming would not attract attention.

Although Calkins would make all the arrangements, he would not be seen at the Kearney station. The deputies would sit separately on the train. The Ketchum brothers and four other deputies would leave the train and be met at Overton, a stop to the east of Plum Creek, so that twelve strangers would not be seen together at the Plum Creek station.

On leaving the train at Plum Creek, three of the deputies would walk directly to a rig waiting in the darkness at the east end of the building. The other three would linger in the dim light outside the station for a rig that would drive up within minutes after the train pulled in. (More than one rig waiting near the station would arouse suspicion.) Reunited at a home in Plum Creek, the deputies would learn from McNamar the whereabouts of each of the six men being stalked, after which a two-man team would be assigned to handle each arrest and would be given instructions on precisely how to carry out their missions. The final step in the delicate coup—removing the outlaws to the Kearney jail—Dilworth had arranged with consistent ingenuity: the Union Pacific Railroad would provide a special train which would come into Plum Creek during the night on Saturday from the railroad yards at North Platte and would be ready on the Plum Creek siding by six o'clock Sunday morning, waiting as long as necessary, steamed up and ready to leave on five minutes' notice.

[20]

GENERAL DILWORTH'S MASTERPIECE

WHEN THE MEETING on December 31 closed, everyone agreed nothing remained to be done before the arrests were made. McNamar and Calkins would handle their jobs as planned and would report immediately to Dilworth if they ran into unexpected trouble. Dilworth asked Judge Gaslin to be in Kearney on Sunday to tell Sheriff Anderson that the arrests had been made—at the last moment. The sheriff would have to cooperate in furnishing an adequate guard at the Kearney jail after the prisoners arrived, but he must not know of the plan for the Plum Creek arrests before Sunday, since he was now regarded as one of the cattlemen's sheriffs.

Print Olive had returned late Thursday with Fred Fisher. Barney Armstrong and Bion Brown were not in Plum Creek on Friday, but they were expected by late Saturday; but with all of the others accessible, McNamar and Dilworth agreed they should go ahead even if Armstrong and Brown should not arrive.

On Friday, shortly after five o'clock in the evening, a telegram arrived in Kearney for Calkins from Plum Creek; its one-word message was "yes." After dark, Calkins rode to the home of each man who would go to Plum Creek and confirmed the mission.

The twelve deputies boarded the Saturday evening passenger train at Kearney, took seperate seats in the three coaches, and carried out every instruction with military precision. The

Ketchum brothers and four other deputies stepped off the train into the darkness of the winter night at Overton, and in minutes each was handed the reins of a saddle horse by two men who led them into Plum Creek.

Before midnight, all twelve of the deputies were assembled in the McNamar home where they were greeted by Dilworth and their host. At Dilworth's request, McNamar reported that all six of their quarry were now in Plum Creek. Baldwin and Green had been in town all week, and Armstrong and Brown had come into town late on Saturday.

Print Olive and Fred Fisher were reportedly planning to leave on Sunday for Texas to help Ira Olive prepare herds of long-horns to be brought up the trail in the spring. Ira's family was already in Texas for the winter, and Ira had remained there after Bob's funeral.

McNamar reported that Print was probably still playing cards at the Baldwin Hotel, where he had joined the regular Saturday night card game earlier in the evening. The players had been discussing the newspaper stories about the lynchings and the threat of legal action against the Olives. Apparently Print was in an expansive, confident mood, and he dismissed the stories, saying that by the time he got back from Texas with the long-horns in the spring everyone would have forgotten about Mitchell and Ketchum.

McNamar told the deputies that he was sure that none of the six men had any suspicions that there was a plan to arrest them within the next few hours. Informants had reported as recently as an hour before that the conversations at the Baldwin Hotel card game and around the bar of Bill Green's saloon gave no hint of concern. The deputies would have the full advantage of surprise.

Dilworth now planned the strategy for making the arrests in detail. The main street, with the railroad paralleling it on the south side and the business buldings lining the north side, was wide and open. The post office was located near the middle of the block, with the Baldwin Hotel a few doors in one direction and the Green Saloon in the other. All four of the cattlemen, Print included, had in recent weeks been coming to the post office early Sunday morning to pick up their mail. They usually came one at a time. Since Print and Fred Fisher were planning to leave for Texas during the day, they would almost certainly pick up their mail early in the morning. Baldwin and Green lived in town and could collect their mail anytime, so the situation in their case was different. Dilworth decided they would have to be arrested where they lived—Baldwin at the hotel and Green above his saloon.

After each arrest, the deputies would bring their prisoner to the back of the post office immediately, to keep them out of sight of those still to be arrested. In this way the element of surprise could be maintained, hopefully until the final person had been taken into custody.

Baldwin would have to be arrested before the others so that the deputies waiting for Olive and his ranch hands could take over the hotel and watch every move on Main Street from a place where they would not be seen. McNamar would go to the Baldwin Hotel so that he could identify the wanted men for the deputies assigned to each. Dilworth would be at the back of the post office to collect the confiscated guns and hold the prisoners out of sight until all were in custody.

Next came the assignment of deputies to make the arrests. Dilworth, recognizing that Print Olive was a gunman known from Texas to Nebraska, asked if any one of the deputies wished to volunteer to disarm and arrest the cattle king. Lawrence Ketchum said that if Print Olive should lose his head and start shooting, he and his brother would take him on with relish. Dilworth turned to Samuel Ketchum. Samuel agreed with his brother. The other assignments were quickly made. Handcuffs were issued to each team of deputies, after which Attorney General Dilworth suggested that everyone get as much rest as he could until six o'clock when breakfast and coffee would be ready.

Shortly before seven o'clock, while it was still quite dark, the two men designated to arrest John Baldwin left for the hotel with McNamar to carry out their mission. As they entered, Baldwin was building a fire in the big stove that warmed much of the hotel's first floor. A tramp was sleeping in a lobby chair. Baldwin, still drowsy, offered no resistance to arrest. In the midst of the proceedings, the tramp awoke, and caused so much commotion that it was necessary to take him into custody along with Baldwin, and the deputies took both men to the back of the post office where General Dilworth was waiting in the warm mail-sorting room.

The deputies going to William Green's quarters found him sound asleep in his bed. After consulting McNamar, who had remained in the hotel following Baldwin's removal, they decided to hold Green where he was. A guard was posted over the sleeper.

By now the time was nearly eight o'clock, and it was light enough to see up the railroad siding and observe that the special train had arrived in Plum Creek during the night. They waited nearly half an hour before any of the Olive cattlemen appeared. Then the first of the outlaws appeared on Main Street. Bion Brown, a member of the hangman's posse, ambled toward the post office. The deputies decided to let Brown enter and to follow him in. As he stepped to his mail box, one of the officers pressed a six-shooter into his back and ordered him to raise his hands. Brown complied as the other deputy took away his gun and snapped handcuffs on him. Without a word, the deputies marched the captive to the improvised marshaling room, where General Dilworth told him he was under arrest for murder. The first of the Olive gunmen had been put in handcuffs and was hidden from sight in less than five minutes.

Ten to fifteen minutes later, McNamar, from his window position on the second floor of the hotel, identified Barney Armstrong as he approached the post office. Armstrong was easily recognized at a distance; he still limped from the serious wound inflicted by Ami Ketchum as the Olive raiding party retreated from the gun battle on Clear Creek in November.

The two deputies assigned to Armstrong moved quietly out of the hotel in time to reach the post-office door before the limping cowboy got there. They wanted to make the arrest outside of the post office since some townspeople had just gone inside to get their mail. Fearing that the wounded Texan might want to make a fight of it, the Ketchum brothers came out of the hotel and followed the other deputies toward the post-office door. Armstrong seemed to be occupied with his own thoughts until he saw two strangers barring the doorway to the post office. One of them ordered Armstrong to put up his hands. Instead, the big Texan reached for his six-shooter. Instantly—and painfully—the butt of Lawrence Ketchum's .45 knocked the gun from Armstrong's hand. Armstrong cried out and cursed, but he surrendered without further trouble. Sam Ketchum helped one of the former old Kearney Guards put the handcuffs on the gunman.

With Armstrong stripped of his gun and in handcuffs, General Dilworth decided to change his strategy. He now had two gunmen, John Baldwin, and a tramp in the mail-sorting room guarded by six armed men. He decided to reduce the guard to three, so that the other three men could help with the remaining arrests. Since Bill Green was under guard, only Print Olive and Fred Fisher remained at large. Dilworth and his agents had to make allowances for the possibility that Olive and Fisher might come to the post office together, or that one of them might pick up the mail for both, since they planned to board the train together later in the day. Dilworth also was beginning to wonder whether anyone had noticed the arrests and had told Print Olive.

As the three guards were leaving, two others brought the saloonkeeper to the back of the post office. A noise had aroused Green from his sleep, and the deputies had placed the Plum Creek businessman under arrest before he could leave his bed.

McNamar now had the Ketchum brothers and five other deputies at his disposal at the hotel. He and the men quickly devised a new plan. Whether Print Olive and Fred Fisher came to the post office alone or together, the Ketchum brothers would be just in front of the post-office door, ready to move inside when the Olive men appeared. The others would station themselves where they could form a semicircle of gun power just outside the post office as either or both entered the door.

At about eight-forty, Print Olive rode onto Main Street from the west. The Ketchum brothers were standing in the street in front of the post office, and only Lawrence Ketchum was in a position to see the cattleman as he rode down the street past the hotel. Ketchum recognized the short, stout, swarthy Texan and motioned to his brother to move into the post-office door even before Olive's plans were clear. Olive rode past the hotel, reining "White Flanks" and dismounting at the corner of the post office. His stalkers advanced behind him unnoticed.

As Print entered the post-office door, the Ketchum brothers closed in from both sides, throwing their arms completely around his body so there was no opportunity for Olive even to reach for his gun. "Mr. Olive, you are under arrest," said Lawrence Ketchum quietly. "Don't move; there are five other deputies with guns drawn just behind you."

The ring closed around the doorway and passed inside before the Ketchum brothers released their grip. Lawrence Ketchum drew Olive's six-shooter from its holster. A second man stepped up to the cattle king, saying, "Mr. Olive, these are the two Ketchum boys." The man who had boasted that "there were not men enough in the state of Nebraska" to arrest him seemed so stunned by what was happening that he mumbled irrelevantly, "That's all right." Samuel Ketchum stepped up and handcuffed the captive's arms behind his body. Thereupon the Ketchum brothers escorted their brother's killer to General Dilworth at the back of the post office.

Minutes later Fred Fisher appeared on Main Street and was easily captured. Six men had been taken into custody without a shot having been fired; the bruise on Barney Armstrong's gun hand was the only injury inflicted. It was nine o'clock.

Emerging from his lookout post, McNamar joined General

PRINT OLIVE, one of the most powerful and richest cattle kings ever to drive herds up the Chisholm Trail. ROBERT OLIVE, Print's brother, lost his life in the gun battle beween the cattle kings and the homesteaders. BARNEY GILLAN—see photo on p. 263   BION BROWN, an eye-witness to the murdering of Mitchell and Ketchum, turned state's witness at the trial of the cattle kings. WILLIAM GREEN, saloon keeper in Plum Creek, witnessed the lynching of Mitchell and Ketchum purely for the excitement. JOHN BALDWIN, hotel operator in Plum Creek, another witness to the killings, was convinced that the cattle kings would rule. *(Langford Collection, Golden, Colorado)*

Dilworth inside the post office, and the deputies formed a guard outside. Dilworth sent one aid to notify the conductor on the special train to be ready to leave for Kearney in a few minutes. He also directed that telegrams be sent to Governor Garber in Lincoln and Judge Gaslin in Kearney telling them about the successful operation.

Dilworth informed the six prisoners that they had been arrested for the murder of Luther Mitchell and Ami Ketchum on warrants issued by Judge William A. Gaslin, Jr., of the Fifth Judicial District of Nebraska. They were being taken at once on a special train to Kearney where Judge Gaslin was waiting and where they would be put in jail. Attorney General Dilworth assured the prisoners that they would be given a fair trial under the laws of the State of Nebraska and that they would be treated with full courtesy as long as they cooperated with the officers. Dilworth then directed the deputies to release the handcuffs that held the prisoner's arms behind them and to handcuff them together in pairs, leaving one hand of each man free. Olive and Fisher were handcuffed together, as were Green and Baldwin, Armstrong and Brown. The tramp was free to go.

General Dilworth asked if the prisoners had any requests to make, specifically whether they wished friends or members of their families to be advised before they boarded the train. Not one of the prisoners wished to see anyone.

However, Print had a sick child at home. He had not come to the post office for his mail but to meet the Plum Creek doctor and get some medicine. He asked McNamar to see that the medicine was delivered to the Olive home, that his saddle horse be taken back to the Olive stables, and that Mrs. Olive be advised it had become necessary for him to make an unexpected trip to Kearney. He would send her a telegram later in the day.

There were people in the post office who saw the deputies take Olive's gun and handcuff him. They had never before seen him without a gun. Word spread across Plum Creek in a matter of minutes, so that by the time the deputies were preparing to put the prisoners aboard the train, at least fifty spectators had gathered at trackside. Now that the Texans were stripped of their weapons some of the men felt free to shout insults, particularly at Print Olive. The crowd pressed in closer, and there were repeated demands to lynch the Texans. Brown and Armstrong were apprehensive. If the crowd became ugly enough, it could possibly overpower the deputies. Olive and Fisher remained sullen and silent.

Lawrence Ketchum helped Olive and Fisher onto the train. Then, turning to the Plum Creek citizens, he said that he had more reason than anyone else to want to take the law into his own hands. However, he added, he had promised General Dilworth to help arrest Print Olive and his men so that they could be tried in court. If the law failed to punish them, Ketchum said, there would be time to deal with the Olives in a more direct way. He added that he believed in giving the law the first chance, and he urged the crowd to see things his way.

On the way to Kearney, Attorney General-elect Dilworth talked with each of the prisoners, offering to answer any questions and explaining that they were all entitled to be defended by lawyers of their choice. He offered to send messages to their families or attorneys. William Green chortled that the trip was really an honor for him. He seldom had an opportunity to travel by train at all, and now he was enjoying a free trip on the "Cattle King's Special." By noon on this fifth day of January, 1879, Print Olive had arrived at the Kearney jail, the same jail from which he had snatched Luther Mitchell and Ami Ketchum only twenty-five days before.

Dilworth was scheduled to leave for Lincoln to take the office of Attorney General on Thursday—the day that Albinus Nance was to be inaugurated as Governor of Nebraska. Before he left, Dilworth and Judge Gaslin decided to ship Print Olive off to the modern and more remote Clay County jail. General Dilworth was worried. He could not trust Sheriff Anderson not to release the men from the Kearney jail. He also worried that the angry townspeople might try to break into the jail and lynch them. Olive and and Fisher were shipped from Kearney to the Clay County jail forthwith.

General Dilworth had arranged a meeting with Governor Garber on Garber's final day in office. Governor-elect Nance was able to join them. In the course of transferring authority from one administration to the next, the fighting between cattlemen and homesteaders along the Platte had come in for more discussion than all the other matters together. Governor Garber complimented Dilworth on what he called probably the finest piece of police work to date in Nebraska. At the same time that aggressive action could break the Olive power along the Platte, he said, it would serve effective notice on all the cattle kings upstream that under the administration of Governor Nance, Nebraska law would be enforced.

Garber and Dilworth tried to size up Albinus Nance. The two older men, senior by twenty years and with great achievement already behind them, viewed the thirty-year-old Nance somewhat apprehensively. Nance, a homesteader whose land north of Osceola was within sight of the Platte, had been a not-too-successful freshman at Knox College in Illinois the year Nebraska achieved statehood. He was an unknown quantity. Circumstances within the Republican party of Nebraska, rather than proven ability in either public administration or statesmanship, had put Albinus Nance in the Governor's chair. He represented the new generation, the first of the young men to come into public life in Nebraska who had not experienced the war as adults. Ruggedly built, mild in his manner, unmarried, and in the state only a few years, there was much that was not known about the new Governor.

But Nance had a keen mind, the ability for hard work, and a certain ruthlessness in attaining what he regarded as worthwhile. He proved these qualities to Garber and Dilworth during their preinauguration talk, and he demonstrated them when they discussed the Olive case.

Sheriff McPeak of Clay County, on learning that Olive and Fisher were to be brought to his jail for safekeeping until their trial in the spring, immediately had asked that the state provide twenty-five special police as guards. McPeak was not sure that the power of the cattle kings would not reach as far east as Clay County. Conceivably a posse of cattlemen might take Print Olive out of the Clay County jail. Nance had a solution for that: bring Olive and his men immediately to the state penitentiary in Lincoln. The transfer had been made during the first week of Nance's administration. The new Governor also made it clear to the satisfaction of Dilworth and Garber that he intended to bring to an end the decade of violence which had raged between the homesteaders and the Texas cattlemen along the Platte.

The *Lincoln Journal* reported in its January 21, 1879, issue,

> The penitentiary was thronged with visitors last Sunday during the entire day, the great attractions being Olive and another notorious outlaw. Olive, acting under instructions from his attorneys, we presume, was not very communicative although civil.
>
> A little girl who was present seemed anxious to see him, but rather timid about approaching the cell door. He called, in a pleasant and winning voice, asked her name and age, and then told her he had a little girl at home that looked very much like her . . . we are informed that the prisoner was visibly affected.

The practice of Sunday visiting-day—of permitting the public to see and talk with the prisoners confined in the state penitentiary—was then in vogue. January 19 had been the first time the curious citizens of Lincoln had had the opportunity to see Print Olive on exhibition. He and Fred Fisher had been brought to the state penetentiary from the jail in Clay County less than a week ago.

Before January came to an end, it had become clear that the Olive case would be handled on both sides by teams of the foremost lawyers in the state. Heading up the prosecution was Attorney General C. J. Dilworth. Although he was not an outstanding orator, he had secured more convictions than any other prosecuting attorney in the state. In addition, Dilworth was perhaps the highest-ranking Union general in a state where great distinction was attached to high rank attained in the Union army during the Civil War.

The Olives brought together the foremost lawyers in Nebraska to conduct the cattlemen's defense. It was a legal staff that only a cattle king could afford. Best known was the cattleman, Judge

Governor Silas Garber, with only a few days of his term as governor remaining, set the stage for bringing the Olive cattle kings to justice. His successor, Albinus Nance, appealed to President Rutherford B. Hayes for U. S. Army troops to guard the Olive trial. *(Nebraska State Historical Society)*

Beach Hinman of North Platte. Helping Judge Hinman were four other top legal minds in the state, including James Laird, attorney for the Burlington Railroad and the one defense attorney who knew Print Olive personally; John Carrigan of Blair, a Union Army veteran, and the only lawyer on either side who did not live along the Platte; and General A. H. Connor, whose record of acquittals rivaled Dilworth's record of convictions.

Best-known of ten Olive lawyers was Judge Beach I. Hinman of North Platte, himself a cattleman with large holdings. *(Nebraska State Historical Society)*

Judge Francis Gregg Hamar of Kearney, another famous Platte lawyer who attempted to defend Print Olive. *(Nebraska State Historical Society)*

The Olive cattle kings were represented by some of the most accomplished lawyers in Nebraska—men who had fought for the Union and men who had or would soon hold the highest positions of public trust.

James Laird of Hastings, an attorney and later a congressman from Nebraska, carried the major burden of defending Print Olive. *(Nebraska State Historical Society)*

H. Conner, a Union general, was retained by the ives largely to plot the n of defense. *(Nebraska te Historical Society)*

General George Crook sent U. S. troops to guard the Olive trial after Governor Nance secured the President's permission.

For all the qualifications of these Olive lawyers, the key man for the defense was Francis G. Hamer of Kearney, the attorney who came to his work with the most convincing credentials of all. It was Hamer who had defended Texas cattle king Jordan P. Smith who three years before, south of Kearney, utterly without justification, had gunned down Milton Collins, a young homesteader and son of Judge Asbury Collins, in the yard of his homestead while his wife looked on. Most observers at Smith's trial had agreed that if the Nebraska first-degree-murder law ever applied against any man, Smith should have been sentenced to death. With Hamer's help, Smith got a jury sentence of only ten years in the Nebraska penitentiary and a recommendation of leniency. Incensed at such a miscarriage of justice, Judge Gaslin, who had presided over that trial, too, as he pronounced sentence decreed that Smith must serve his term in unbroken solitary confinement.

Faced with such formidable opposition, General Dilworth recruited a battery of assistants that with but one exception could not match the glamor and renown of the defense team. The exception was attorney John M. Thurston of Omaha, one of Nebraska's most eloquent speakers. The others were men who had been acquainted with Luther Mitchell and Ami Ketchum and who felt strongly that their murderers should be brought to justice. Dilworth's former colleagues, Fifth Judicial District Court prosecutors T. D. Schofield and A. T. Ash, joined the lawyers who had volunteered to represent Luther Mitchell and Ami Ketchum after their gun battle with the Olives in November, Captain C. W. McNamar of Plum Creek, Captain E. C. Calkins of Kearney, Judge Aaron Wall of Loup City, and Thomas Darnell of St. Paul.

[21]

TRAVAIL AT HASTINGS

In January Judge Gaslin obtained the arrest of several additional Olive accomplices, and secured a change of venue. First of all, Gaslin issued warrants for six men who further investigation showed were involved either in the gun battle on Clear Creek or in the murder in Devil's Canyon. Three of them were Olive-hired Texans: Dennis Gartrell, Pete Beeton, and Pedro Dominicus. Three of them lived on the Platte: Sheriff Barney Gillan of Ogallala, also a Texan; Deputy Sheriff Phil DuFran of Cottonwood; and Jim McIndeffer of Mason City. The warrants were served and arrests made again without a gun being fired. The prisoners were held in the county jails at Plum Creek and Kearney. Before the trial began in the spring, Sheriff Gillan escaped under circumstances never fully explained, creating the suspicion that cattlemen's power and money had been used to prevent a cow-country sheriff from being tried as an outlaw. Certainly, after Gillan escaped, it was generally known that the big cattlemen, including perhaps the biggest of them all, Russell Watts from Texas, provided a haven for the renegade officer, hiding him until he could escape to Wyoming. He never returned to Nebraska.

There were no indictments against Olive veterans Jim Whitehead, Calico John Gatlin, Sam Carr, Will Steers, John Wheat, Ricardo Moreno, or Jim Kelly. The prosecution had discovered that these longtime associates of the Olive brothers, the men

315

who had made them cattle kings and had precious little to show for it, had refused to deal in homesteader gun whippings and murder.

Judge Gaslin's second step was to move the trial from Kearney to Hastings, in Adams County, some fifty miles east. Feelings in Kearney were so high and the atmosphere so tense that he believed a fair trial there would be impossible. He also believed that, since the Fifth Judicial District over which he presided included Sherman County and the area "west of Sherman County," the southern half of Custer County where both the gun battle and the murders took place was within his jurisdiction— at least until the legislature assigned it specifically to some other judicial district. The way was now open to hold the trial in Hastings at the spring term of court, which meant that the case would be heard about April 1.

Late in January, Ira Olive returned from Texas and immediately came to the state prison in the company of one of the Olive attorneys to see his brother. The men asked Deputy Warden Nobes if they could talk with Print Olive privately, the *Lincoln Journal* reported. "Both gentlemen, we understand, desired private interviews with the prisoners [Olive and Fisher] but were refused," the story read. "An order from the Governor or Warden Dawson is the only authority that will allow Mr. Nobes to depart from the established rules of the prison."

The week before the grand jury met in Adams county, lawyers for both sides swarmed into Hastings. The *Hastings Journal* in its weekly issue published February 20, 1879, commented, "F. G. Hamer, Esquire, of Kearney, one of the attorneys for Olive and his gang, was in the city today and made the *Journal* a pleasant call. He informs us that a change of venue has been taken in the Olive case from Buffalo County (Kearney) and the court will convene here about the 26th . . . and that the trial will be at the next regular term of court in this county."

In a series of grand-jury actions, indictments were returned on February 19, 23, and 27, announced in the press vaguely as "against the Olive gang."

The grand-jury findings officially linked the November raid and the December lynching, and General Dilworth asked for indictments against the Olive henchmen who took part in either the battle on Clear Creek or the murders. He hoped not to have to prosecute those who took part in only the gun battle; yet he wanted to show prolonged and deliberate malice on the part of the gang of outlaws and their leader. As a result, the true bills named each man who took part in the Clear Creek battle except the dead Robert Olive. The grand jury was so thorough that it included the Comstock cattleman-homesteader who guided the posse to Clear Creek even though his first name was not known and the spelling of his last name was vague. Thus "one Macenduffer," Armstrong, Fisher, and Beeton were named, though only Fisher was implicated in the murder.

Dilworth resolved at the onset to seek a verdict of first-degree murder. He especially wanted the death penalty for Print Olive and the others directly involved in the murders of Luther Mitchell and Ami Ketchum. Unless the prosecution could produce witnesses to testify that specific persons were present, however, his chances of success were remote. From testimony before the grand juries, the prosecution knew exactly how Mitchell and Ketchum met their death, who was present, and what role each performed, but the information was all secondhand. No witness had admitted even being present. Dilworth wanted desperately to obtain something more conclusive than hearsay.

Nor was all the intense activity on one side only. The defense was as determined to free the men as the prosecution was to convict, and they went to great lengths, as was suggested by a story in the *Hastings Journal* of February 27:

> There have been rumors in circulation for several days
> that an attempt had been made to bribe certain per-
> sons connected with the Olive trial. One rumor even
> went to the extent of declaring that a definite offer
> had been made to a member of the petit jury, pro-
> posing to pay him $1,000 if he should be one of the

twelve men to try Olive. As a consideration he was to pledge himself to vote each and every time in favor of acquitting Olive and in so doing compel a disagreement of the jury even if an acquittal could not be obtained.

These, as we have said, were mere rumors until this morning when Judge Gaslin, when addressing the grand jury, said that he had a case to present to that body which was different from anything that had ever come to his judicial knowledge since he had been upon the bench. Evidence had been presented to him, making it appear that an attempt at bribery had been committed and that they (the grand jurors) should examine the evidence and take the action indicated in the grand jury. Gaslin immediately summoned witnesses in the afternoon and there was returned an indictment which confirms the rumor mentioned above. In order not to defeat the ends of justice, we refrain from publishing the names of the agents who attempted this bribery until they shall have been placed under arrest.

The cattle kings had launched a battle as ruthless as any they had previously waged. Now gold would be their major weapon.

In its March 6 issue, the first following the grand jury action, the *Hastings Journal* reported under the headline, "Olive and Party Indicted for Murder in the First Degree":

The absorbing event of the past week was the sitting of the grand jury to inquire into the alleged murder of Mitchell and Ketchum by the Olive party. . . . After examining a large number of the witnesses, the jury on Thursday found an indictment against I. P. Olive, John Baldwin, William H. Green, Frederick Fisher, Barney C. Gillan, Bion Brown, Pedro Dominicus, Philip DuFran and Dennis Gartrell charging them with the murder of Luther Mitchell. . . .

The trial is set for the 31st of March and will undoubtedly attract more attention than any case of its
kind ever heard in the state.

General Dilworth and his colleagues had won the first round.

While the defense attorneys hoped for acquittal, their minimum objective was to avoid the death penalty. They relied
heavily on the prosecution's not being able to get anyone who
actually observed the killings to take the stand. Witnesses to the
good character of Print Olive were of the utmost importance to
the defense, and these were not hard to find in Texas or along
the Chisholm Trail. They acknowledged that Olive actions were
sometimes brutal but maintained that such brutality, at least in
the early days, was usually of a retaliatory or defensive nature.
An Olive's word given was scrupulously honored.

Attorney Hinman asked Ira Olive if his elderly parents were
physically able—and could be persuaded—to make the long
trip north to attend the trial. Ira thought this could be arranged
though he would have to go to Texas and discuss the matter
with them. Ira's success was reflected in the columns of the
Lincoln Daily Journal on the eve of the big trial:

Among the passengers on the West bound train today,
were Mr. and Mrs. James Olive, and Mr. I. W. Olive,
the father, mother, and brother of I. P. Olive, of Plum
Creek. They came up from the South this morning on
the K.C., St. Joe & C.B. Railroad, and came over to
this side to wait for their train. Accompaning them
was Mr. J. Wood, better known to his friends and ac-
quaintances as "Happy Jack," a herder from the
vicinity of Plum Creek. From a member of the party
we learned that they had just come from Williamson
County, Texas, where on the Little Brushy Creek, the
old gentleman owns thousands of cattle and hundreds
of horses. The father is a fine old gentleman, short
and slightly bent with age. He has passed his seventy-

eighth birthday anniversary, but is still a hale, hearty, man, and says he can still drive a knife to its hilt, if necessary. Mrs. Olive is 14 years younger than her husband, while Ira W. Olive, the brother of Print, is a man in the prime of life.

We were informed that but for the recent fire, which nearly destroyed the town of Taylor, in Williamson County, there would, ere this, have been published and circulated, a testimonial of the past life of I. P. Olive, the accused, which would entirely disprove the reckless and extravagant stories which have been freely sent broadcast to do him injury. The testimonial had been prepared and was attested by the county officials under seal. The story of his troubles in his own State, which finally resulted in his removal to Nebraska, was thus related.

Mr. Olive has gathered together a large number of cattle and about 700 horses, which have been started on the trail for this State. He will spend every cent of their value, if need be, in clearing his son.

With Print in prison and unavailable for private conversations of any kind, his mantle settled for the first time on the shoulders of Ira. Some of Ira's decisions, such as the one to bribe the juror in Hastings, backfired badly; but for the most part, he was becoming an effective head of the Olive cattle empire.

The stage was now set for the trial that received more attention than any other arising from the cattleman-homesteader troubles on the plains. The editor of the *Lincoln State Journal* noted that practically every one of the eight thousand newspapers in the United States gave some attention to the Olive case. The power of the cattle kings vied with the State of Nebraska to determine the future of the Platte country west of Kearney: would the Chisholm Trail Texans or the immigrant-car homesteaders prevail?

Aware that none of the public buildings in Hastings or Adams

County could accommodate the people who would come to witness the legal showdown, the Fifth Judicial District arranged to conduct the trial in Liberal Hall, a brick structure erected by the Unitarians of the Hastings community and used by them each Sunday. The seating capacity of the main floor was augmented by a spacious balcony across the back of the auditorium. In front was a large stage. For the trial, seats were placed on the stage as well, so that it was possible to seat up to four hundred persons, with standing room for another one hundred.

Shortly after eight o'clock on the morning of Tuesday, April 1, Judge Gaslin entered Liberal Hall. Already a scattering of persons occupied the front seats. Within a few minutes Attorney General Dilworth and Prosecuting Attorney T. D. Schofield arrived. By eight forty-five the size of the press corps attested to the intense interest the trial had generated. In addition to the Lincoln paper and those from smaller towns, the *Daily State Journal,* the *Omaha Herald,* and the *Omaha Republican* each had special correspondents covering the trial. These writers, in keeping with newspaper practice of the day, signed their articles with pen names; the correspondent for the *Journal* in Lincoln signed his stories "Cymon," and the writer for the *Omaha Republican,* "Lino."

The defense lawyers were the last to put in an appearance. Then at exactly nine o'clock, Judge Gaslin rapped for order and announced that his court was in session for the purpose of hearing the case of the State of Nebraska *vs.* I. P. Olive *et al.* The prisoners had been indicted separately for the murders of Mitchell and Ketchum, and the Attorney General had decided to try them first for the murder of Luther Mitchell. If they were convicted, there would be no need to try them for killing Ami Ketchum. The attorneys had begun their opening statements before nine-thirty, when Sheriff Richard James of Plum Creek and Dawson County entered with the defendants who had been held in the Kearney jail. About ten o'clock Sheriff S. L. Martin of Hastings and Adams County ushered in Print Olive and Fred Fisher, prisoners from the state prison in Lincoln.

Dilworth's opening statement for the prosecution was brief and to the point. The state was charging I. P. Olive and his associates with the murder of Luther Mitchell and would seek to convict them of first-degree murder. By agreement with the counsel for the defense, I. P. Olive and Fred Fisher would be tried together first. After this trial, John Baldwin and William Green of Plum Creek would be tried together. All others would be tried individually. Dilworth gave no clue as to the nature of the case his associates would press against I. P. Olive or his men. He spoke in conversational tones and left the impression of a man leading from strength.

John Carrigan opened for the defense, and in the first ten minutes of his remarks, the defense tactics became clear to everyone. Fearful that no solid defense existed, the lawyers would delay, harass, and attack. No one remotely connected with the case would be free from attack. The *Journal* reported, ". . . Carrigan then proceeded with his argument to sustain the motion to 'quash.' He did not indulge in very flattering language relative to the press, stating that they had misrepresented every feature of the case, and called them 'penny-a-liners,' etc. He denounced the Grand Jury impanelled, which found an indictment against Olive and others, as a 'mob' selected in and around Hastings . . . a stranger to the requirements of the laws."

Of Print Olive's and Fred Fisher's first day in court, one of the newspapers said, ". . . a study of their countenances did not reveal the brazen effrontery which characterizes the desperado. They gave their undivided attentions to remarks of counsel and the court and gave no heed to outward surroundings." On Friday, the fourth, Print Olive and Fred Fisher, after hearing the indictments read, pleaded "not guilty."

One newspaper account referred to an uneasiness that had permeated the courtroom: "The uneasy restlessness that was felt by many in consequence of the presence of these men, arising from vague rumors of rescue by outside friends, has given way to a feeling of perfect security, and I have no doubt the citizens of Hastings will repose tonight without being interrupted by dreams of a town invaded by desperados seeking whom they may devour."

The remainder of the week, through the Saturday session of court on April 5, was given over to hearing objections and petitions of the defense attorneys. Olive's lawyers asked that the trial be moved to another location. This petition was denied. The defense challenged the indictment returned by the two grand juries that had considered the Olive case. In order to avoid further delay, the matter was submitted to the Adams County Grand Jury then in session in Hastings. This Grand Jury returned the same indictments against Olive and his men. Judge Gaslin maintained a calm attitude in spite of the tactics of the defense, though on one occasion he did observe that "one of the prominent attorneys for the defense had asked a great many questions unknown to the law and would he ask some which were contemplated by it."

All during the week the likelihood that cattlemen and cowboys might attempt a rescue of the accused came up again and again. Sheriff Martin confided his suspicions to Judge Gaslin that a rescue plot did exist, adding that he did not have enough guards to preserve order against a large posse of armed men. "Cymon" of the *Journal*, who tended to consider the rescue reports as stupid, ended his dispatch for Sunday, April 6, by saying, "I can say without fear of contradiction that the attempt would fail, as the authorities are fully prepared to meet an emergency of that kind."

During the early part of the week of preliminary skirmishing, the big courtroom was not always filled; but by the end of the week all four hundred seats were filled at most sessions. The *Lincoln Journal* took the opportunity to rebuke the *Omaha Republican* for reporting that no vacancies existed in the Hastings hotels. However, "Cymon," returning from Lincoln at the beginning of the second week, was unable to get into a hotel and had to seek lodging in a private home.

The first three days of the second week were devoted to selecting a jury and serving subpoenas on the long list of witnesses sought by the defense. Despite the danger that summoning an unlimited number of witnesses and subjecting them to unrestricted questioning could easily exhaust the $20,000 granted by the state, Judge Gaslin authorized the process. There were forty-five names on the list, several of them out of state. Under Gaslin's ruling they would all be reimbursed for travel and living expenses in Hastings so long as their presence was required in the conduct of the trial. The picking of the jury was taking so much time and the expenses of the trial were mounting so high that Judge Gaslin ordered night sessions.

Finally, at three o'clock on Wednesday afternoon, April 9, the selection of the jury was complete. Half of the panel testified that they had never heard of the "Custer County sociable on the tenth of December."

Immediately after the selection of the jury was completed, Judge Gaslin requested the newspapers in Adams County not to publish the evidence presented to the jury until after the trial was over. The editor of the *Hastings Journal* immediately announced its determination to publish anything it pleased, regardless of the consequences.

By Wednesday evening the public facilities of Hastings were exhausted, and travelers were applying to private homes for lodging. One of the newspapermen related that he found forty applicants ahead of him at the Lepin Hotel—and it was already full. One hundred Texas cowboys were said to be in town—armed, courteous, and sober. But they were a disturbing delegation, nevertheless.

On Thursday morning Judge Gaslin opened court exactly at eight-thirty. The Olive family, including Jim and Julia, were present. Jane Mitchell and Tamar Snow arrived during the morning and had to be seated on the stage, all seats on the main floor and in the balcony having been taken. In the crowd were many cowboys not previously seen at the trial. Jane's face bore new lines. Tamar, intensely alert, was said by one reporter to be as attractive as any woman at the trial. Both the prosecution and the defense exhibited families calculated to influence jurymen and observers alike.

The prosecution opened its case by stating that upon inquiry it had been found that "county officers of said Custer, so-called county, when called to take some action in respect to the crime could get no officers of said so-called Custer County to act in respect of bringing to justice the guilty . . . that no officers were in said county willing to serve the provisions of the court in said county on account of fear and terrorism which reigned in said so-called Custer County which is sparsely settled and that there are not lawful men sufficient in said so-called county to enable the prosecution of criminals for acts done in so-called county to be availing."

The first witness to be called by the prosecution was C. W. McNamar of Plum Creek. General Dilworth questioned the witness himself. McNamar told the jury of his experience on December 10 and he identified Sheriff Barney Gillan of Keith County and Deputy Sheriff Phil DuFran of Custer County as the two men who had the prisoners in custody. He told of seeing Gillan and Print Olive confer, and he recounted fully what happened up to the point where the wagon and the men were lost in darkness along the South Loup trail at a point about twenty miles north of Plum Creek.

Then, over the violent objections of defense attorneys, McNamar told the jury of his encounter with three horsemen, one of whom left the others and rode back to see who was in the buggy. The man was Print Olive. McNamar related how, having spent the night at the ranch of Lewis Wamsgans, he left at sunup the next morning and went to the Olive ranch on the South Loup where I. P. Olive professed to have no knowledge of the whereabouts of Mitchell and Ketchum, suggesting that Judge Roblits had the particulars. McNamar reported to the Hastings jury how he and five small-ranch neighbors of the Olives went to Devil's Canyon and found the bodies of Mitchell and Ketchum hanging from a tree.

McNamar completed his testimony shortly after noon on Thursday the tenth. General Dilworth then called in rapid succession witnesses who confirmed the McNamar testimony and added details that made the work of the defense much more difficult. Donald McLain (referred to as John in the record) told the jury under oath that he saw Fred Fisher ride north past his place at about three o'clock in the afternoon of December tenth.

"About an hour after he went by, I saw a buggy or wagon drive into my place to water the team," McLain reported. He knew Phil DuFran to be one of the men. He did not know Sheriff Gillan nor did he know the two men chained to the wagon. He saw McNamar pull into his ranch and talk to the prisoners. McLain thought both the wagon and the McNamar buggy left his place and moved on north at about four o'clock. Half an hour later McLain testified that he saw Print Olive ride past his place alone, but he observed that Olive was joined by two other horsemen about half a mile from his place. Together they rode on north up the South Loup trail.

Dilworth then called P. G. Wilson who lived on a farm two and one-half miles north of Plum Creek. Wilson was in Plum Creek on the afternoon of December 10 and saw Olive confer with DuFran and Gillan. Wilson went back to his farm in time to see Fred Fisher riding north to be followed later by the wagon and the buggy, and still later by Print Olive on horseback. Next E. O. Carpenter, the Plum Creek livery-stable operator, was called. He testified to the jury that he witnessed the bringing of the homesteaders into Plum Creek on the train, saw DuFran and Gillan confer with I. P. Olive, after which Gillan and Du-Fran engaged his fast team of bays and a light wagon for a trip north. Carpenter testified that he had charged the rental to I. P. Olive and that the bill had been paid by Mr. Olive.

Dilworth introduced two employees of the Olives, one working at the barn in Plum Creek and the other at the Olive corral on the South Loup, establishing that the horses ridden out of Plum Creek by Fisher and Olive on December 10 were checked in at the South Loup within exactly the time that it would have taken to make the trip into Custer County.

Louis Wamsgans testified that McNamar did come to his ranch to spend the night of the tenth. Anton Abel confirmed for the jury that he was with McNamar when the bodies of Mitchell and Ketchum were found. George Sandford, the man who first discovered the bodies in Devil's Canyon, corroborated all that the previous witnesses had said.

General Dilworth then called James Kelly over the violent

objections of the defense. Kelly said he had been at the South Loup ranch the afternoon of December 10. Kelly acknowledged that Judge Boblits had come to the Olive ranch hoping to see Print Olive regarding the transfer from Kearney of the homesteaders who killed Bob Olive. Dilworth next asked Kelly if he saw Fred Fisher come to the ranch that afternoon. Kelly was slow to answer and finally said he did not remember. At this point Judge Gaslin asked Kelly if he knew that he did not have to answer self-incriminating questions. Kelly said he did know that, but the judge had one final question: "Did you come in here to testify of your own free will?"

"No sir, I did not," Kelly replied.

"You may step aside," Gaslin returned.

Before adjournment on Thursday, General Dilworth introduced two surprise witnesses, one B. F. Hassen of Plum Creek who told the jury that he had ridden down from the South Loup with Print Olive the Saturday before the murder of the homesteaders. He reported that as they rode toward Devil's Gap, near the large tree in Devil's Canyon, Olive said to him, "I wonder how they [Mitchell and Ketchum] will feel when they ride under that tree." The cattle king had the tree picked out for the hanging even before he knew when he would be able to lay hands on the homesteaders.

Dilworth was moving rapidly in spite of the constant objections of the defense lawyers. Hassen was on the witness stand less than twenty minutes when Dilworth sought to introduce one more surprise witness before adjournment. Judge Gaslin consented on condition that testimony could be taken within the hour.

General Dilworth motioned to Sheriff Martin to call the next witness. Consternation prevailed among the defense lawyers when the door back of the jury box opened revealing one of the defendants, Phil DuFran.

"Cymon's" account in the *Lincoln Journal* read:

A sensation was created when Philip Dufran [sic], a large boyish looking person, who has turned State's evidence and knows the whole story, came on the stand, pale and trembling, and with reluctance, and hesitatingly told his story, substantially as follows:

"I reside in Custer County; am the foreman for Durfee at his ranch. On the 10th of December, I arrived in Plum Creek from Kearney, with Sheriff Gillan, who had Mitchell and Ketcham [sic] in custody. About 3 o'clock I started for the Loup in a wagon, with the prisoners chained together to the wagon. Between 8 and 9 o'clock that night some men came up with guns and said they wanted the prisoners. Gillan said it was rough, and he ought not to give them up. We were told to get out of the wagon, and did so." Mitchell and Ketcham's shackles were taken off. The teams, with the prisoners, were driven back on the road. Dufran and Gillan walked along the road. Soon after, Gillan said he heard a shot. Gurtrel [sic] brought back the teams, and Olive came up and inquired what had become of the prisoners? Gillan said: "I thought their friends had rescued them." Olive and Gillan had a talk by themselves. The whole party then proceeded along the road until they came opposite Olive's ranch, and the Olive party went in. Dufran and Gillan went to Durfee's ranch.

Dufran swears that he recognized the men who took Mitchell and Ketcham from them as Olive, Brown, Pedro Dominicus, and Dennis Gurtrel. His cross-examination will begin tomorrow. The prosecution will close tomorrow, unless Dufran's testimony is shaken. The defendant's future looks woefully gloomy.

Olive's wife, with her baby, created quite a sensation, crying aloud in the court room when the damaging testimony was adduced.

The testimony against the Olive hirelings and Print himself had been damaging throughout the day. By the time court adjourned, Hastings was choked with cowboys—about two hundred, by Sheriff Martin's reckoning—some declaring openly that the cattlemen had just about had their fill of this trial: that if things didn't start looking more sensible on Friday, the cowboys figured they might just step in and take Print Olive and Fred Fisher back to Custer County. Some of them proposed that in the process they put the torch to Hastings. Some were not interested in waiting until tomorrow. Why not tonight? Hastings, they said, deserved to burn for letting Gaslin hold such a trial against Texans. Sheriff Martin had but thirty-five deputies. Clearly the future of the town and its citizens was hanging in the balance.

At nine-thirty Sheriff Martin went to see Judge Gaslin and General Dilworth. He pleaded with the judge to issue a statement recessing the trial for at least one day until they could get help. Not having been out on the streets, neither Gaslin nor Dilworth was fully aware of the danger. Martin demanded that they go into the streets of Hastings, make their own judgments, and meet him again within the hour. He ordered deputies to stay close to the judge and general, fearing for their lives. Half an hour amidst the turmoil and threats on the streets and in the bars convinced Gaslin and Dilworth that the crisis was real. They did not think recessing the trial would help, but they authorized Martin to appeal to Governor Nance to send a full company of U.S. Army troops. At the telegraph office, Martin filed this message:

HASTINGS, April 10, 11:20 P.M.

His Excellency, Albinus Nance, Governor of
Nebraska, Lincoln.
SEND COMPANY OF TROOPS IMMEDIATELY,
THE CRITICAL TIME HAS ARRIVED. DO NOT
FEEL SAFE WITH SUCH GUARDS AS I CAN
GET. SEND TROOPS FROM OTHER POINTS
THAN THIS COUNTY, FOR REASONS THAT
YOU KNOW. HAVE THEM HERE BY SPECIAL
TRAIN AT NOON TOMORROW (FRIDAY). FOR
GOD'S SAKE DON'T FAIL—S. L. MARTIN,
SHERIFF OF ADAMS COUNTY.

[22]

ENTER THE U.S. ARMY

———◆◆◆———

GOVERNOR NANCE was not in Lincoln, so the message had to be delivered to S. J. Alexander, secretary of state and adjutant general of the Nebraska militia. In the Governor's absence, Alexander had been following the trial closely, but shortly before midnight, thinking matters were under control, at least for the night, he had gone home to bed. By two A.M. he was back at his office. Members of his office staff, aroused from their beds, were already reporting at their desks.

Alexander was willing to act in behalf of Governor Nance, but he first wanted confirmation from General Dilworth that a crisis was indeed developing at Hastings. He sent a telegram to Dilworth and began to map a plan of action. First he would request from General George C. Crook, commandant at Fort Omaha, a full company of U.S. Army troops to be sent to Hastings by special train. Next he would call up one hundred state militiamen; and finally he would send a telegram to the home guards of each of the towns along the central Platte, including Central City and Grand Island, asking how many men they could put into action immediately if called upon.

General Dilworth's reply came:

HASTINGS, April 11, 3:10 A.M.
LATE LAST EVENING IT WAS LEARNED THAT
MEASURES WERE BEING INAUGURATED BY

COWBOYS AND OTHERS TO RELEASE OLIVE
AND HIS GANG. SHERIFF MARTIN CALLED
ON GOVERNOR NANCE FOR TROOPS. . . .
TROUBLE IS EXPECTED AT AN EARLY HOUR.
GREAT EXCITEMENT AMONG OUR CITIZENS,
AND MANY EXPRESS THEIR FEARS OF SEEING
THE CITY IN ASHES IF ASSISTANCE DOES
NOT SOON REACH US.

The Secretary of State had the confirmation he needed. He immediately wired General Crook at Fort Omaha:

LINCOLN, April 11, 3:30 A.M.
SHERIFF MARTIN, OF ADAMS COUNTY,
NEBRASKA, HAS CALLED ON GOVERNOR
NANCE FOR MILITARY ASSISTANCE TO AID
HIM IN GUARDING THE OLIVE GANG FROM
OUTLAWS, WHO, FROM OFFICIAL AUTHORITY
RECEIVED AT THESE HEADQUARTERS, WILL
ATTEMPT THE RESCUE OF THE PRISONERS
NOW IN SHERIFF'S CUSTODY. CAN YOU
FURNISH THE STATE WITH A COMPANY OF
U.S. TROOPS FOR DUTY AT HASTINGS,
NEBRASKA, AND HAVE THEM THERE THIS
MORNING BY SPECIAL TRAIN THAT WILL BE
FURNISHED YOU AT OMAHA? PLEASE ANSWER
IMMEDIATELY.
S. J. ALEXANDER, ADJUTANT GENERAL
BY ORDER OF THE GOVERNOR.

The telegrams to the home-guard units were filed immediately after the telegram to General Crook. At four-fifty A.M., an hour and twenty minutes later, General Crook's reply reached Alexander and his deputy, Edward Roggen. It read:

OMAHA, April 11, 4:45 A.M.
A COMPANY OF TROOPS WILL BE SENT TO
HASTINGS AT ONCE.
GEORGE C. CROOK, BRIG.-GEN.

The Union Pacific placed the fastest train available at General Crook's disposal. Engine 119, holder of most speed records on the Platte run, was coupled to one large passenger car loaded with thirty-five soldiers and all their equipment.

The engineer, assured of open track all the way, was directed

Engine 119 with band, railroad officers, and crew at Promontory Point, Utah, on May 9, 1869, linking Union and Central Pacific Railroads. *(Union Pacific Railroad Museum)*

to set aside the usual regulations and take the train into Hastings at the highest speed he considered safe. On leaving Omaha, about nine-fifteen A.M., the troop train immediately reached record speeds. From Omaha to Bellevue-on-the-Platte, instead of the average forty miles per hour, its speed ranged from fifty-five to sixty-five miles per hour. Across the Platte on the way to Lincoln, the grades forced the engineer to reduce his speed, but on the flats from Waverly to Lincoln he accelerated to seventy miles per hour across a region where a dozen years before no man had traveled faster than a horse could run. The April 12 issue of the *Lincoln Journal* reported:

> The best railroad time ever made in Nebraska was made yesterday by the special train that conveyed the troops from Omaha to Hastings. From Omaha to Bellevuo thc train passed over the ground at the rate of a mile a minute. From Ashland to Waverly, twelve miles in-seventeen minutes, and from Waverly to Lincoln, scventeen miles in sixteen minutes.

William Gaslin, a Maine judge before settling on the Platte, presided over the Olive trial with a six-shooter in his lap. (*Nebraska State Historical Society*)

333

Shortly after eight o'clock in the morning, Judge Gaslin, the attorneys, jurors, witnesses, and the defendants entered Liberal Hall as crowds of armed cowboys looked on, all of them sober, some of them sullen. By eight-thirty every person whom the bailiffs would admit to the courtroom had entered. All the chairs were filled and a few spectators stood at the rear of the hall.

Promptly at nine o'clock Judge Gaslin called for order. It was his practice to keep his six-shooter in his lap; this morning he laid the .45 on the bench in plain view.

Secretary of State Alexander, meanwhile, had reached Nance at his home in Osceola, reporting that he had dispatched the request for troops in the name of the Governor.

The special train pulled into Hastings at 2:19 in the afternoon, its arrival still a closely guarded secret. Only the sheriff and two of his bailiffs were at the station to meet it. Within the hour, Company H of the 9th U.S. Infantry stood guard at both the jail and Liberal Hall, Gatling guns mounted and manned before the doorways of both buildings.

The cowboys, who were in evidence everywhere, had heard that additional guards were being sought, and they would not have been surprised had the state militia made an appearance; but the arrival of troops of the United States Army startled them.

By evening the number of cowboys had thinned, swelling again the next morning as cowboys who had been traveling to the trial arrived, unaware of developments within the city.

Although General Crook had dispatched the troops to Hastings, he recognized the unusual, if not unique circumstances. Murder trials were in progress almost constantly at one place or another, but the use of federal troops at such trials was hardly the rule. Consequently he sent a second telegram:

Headquarters Department of the Platte
Fort Omaha, Nebraska, April 11, 1879. 11:30 A.M.
GOVERNOR NANCE
Lincoln, Nebraska
IN ACCORDANCE WITH REQUEST OF YOUR

ADJUTANT GENERAL I HAVE SENT A
COMPANY OF TROOPS TO HASTINGS TO
MEET THE EMERGENCY STATED BY HIM. I
WOULD LIKE YOU TO OBTAIN AUTHORITY
WITHOUT DELAY BY TELEGRAPH FROM THE
PRESIDENT OF THE UNITED STATES FOR
THIS USE OF UNITED STATES TROOPS.

[signed] George Crook
Brigadier General Commanding

Governor Nance wired Washington, his request reaching the desk of President Rutherford Hayes the morning of the thirteenth. President Hayes, acting through his Secretary of War, declined to approve the use of federal troops as guards at a trial involving no federal issues, and the commander at Fort Omaha sent still another telegram to Governor Nance:

Fort Omaha, Nebraska, April 14, 1879, 10:45 A.M.
GOVERNOR NANCE, Lincoln Nebraska
THE PRESIDENT HAS REFUSED THE USE OF
U.S. TROOPS AT HASTINGS AND THEY HAVE
BEEN ORDERED TO RETURN WITHOUT
DELAY TO THEIR STATION.

[signed] George Crook
Brigadier General Commanding

Having telegraphed the Governor, General Crook elected to recall the troops by written communication, delivered by courier. Thus the soldiers would remain on guard at least another day. Governor Nance used the respite to wire the President once more. Nance's telegram of April 14, relayed through his Lincoln office, brought the following response:

Fort Omaha, Nebraska, April 15, 1879, 11:15 A.M.
GOVERNOR NANCE, Lincoln Nebraska
YOUR TELEGRAM OF THE FOURTEENTH
RECEIVED. THE SECRETARY OF WAR NOW
DIRECTS NOT TO WITHDRAW TROOPS FROM
HASTINGS AT PRESENT, BUT TO LET THEM

REMAIN THERE A FEW DAYS FOR THE SAKE
OF MORAL INFLUENCE WHICH THEIR
PRESENCE WILL HAVE IN KEEPING THE
PEACE, AND THAT THEY WILL BE
CONVENIENT IN CASE A CALL FROM THE
GOVERNOR UPON THE PRESIDENT FOR AID
TO SUPPRESS DOMESTIC VIOLENCE.

[signed] George Crook
Brigadier General Commanding

Young Governor Nance had averted what could have become a catastrophe, Omaha citizens read in their newspaper, "There will be no more trouble or attempt to rescue. Governor Nance and General Alexander are here."

[23]

DEATH WITHOUT WORDS

THE GOVERNOR ARRIVED at Liberal Hall near the climax of the Olive trial's most dramatic development. The day had begun with the cross-examination of DuFran by Hamer for the defense, who tried to get DuFran to say that the posse included many men besides the ones arrested for the crime. DuFran stated:

> The moon was shining where these men [Mitchell and Ketchum] were taken from us. It is bluffy on either side of the road where they came upon us. They rode right up and put their guns close to our heads. I recognized Olive by his voice, not seeing him in the crowd. I could not tell how many men were in the party, might have been ten. I was excited.

Then Dilworth asked for a brief recess before presenting testimony of a man not named on the original list of witnesses. Judge Gaslin showed his surprise, but he granted Dilworth's request as a buzz of excitement ran through the crowd that had come to expect each day a development more sensational than the last.

As court reconvened, General Dilworth and Sheriff Martin returned escorting one of the defendants, Bion Brown. Instantly the defense attorney Hamer was on his feet objecting. "This man is my client. I demand to know if he is brought into this court-room against his will."

Judge Gaslin turned to Brown, directing him to answer Hamer's question.

"I am here of my own accord and free will," Brown responded, raising his hand to be sworn—to give an eyewitness account of the killing of Luther Mitchell and Ami Ketchum. Leaning forward in their chairs as Dilworth began his questioning, members of the jury frequently exercised their right to cut in and question the witness directly, impatient to get direct answers to questions that had long haunted them about the lynching.

"Who demanded these prisoners first from Gillan and Du-Fran?" one of the jurors asked, turning Dilworth aside.

Brown hesitated, turned deliberately to the speaker, and answered, "Mr. Olive."

"Were Mitchell and Ketchum in the wagon when the rope was put on their necks?" questioned another juror as Dilworth stepped back.

"Yes sir," said Brown to a courtroom now so still that even the rustling of papers was an annoyance, adding, "and they were hung by driving the wagon out from under them."

"Who tied the ropes?" the juror continued before Dilworth could put in a question. "Who provided the ropes?"

"Mr. Olive carried the rope used for Mr. Mitchell on his saddle. Fisher furnished the other," Brown explained. "Gartrell tied one, and the Mexican [Pedro Dominicus] tied the other, and it was a long rope wrapped once or twice around the neck and taken to a root of the tree and tied," Brown replied.

"How did the fire occur?"

"From a gun fired," replied Brown, at which point Dilworth resumed his questioning.

"Just name who were present at that time."

"Mr. Olive, Fisher, myself, Baldwin, Green, Gartrell, and the Mexican," Brown stated as a juror demanded, "These were all you saw?"

"Yes sir, these were all I saw—all there were."

"Cymon's" account of Brown's testimony included many interesting sidelights not recorded in the official transcript. According to the *Journal,* there was no struggle before Olive shot

Mitchell. "Olive asked the prisoners if they had not drove off his cattle and, immediately after, without waiting for an answer, he fired on Mitchell. Olive said, 'Boys, put the fire out.' I thought I put it out. I could have reached the fire with my hands, but I used the butt of my gun. We all supposed the fire was out when we left.

"I went with the others to the scene of the tragedy of my own accord. The reason that I did not object to going was that I was afraid to go back on the crowd. I was afraid of my life."

Even after direct testimony and cross-examination, the questions continued.

Q. Where did Mitchell sit?

A. At the right-hand side of the wagon in the bottom between the front seat and the dash, near the front wheel.

Q. How close was Mr. Olive to that wheel when he shot Mitchell?

A. So close that the gun touched the side of the man.

Q. Did the point of the gun touch Mr. Mitchell when the shot was fired?

A. I think it did.

Q. Was there any attempt to get the prisoners out of the wagon at any time before they were hung to the limb?

A. No sir, there was no attempt.

Q. Was there no struggle of any kind?

A. There was no struggle, but when he shot Mr. Mitchell the man kind of fell back.

Q. What did Mr. Olive say when the shooting was done?

A. Mr. Olive asked the men if they drove off his cattle, and I understood Mr. Olive to say "see."

Q. Do you remember Mr. Olive saying anything about them killing his brother?

A. I do not.

Q. Don't you remember Mr. Olive said, "I will show you how you shot Stevens"?

A. I do not remember anything of that kind.

Q. Do you not remember talk about hanging these men because they were cattle thieves?

A. No sir, I do not.

Q. Do you remember whether or not the prisoners, either of them, said anything in regard to what Olive said about them?

A. I do not think there was any one of them said anything.

Q. You had not been drinking much?

A. I had not had a drop of whiskey before I went there.

Q. Did you drink going out there?

A. No sir.

Finally, the whole story had been told. Print Olive, the cattle king, was revealed to have degenerated into a lying, cheating drunken murderer of men unarmed and in chains, his own role the more despicable when seen against the courage of his victims. Luther Mitchell and Ami Ketchum had ridden to their deaths maintaining a frigid silence that enabled them to rise above their antagonists and emerge as the dominant figures at their own lynching. They had maintained absolute silence, Brown said, from the time the Olives took them over from Gillan and DuFran until their lives ended in Devil's Canyon. Brown called the homesteaders, "the best-nerved men he ever saw," adding that even Olive, confiding that he "had attended a dozen such weddings," credited these men with the most guts he had ever encountered.

During the testimony of the Ohio herder, old Jim Olive, sitting behind Fisher, gazed down at the sawdust-covered floor. Tamar Snow cried, her face buried in her handkerchief, while Jane Snow Mitchell, sitting impassively through the recitation, shed tears of pride when Brown told of the bravery with which the

340

two men met death. As for Print Olive, he seemed detached, staring at his cowboy with the same degree of attention shown by the fascinated spectators, but no more. Of Louisa Olive one reporter wrote, "Mrs. Olive, wife of the prisoner, sat at the side of her husband holding in her arms a six month's babe. She is a large woman, neatly dressed in black. Her face was the picture of distress and sorrow, and her eyes have shed a constant stream of tears."

With Bion Brown's testimony, the prosecution rested its case. The defense presented a large number of witnesses, most of whom testified to the good character of I. P. Olive before the murder of the homesteaders. Through their questions, the defense attorneys attempted to portray Print Olive as the avenger of his brother Robert who, although he was sought by the Texas Rangers for several murders, and consequently lived on the Platte under the alias of Bob Stevens, had nonetheless been acting as a deputy sheriff attempting to arrest Ami Ketchum on Clear Creek when he lost his life. The prosecution objected to the introduction of evidence regarding any murder other than those for which the grand jury had issued indictments. Judge Gaslin upheld every such objection.

The last witness for the defense, Sheriff David Anderson of Buffalo County, was expected to establish the fact that Bob Olive, alias Stevens, had been deputized for the specific purpose of arresting Ami Ketchum for cattle stealing. The prosecution objected to every question put to Anderson, and Judge Gaslin sustained each objection, so that after nearly an hour on the stand Anderson had not been permitted to answer a single question regarding his relations with Bob Olive. With Anderson's testimony the last defense maneuver collapsed. Only the closing arguments remained to be entered, beginning on the sixteenth of April and ending at noon on the seventeenth. Hamer for the defense struck on a personal note:

This trial has been a good opportunity for somebody. Thurston thought he would go to Congress, and Dil-

worth would go on the Supreme Bench and then Mc-
Namar—well, he would like something of the kind.
It would be a great thing to say "I was in the Olive
case and we got away with those fellows."

On the final morning Defense Attorney Laird spoke for three
and one-half hours. His address, carried in full by several
Nebraska newspapers, revealed how severely the cattlemen's
threatened intervention had damaged their own cause. The defense also lamented at length the fact that the prosecution and
the judge had generous state funds at their disposal, portraying
the Olives as too poor to defend themselves adequately against
such wealth and power.

For the state, Judge Thurston answered the implications of
the defense that somehow the funds made available to the prosecution represented an irregularity and the troops a violation.
"The reference to the $10,000 appropriation was only to prejudice
you against lawyers. This money goes to pay your clerk, sheriff,
witnesses, and yourselves," he told the jury. "If there is any left,
a part of it goes to the lawyers. . . . I say, speaking for General
Dilworth, Mr. McNamar and myself, had the Governor asked
us to appear here, we should have willingly accepted the call
without promise or hope of compensation. . . . They cry out
about the soldiers. I never look upon Uncle Sam's boys, or hear
the bugle sound, without feelings of joy."

General Dilworth pleaded, "We are living in an age and in a
community where law and order must prevail. If this man Olive
is guilty, he should be punished; if innocent, he should be
released. Your verdict must be in accordance with the evidence.
There is no juryman among you but would rather be somewhere
else today. Somebody must be the representative of the community and you have been chosen to act."

The jury received its instructions shortly after noon. An hour
later it returned its verdict: guilty of murder in the second
degree. The Olives' small baby began to cry so loudly that
Louisa had to leave the courtroom. General Dilworth expressed

disappointment that the jury had not declared the crime to be first-degree murder. The Ketchum brothers looked on soberly as, for the first time in the long trial, Jane Mitchell cried aloud. Tamar, now dry-eyed, attempted to comfort her mother. Jim

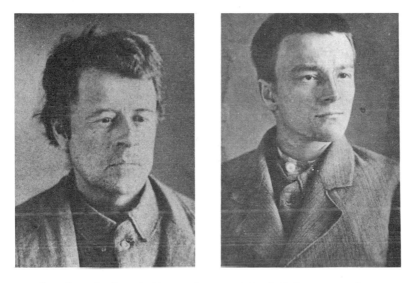

Their beards shaved, Print Olive and Fred Fisher were photographed at the Nebraska State Penitentiary as they began serving life sentences in April 1879. The Olive family contended this was not a picture of Print Olive. *(Nebraska State Historical Society)*

Olive put his head in his hands, but Julia went to her son and put her arms around him.

Before dismissing the jury, Judge Gaslin warned that no member could discuss what went on in the private deliberations, and that he would take harsh measures against anyone who did. He then pronounced the maximum penalty under the law; he sentenced I. P. Olive and Frederick Fisher to life imprisonment in the Nebraska penitentiary. The next morning, while elements of

343

the Ninth U.S. Infantry and the Ketchum brothers looked on, Sheriff Martin and his deputies removed Olive and Fisher from the Adams County jail. Before evening the cattle king and his young lieutenant were back in their cells at the state prison at Lincoln. They had been away only eighteen-and-a-half days and were back in time for Sunday's public visitation.

[24]

NEW EMPIRE OF THE PLATTE

IRA OLIVE made arrangements for continued operations along
the Platte immediately after the trial. A month later he accompanied Jim and Julia home to their ranch at Thrall. There
he took over as trail boss for the herd of longhorns and horses
the Olive stalwarts had assembled to move up the Chisholm
Trail. With so many of the cowboys in jail up north, it was
necessary to hire several new men to work with Jim Kelly and
a few other oldtimers. One of these new men was "Teddy Blue"
Abbott, a native of the Platte who had come to Texas during
the winter to join some Texas outfit sending an early herd
back north.

Teddy Blue at nineteen was already an experienced cowboy.
He had begun herding longhorns on his father's ranch near
Lincoln at about the age of twelve and had made two previous
trips up the Chisholm Trail. He had long wanted to ride with
the Olives because they were regarded as a tough outfit; and
Teddy Blue thought of himself as being a pretty tough customer.
So when he was offered an opportunity to join Ira Olive and
Jim Kelly in the spring drive of 1879, Teddy Blue came to terms
at once.

The herd was large—seven thousand horses and about as
many cattle. Things went well during the early part of the
drive, but one morning when the herd had moved into southern
Kansas, Ira found some occasion to fault Jim Kelly's work.

Jim had not really intended to stay with the Olives after he had had to separate Print and Judge Boblits the December before, but the other cowboys had talked him into returning south to help bring one more big herd up the trail, and he had not known that Ira would be the trail boss when he agreed to handle the job.

On this particular spring morning, Teddy Blue Abbott saw that Ira was obviously goading the Negro in hopes that Kelly would make some move to defend himself and give Ira an opportunity to use his six-shooter. Kelly, who had been with the Olives long enough to know what Ira was doing, was giving Ira no opening to kill him. Suddenly Ira pulled his six-shooter. Slugging Kelly across the face with the butt, he forced him to the ground, knocking out several teeth in the process.

Ira scarcely knew Teddy Blue, and he was not aware that Abbott was watching. But Kelly had hardly hit the ground when Abbott sprang at the cattle king like a panther, knocking the surprised Olive off-balance and spinning him to face his assailant at a distance of no more than three feet. Before Ira could move or utter a sound, Teddy Blue, six-shooter in hand, shouting loudly enough for a number of the Olive men to hear, ordered Olive to leave Jim Kelly alone, "Or I'll shoot out both your eyes!" ("The strange thing about it," said Abbott later, "was that I would have done it.")

Ira Olive stood stunned for a long moment, then turned, got on his horse, and rode out of sight to the north. He went directly on to Plum Creek, leaving the herd in charge of the trail crew. Ira Olive did not raise his hand against any man, white or black, again.

Soon after he returned to the Platte, Ira went to Lincoln to visit Print, who was behaving like a caged animal in prison. Print demanded that Ira see his lawyer, James Laird, about preparing an appeal to the Nebraska Supreme Court at once. Laird said grounds might be found for appeal, but at best it would be a costly undertaking. Ira directed Laird to begin at once.

Just two years after Print Olive's arrest, the Nebraska Supreme

Court ruled in a two-to-one decision that the trial had been improperly organized by Judge Gaslin: the case should have been tried in Custer County. Chief Justice Samuel Maxwell dissented, arguing that a county where the courts and other administrative agencies were still in the process of organization could not guarantee to its citizens the privileges and protections of the Bill of Rights. Until the legislature acted, "be it two or ten years hence," he maintained, remanding the case to a non-existent jurisdiction had the effect of robbing the Bill of Rights of all force. He also contended that a county could not be a county, in fact, until it was entirely organized, since the primary purpose of organization was the administration of justice. Nevertheless, Olive and Fred Fisher were freed, subject to a new trial to be held in Custer County.

Judge Boblits brought the case to trial but he lacked Judge Gaslin's legal training. In embryonic Custer County, court procedures were inadequate, and there were no Darnells, Calkins, or McNamars, no Judge Wall—no one willing to give time and money to prosecute the Olives. Attorney General Dilworth could not come from Lincoln to prosecute a county case. The Olive might in Custer County was such that no one appeared to testify against the cattle kings. Judge Boblits had no choice but to continue the case and release the prisoners. The trial was never reopened.

Although Print was free, the price of his freedom came high. Ira Olive confided to friends shortly after the release of his brother and Fisher: "Getting Print out of the penitentiary cost all the longhorns two Union Pacific engines could haul out of Plum Creek. I gave all the money to Jim Laird. He said when I first asked about getting Print released that it would cost a 'very great deal of money.'

"I used a lot of my own cattle to round out those two train loads; I never asked Print for them back, and I was always glad to have done it," Ira continued. "The one thing that surprised and hurt me was that Print never did seem to appreciate what I had done for him."

The cattle roundups each spring were presided over by a

marshal elected by all owners of cattle on the range. Print had been marshal the spring before the murder of Mitchell and Ketchum. That he would be marshal again, he never seemed to question, and he looked forward eagerly to the election in 1882. The big day came, and the post did go to an Olive— Ira Olive—in deference to the size of the Olive herds. Fellow cattlemen had observed during Print's absence that Ira was as efficient as his brother in his operations and less ruthless. Moreover, the ranchers might share Print's objectives, but they could never again afford the risks inherent in his methods.

Shortly after spring roundup Print, struggling for the first time in his life with debts and feeling rejected by his peers on the Platte, announced that he was going to sell out his Nebraska interests and move to the free range in western Kansas and eastern Colorado.

Ira stayed in Nebraska and made the Platte his permanent home. He became an example of how the Texas cattle kings learned to live within the law while they prospered as never before. Ira turned his back on the free range, liquidating his cattle interests north of the Platte. South of Plum Creek and the river, he bought nine thousand acres, maintaining the range and improving his herds until those acres were producing more meat than they ever had in the best years of the buffalo. Ira and Lou Westbrook Olive lived in the largest house in town. Ira became president of the bank and a leading citizen of the Central Platte town whose name was eventually changed from Plum Creek to Lexington, its present name.

In October 1882, Print and his family, with a small remnant of the Olive cowboys and his thinned herds, crossed the Platte for the last time and headed for Kansas. He had made his new home in Dodge City, though the center of his new operations was farther west, at Trail City. Within four years he had established a number of other enterprises in Kansas and Colorado.

Late in the Summer of 1886 the cattle baron had been in Trail City, Colorado, on business and was waiting for the eastbound train to Dodge. His luggage was packed—his six-shooter inside—when he strolled to the open door of the saloon he owned. Through the door, he saw Joe Sparrow at the bar. The young Texas cattleman had borrowed a substantial sum from Olive the previous year, and earlier in the day Olive had pressed him for repayment of the final ten dollar balance.

In an instant and without notice, Sparrow reached for his gun. Print Olive could not draw in self-defense. He wasn't even armed. A slug from Sparrow's Colt .45, fired point-blank, crashed into Olive's chest. He never felt the others, as the enraged gunman emptied his six-shooter into the lifeless body on the floor.

Once the cattleman-sodbuster conflicts were resolved, homesteaders came to the Platte Valley in great numbers, occupying all the good land within a decade. Here they raised the corn and the other crops needed to fatten the cattle coming off the grasslands of the valley. Together the homesteaders and cattlemen devised new ways of producing more, eventually damming the Platte to store its water in the winter and spring for irrigating crops in the summer and fall. It is said that each year fewer people produce more food in the Platte Valley than in any other area of comparable size on earth. Thus, three generations later, the people of the Platte, heirs of both cattlemen and homesteaders, profit from the courage and perseverance of their forebears who carved from the wilderness a bounteous empire.

IF YOU WOULD LIKE TO KNOW MORE

WE DROVE INTO OSCEOLA, Nebraska, late on a spring afternoon. We were there to have a firsthand look at the country where the young homesteader from Illinois, Albinus Nance, had lived. In 1878, when he was only thirty years old, Albinus Nance, through a strange set of political circumstances, was elected Governor of Nebraska. Although some thought he was too young and inexperienced to deal with the difficult problems of the Nebraska frontier, it was Nance's sharp judgment and iron nerve that brought the lawlessness of the cattle kings against the homesteaders to an abrupt end. At the critical hour, he convinced the President of the United States of the need for U.S. Army troops to maintain order.

Research probing can walk on very common feet at times. Such was the case that afternoon going into Osceola. We had hoped to locate Governor Nance's homestead near Osceola. We had no specific information as to where the Nance homestead had been, nor anything specific about Nance's life at Osceola. We did know he was unmarried during those years and suspected this would make our probe more difficult. When you are up against it, a historian has to reach deep to come up with something original. We looked up the gasoline service station with the sign out front, "As you travel, ask us," and announced to the attendant, "We are seeking information about Albinus Nance who was Governor of Nebraska in 1878 and lived near Osceola."

"Go up the street and talk to our barber. He knew him," the man said quite casually.

"I dont think you understood," I answered. "He was Governor back in 1878. A man by the name of Nance."

With a glint in his eye revealing a degree of satisfaction the Standard man replied, "Just like I said Go up and see the barber. He knew him." The man knew he had completely confounded us.

We found the barber, still agile with his scissors and comb, despite his ninety-two years. We explained our mission.

"Better go on up the street and talk to the bee man. I knew Governor Nance but the bee man knew him much better, but, then, he's older than I."

So we drove to the bee man's house. Our hopes began to mount. We knocked at the door. The bee man's daughter, herself a grandmother, answered. She was sorry her father was not home but he had just walked downtown to the drugstore. He would be right back and we were invited to wait.

Shortly, John Wilson entered through the back door of the house. He was all apologies. It was stupid of him not to be at home when we arrived. He had already been downtown twice before that day and had forgotten a promise to Mrs. Wilson to pick up something at the drugstore. He had walked six blocks to make the promise good.

Yes, he knew Governor Nance quite well. Fine man, Governor Nance. Great to have as a neighbor. Mr. Wilson particularly remembered the year the drought knocked out the corn. There was not enough corn for seed the following year. The Governor, who had a small field close to the Platte where he could get enough water to produce a fair crop, gave the corn to his neighbors so they would have seed to plant.

Yes, the bee man did realize that when he was born in 1867 there was no railroad built up the Platte Valley and the primary vehicles of commerce were still the stagecoach and the wagon train.

This Osceola experience points up the rapid progress experienced in America. In one man's long lifetime, we have passed from the stagecoaches to the jetliners. This fact alone places a great urgency on the historian. There are, still living, men and women and their children who struggled to convert the plains and the West into a bastion of American strength and progress.

Empire on the Plate largely depended on the person-to-person reporting of historians. The Burt Sell Platte Valley Documents,

Burt Sell, a homesteader in his own right and one of those rare persons who was a historian even as a child, has over a period of more than seventy years collected *The Burt Sell Platte Valley Documents,* a historic collection of written statements, pictures, and tape recordings. Available for the first time, important elements of this book are based upon his reports.

available after January 1, 1968, at the Nebraska State Historical Society, 1500 R Street, Lincoln, Nebraska, are the result of this research. These documents have roots going back more than seventy-five years and are still being developed by Burt Sell and others, such as myself, associated with him. Writers and researchers of the future, seeking to understand the history on the plains, will be consulting these documents in the years to come, perhaps many centuries from now. They now can listen to the voices of people who were part of the story and who took part in the development of the West.

Burt Sell is a remarkable chronicler of the plains and the Platte story. Now in his eighty-second year, he began collecting his amazing plains history at an early age. He was five years old and living on his family's Nebraska homestead when he learned about the neighbors who were going to Oklahoma to take part in the historic land race of 1889. As it turned out, some of the neighbors who went to the Oklahoma Territory did so well that they stayed. Others came back to sing for Burt a song the settlers had composed over campfires while waiting for the appointed hour to enter the Cherokee strip. No one has mentioned these Oklahoma campfire songs to him for half a century and more but he still recalls the tunes and the most colorful lines.

There is a tendency to discount human memory in favor of published references, particularly if the memories and printed reports do not agree. The memory can be, and often is, more accurate. Newspaper references and local histories have given the date of the death of the cattle king, Robert Olive, variously as November 28, November 30, and even December 1 and 2. Burt Sell had an opportunity to confirm the exact date in 1924. Over the next forty years he maintained that, regardless of what the printed reports said, he knew it to be a fact that Robert Olive died shortly after noon on November 27, 1878. Because a gun battle and other important incidents were tied into the hour of the cattle king's death, the accuracy of the date became extremely important.

In the spring of 1966, Burt Sell went to Texas on a fact-finding mission. He visited the Olive family burying grounds near Thrall, Texas, and found the headstone of Robert Olive, placed there by his father and mother. The legend is still clear. The date of death is given as "November 27, 1878."

For those who would like to know more, the Burt Sell Platte Valley Documents offer many important records. Only a small part of the information contained in the Platte Valley Documents is used in *Empire on the Platte.* The documents cover a wide number of subjects, including an excellent account of the effort of Jesse James and his brothers to establish a hideout and settle down on a homestead near the Platte. Their first sally, using their Platte homestead as a base of operations, proved to be the ill-fated effort to hold up the bank at Northfield, Minnesota. They did not bother to return to the Platte and pick up even personal possessions left there.

There is little in the Burt Sell Platte Valley Documents dealing with matters in the first three chapters of *Empire on the Platte.* For students and others seeking to learn more about matters described in these three chapters I refer them to the following publications.

Concerning the military operations before and during the Civil War, especially helpful is *The Civil War Dictionary* by Mark M. Boatner, III, published by David McKay Company, Inc., in 1959. *Personal Memoirs of U.S. Grant,* published in two volumes by Mark Twain in New York in 1885; *The War of the Rebellion: A Compilation of the Official Records of the Union and Confederate Armies,* published by the United States Department of War, 130. volumes, Washington D.C., 1880–1904; the biography of Albert Sidney Johnston by W. P. Johnston, published in 1885; and *Grant Moves South* by Bruce Catton, published by Little, Brown and Company, Boston, in 1960 will collectively provide a great deal of additional information.

Two books, published on the One Hundredth Anniversary of the Act of Congress providing for a transcontinental railroad, are excellent in themselves and also provide scores of references. One of these books is *The Great Iron Trail* by Robert West

Howard, published in 1962 by G. P. Putnam's Sons of New York. The other is *A Work of Giants* by Wesley S. Griswold, published in 1962 by the McGraw-Hill Book Company, New York. A third small book that warrants special attention for anyone doing extensive research is William Lightfoot Visscher's *A Thrilling and Truthful History of THE PONY EXPRESS or Blazing the Westward Way and Other Sketches and Incidents of Those Stirring Times,* published in 1946 by Charles T. Powner Company of Chicago. Visscher was a reporter and editor on plains' newspapers during the heyday of the wagon trains up the Platte and the building of the transcontinental railroad. As did many of his contemporaries, Visscher regarded the organizing and running of the Pony Express as the epic achievement that proved the Platte or central route was a practical means of moving people and goods from the eastern to the western United States.

There are three publications that will provide information and references in greater depth on the Texas cattle kings and the Olive operations on the Chisholm or Texas Trail and in several plains states and territories, including the Platte Valley. *The Cattlemen* by Mari Sandoz, published in 1958 by Hastings House of New York, is of special interest. Miss Sandoz was reared in a homesteader dugout in the Nebraska cattle country and this book, as well as a number of her other books, constitutes a firsthand account of what happened by those who took part in the high drama of the taming of the plains. *The Ladder of Rivers* by Harry E. Chrisman, published in 1962 by Sage Books in Denver, is a biography of Isom Prentice Olive and an account of the Olive family's rise to cattle king status. *We Pointed Them North* by Helena Huntington Smith, published by the University of Oklahoma Press, of Norman, Oklahoma, in 1939, is a preservation of the recollections and experiences of E. C. "Teddy Blue" Abbott, a Platte cowboy who himself became a Montana cattle king with longhorns siphoned up the big trail from Texas.

The completion of this manuscript was delayed several months

355

by rewriting made necessary as the momentum of the research inquiry unearthed a series of facts never before available to any writer. I shall mention three.

ONE: In the late stage of manuscript development, a writer's research has confirmation as its primary objective. During this time, many things are investigated in the hope of securing further confirmation of matters already established, but also in the hope of enriching the account. In *Empire on the Platte,* the weather during December 1878 was of the greatest importance. An eye-witness had reported that the Mitchell and Ketchum bodies were frozen and were cut down at about 3:00 A.M., in temperatures well below freezing. There were two to three inches of fresh snow on the ground. There had been no snow at 9:00 P.M. the evening before. The United States Weather Bureau was consulted as a routine matter but with little thought of securing additional information. It could hardly be expected that the weather bureau could provide much information about temperatures and snowfall at Devil's Canyon in 1878, forty miles from the nearest telegraph station. But it was fortunate that we probed this unlikely source. We were referred to the Nebraska climatologist, a Weather Bureau expert, located at the University of Nebraska. The Nebraska climatologist, R. E. Myers, provided a detailed study that clarified the circumstances. In 1878, there was a paid weather bureau observer at North Platte, forty miles to the west of Devil's Canyon, plus an outstanding voluntary observer at Ravenna, thirty miles east. The reports of the two sources checked exactly with an account in the Burt Sell Documents from one of the men, Si Hagadorn, who cut down the bodies.

There was a space on the 1878 U.S. Weather Bureau forms for "remarks." On the night in question, the observers at both North Platte, to the west, and at Ravenna, to the east, reported .14 and .10 of an inch of moisture fell as snow, the first reported in December of 1878.

"Our man in Ravenna" wrote under remarks, "the snow began to fall at 1:00 A.M." Si Hagadorn said, "There was no

snow until that night. There was none at 9:00 P.M. when Print
Olive ordered us to bed, so we could be at Devil's Canyon
at 3:00 A.M. to cut down those bodies. I was surprised when I
put my head outside the bunkhouse door to see the ground
all white with snow."

TWO: *Empire on the Platte* presents the first eye-witness account of the murder of Mitchell and Ketchum. Recently, the
Nebraska State Historical Society found the voluminous official
transcript of the Olive trial and placed it on microfilm. Through
the years, there have been about as many versions of the lynching of Luther Mitchell and Ami Ketchum as there were writers.
Some of the statements attributed to Mitchell and Ketchum and
Print Olive by early writers have become legends. The account
of an Olive man, who told the story under oath, revealed that
Mitchell and Ketchum had said nothing. Print Olive made one
brief and pointless statement which could have been a question
directed to the homesteaders. If it was, he did not want a
reply. Instead, he immediately murdered Luther Mitchell.

THREE: To this day, cattlemen on the Platte vigorously contend that Print Olive and his associates were tried unfairly.
They contend that the use of U.S. Army troops to guard the
trial was merely a shrewd maneuver on the part of Attorney
General Dilworth. They feel Dilworth purposely created the
impression that cattlemen would break up the trial and perhaps
destroy the town of Hastings at the same time, rather than accept a death penalty or even less severe conviction of the Olives.
After several years of probing deeply into the events that had
always been available to any writer, it was clear the U.S.
troops were brought in by the intervention of Governor Nance
who wanted assurance that the Olive trial would be conducted
in an orderly fashion. Had the use of U.S. Army troops been
for effect, Governor Nance's office would not have delayed the
request nearly three hours, particularly in the middle of the
night of April 10–11, 1879, in order to secure confirmation of
the urgency from Attorney General Dilworth. Governor Nance
would not have appeared at the trial. The Governor also ordered

357

his Secretary of State to meet him there, in the shortest possible time, in order that the two highest elective officers in the State of Nebraska could be present to exert a stabilizing influence. General George Crook, at Fort Omaha, would not have assumed the sole responsibility for use of U.S. troops if he had not thought the situation to be critical. The Union Pacific would not have moved the troops at speeds never before attempted, traveling in excess of a safe speed, for mere propaganda purposes. Sheriff Martin at Hastings, who originated the request for troops at 11:20 P.M. the night before, would not have kept the coming of the troops a secret until the Union Pacific special train pulled into Hastings if propaganda had been his aim. Had that been the case, he would have announced the troops coming at the time they left Fort Omaha, hours before. He did not announce the use of U.S. troops for fear the news would trigger immediate action from armed cowmen.

The case for extreme urgency was overwhelming by the time the research was completed for *Empire on the Platte.*

I went to Lincoln, Nebraska, to deliver the manuscript to Governor Morrison. After leaving the Governor's office, late on the afternoon of August 24, 1966, I stopped at the Nebraska State Historical Society to thank personally the historians for their encouragement and assistance over a period of several years.

Neither Director Marvin Kivett nor State Historian Dr. Donald Dankers were present, but I did have a chance to meet historian Paul Riley. As I conveyed my thanks, Riley asked, "Mr. Crabb, did you ever have an opportunity to examine the private correspondence of Governor Nance? I looked at it briefly not long ago and there are a number of matters in it relating to the Olive trial." I had not known of the special file of Governor Nance's private correspondence.

"Would you want to see it or is the production of the book too far along should there be something of interest?"

We went to the archives and studied the Nance correspond-

ence. We were elated when we found the previously unreported
telegrams between Governor Nance and President Rutherford
B. Hayes regarding the use of the United States Army troops.
President Hayes first turned down the use of U.S. troops to
guard the Olive murder trial. When Governor Nance further
explained the urgency, the President reversed himself and
ordered the troops be made available to Governor Nance inde-
finitely and as long as the Governor judged they were needed
to "suppress domestic violence."

There are many people who played essential roles in the
writing of *Empire on the Platte*. The many others will understand, perhaps even applaud, if I first express appreciation to
Mrs. C. R. Crabb, my mother, who despite her more than three
score and ten years, is still an active newspaper publisher, a
historian, and a better writer than any of her several children.
Her manuscript suggestions have been invaluable, especially
those graceful phrases that better describe the situation and
usually eliminate the need for a sentence or even a paragraph.

It is with a deep pleasure that I convey my gratitude for
manuscript appraisal by Dr. Allan Nevins, Mrs. Nevins, and
Dr. Raymond Billington of the Huntington Memorial Library at
San Marino, California. Mrs. Nevins grew up on the Platte.
To Burt Sell; Governor Frank B. Morrison; and Nebraska historians Kivett, Dankers, and Riley my special thanks. A special
appreciation is due to my agent, Roy E. Porter of Evanston,
Illinois. He must be saluted for service over and beyond that
of an agent and editor. It was through his guidance that *Empire
on the Platte* was transformed from a regional story to one of
national interest and significance.

Many of the pictures in this book have never been published.
Special recognition is due Evelyn Sell Camp from San Diego,
California. After there was reason to believe that no picture
of Tamar Snow existed, Mrs. Camp organized a detective-like
probe, extending from Nebraska to Texas to California. Finally,
Mrs. Camp found the picture of Tamar Snow taken in San
Antonio, Texas, three quarters of a century before. In the

breakthrough Mrs. Camp also brought to light the Civil War letters of Peter Snow to his family and pictures of Tamar's mother, Jane Snow Mitchell, and Tamar's sister Lydia, who became the mother of eleven children, giving birth to one of them in a small Nebraska dugout attended only by a Sioux Indian squaw who understood no English and who stopped at the dugout only minutes before seeking food.

Almost every reader of this manuscript, and they were numerous, urged me to reveal what happened to Tamar Snow, Johnny Bryan, Mrs. Luther Mitchell and others who took key roles in this book.

Johnny Bryan farmed in Custer County all his life. His second wife died and left Johnny five small boys to rear.

Jane Snow Mitchell eventually married again. She and her husband, William Marvin, went to California and lived long and useful lives.

None of the men indicted for murder along with Print Olive and Fred Fisher were ever tried. Brown and DuFran turned states' evidence. Charges against Green and Baldwin were eventually dismissed.

Governor Nance served two terms as Governor and shortly thereafter returned to his native Illinois to enter business.

As might be expected, Tamar remained close to her mother for a long time after the murder of her fiancé, Ami Ketchum, and her stepfather, Luther Mitchell. Four years after the tragedy, Tamar Snow married William Wall, brother of Judge Aaron Wall, and moved to Texas. There followed six happy years, mostly in San Antonio, during which time Tamar became the mother of two daughters, Nora and Agnes. When the little girls were six and four the family realized that Tamar was incurably ill with tuberculosis.

Thirty days after Tamar died, the little girls' father, William Wall, became ill with smallpox. At this time in San Antonio, smallpox sufferers were treated as lepers. They were required to leave their homes at once and live in a colony outside of town.

Those who recovered returned to their homes; those who did not were buried, without funeral services, in a common grave kept in readiness.

As he was leaving for the smallpox colony, William Wall arranged with a Catholic priest to care for the daughters until he returned. If he did not survive the ordeal, the priest was to notify Judge Aaron Wall of Loup City, Nebraska.

Tamar Snow, as she appeared at the time of her wedding to William Wall, four years after her decisive role in the gun battle with the Olives.

361

William Wall was buried in the unmarked mass grave. The San Antonio priest notified Judge Wall of the plight of the daughters of Tamar and William Wall. Judge Wall traveled to Texas immediately and took the little girls to Nebraska. They were reared by Agnes Wall Hottinger, Judge Wall's oldest daughter, who later moved to California and took the girls with her. They lived in California the remainder of their lives.

The youngest daughter, Agnes, who often demonstrated the courage and determination of her mother, became one of the first women in California to pilot an airplane. In the first critical days of World War II, when she was more than fifty years old, she was perhaps the only woman, or certainly one of a very small number, active as a pilot in the United States Air Force Auxiliary. The Auxiliary helped ferry war planes from California to the East Coast of the United States, from where they were sent to the fighting fronts in Europe.

In a sense, Tamar's daughter acted in her mother's former role; delivering weapons in another crisis between order by law and order by tyrants. Tamar would have been proud of her daughter. Peter Snow, the man who did not make it all the way to Atlanta with General Sherman, would have been proud of both his daughter and his granddaughter.

RICHARD CRABB

Wheaton, Illinois
October 1966

INDEX

Teton Dakota

Red Cloud Ageny

Niobrara River

Spotted Tail Agency

Ponca

Ft. Robinson

No

Dismal River

North Platte

South B.

Chimney Rock

Pawne

U. P. R. R.

Platte

Ft. Sedgwick

South Platte